I0793064

IMAGES
of America

OWYHEE COUNTY

On the Cover: See pages 12 and 13.

IMAGES
of America

OWYHEE COUNTY

Robert L. Deen

ARCADIA
PUBLISHING

ISBN 978-1-4671-3309-8

Published by Arcadia Publishing
Charleston, South Carolina

Printed in the United States of America

Library of Congress Control Number: 2014951062

For all general information, please contact Arcadia Publishing:
Telephone 843-853-2070
Fax 843-853-0044
E-mail sales@arcadiapublishing.com
For customer service and orders:
Toll-Free 1-888-313-2665

Visit us on the Internet at www.arcadiapublishing.com

To the pioneers of Owyhee County and my grandsons Landon and Carter

Contents

Acknowledgments

The book would not have been possible without the support and cooperation of the Owyhee County Historical Society and Museum (OCHS). Unless otherwise noted, photographs are from the collection of the OCHS. I would also like to recognize the historical work of Mildretta Adams (1907–1987). An Owyhee pioneer herself, her writings were an invaluable resource. She made a unique contribution to capturing and preserving the history of Owyhee County. Special thanks to OCHS board president Mary O'Malley and former staff member Brittany Lindstrom.

Introduction

Owyhee County is a sprawling, slightly mysterious and relatively unexplored region of high intermountain desert located in the southwestern corner of Idaho. Although larger than the state of Vermont—7,697 square miles—there are fewer than 12,000 residents. At its height in the 1880s, during the mining boom, Owyhee County was among the most populous places in Idaho. Today, it is among the least, at 1.4 persons per square mile. Few roads penetrate its interior, and visitors are largely restricted to the hardy and adventurous. Travel beyond the few paved highways is by four-wheel drive, all-terrain vehicle, dune buggy, motorcycle, and horseback.

The county is part of a larger desert region referred to by locals as "ION country," an acronym of Idaho, Oregon, and Nevada, where the three states meet.

The Owyhee Mountains dominate a landscape of sagebrush and basalt canyons, with Hayden Peak reaching 8,403 feet above sea level. The Snake River forms the county's northern border from Oregon to just west of Glens Ferry.

The Owyhee Wilderness Area, created by the Omnibus Public Land Management Act of 2009, is the second-largest US Wilderness Area (that is not located within a National Forest, National Park, or National Wildlife Refuge).

Owyhee County has a rich history that began with Native American culture stretching back more than 10,000 years, interrupted by a massive influx of whites drawn by the discovery of silver and gold lodes exceeded only by the Comstock discovery in Nevada. Silver City was one of many gold rush–era mining towns, but it remains today as possibly the largest intact ghost town in the West. Mining followed a boom and bust cycle into the 1920s. A few mines remain active to this day, but mining was replaced by ranching, agriculture, and the building of major water projects in the early 20th century.

Interestingly, the name Owyhee is not a Native American term; it comes from an early anglicization of the native Hawaiian word for Hawai'i.

When Europeans first interacted with the Hawaiian Islands in the late 1700s, they referred to the natives as Owyhees. Much admired for their strong physiques and skills on the water, many were recruited to serve on European sailing ships. This brought them to the American Northwest coast and the Columbia River, participating in the fur-trapping trade.

During the early 1800s, Donald Mackenzie of the Northwest Company annually led a trapping party into the Snake River country of Oregon and Idaho. In 1819, three Owyhees joined the annual expedition, and during that winter they left the main party to explore the unknown area of what since has been called the Owyhee River. They disappeared and were presumed dead. Their fate remains a mystery. In memory of their lost comrades, British fur trappers began to call the region Owyhee.

During the 1840s, the Oregon Trail followed two routes through Idaho, one of which was the southern bank of the Snake River along what is now Owyhee County's northern border. Hundreds of thousands traveled the Oregon Trail, and many novices who used it to reach the California gold fields in 1849 would return to Idaho in later years as experienced miners.

Native Americans had populated the region for thousands of years, and whites encountered the Paiute and Shoshoni Bannock tribes. The Bannock War of 1878, which cost of lives of more than 40 settlers (three in Owyhee County), climaxed locally at the battle of South Mountain in the Owyhees. Local volunteers from Silver City engaged a force of approximately 50 Bannock warriors on the slopes of a mountain near the mining communities. Bannock War Chief Buffalo Horn was killed during the struggle, and the hostiles moved southwest to join their Paiute allies, who together continued hostilities in western Oregon.

In 1863, Michael Jordan discovered gold on the creek that bears his name. That led to the discovery of gold and silver lodes higher up, most notably at War Eagle Mountain, and a mining boom spawned the cities of Ruby and Silver City, DeLamar, Wagontown, Dewey, Boonetown, and Fairview.

The mining towns became the home of colorful characters and events. When the shafts of two competing gold mines inadvertently intersected in 1866, the "War under the Mountain" commenced, resulting in several deaths and requiring the intervention of Idaho's governor and federal troops.

Col. W.H. Dewey, who as a young man walked to Silver City all the way from Virginia City, Nevada, became a leading figure and promoter of the mining industry. He founded the town of Dewey and was briefly imprisoned after shooting a local bartender in what supporters claimed was a plot to take over his mining interests.

Mining magnate J.R. DeLamar, the "Monte Cristo of Idaho," founded the town of DeLamar and operated the famous Trade Dollar Mine, which extracted millions of dollars of gold and silver bullion. After serving as a state senator in Idaho's first legislature, DeLamar moved to New York, where he was known on Wall Street as the "man of mystery." The New York mansion he built was thought to be an inspiration for Gatsby's house in F. Scott Fitzgerald's *The Great Gatsby*.

During the 1800s, the mining region quickly became one of the most populous areas of Idaho, but as the ore played out the towns faded and for the most part disappeared. Today, the region is one of Idaho's most sparsely populated regions, with the remaining residents scattered on small homesteads, ranches, and farms. Today, most of the county's population of 11,500 lives in a handful of small towns along the Snake River, including Homedale, Marsing, Murphy, and Grand View.

Owyhee County is a remote, beautiful, little-visited corner of America's West. It is indeed off the beaten path. Historical photographs capture a land of excitement, drama, and surprising richness—even grandeur. It is hard to believe that the bustling towns that covered the slopes of War Eagle Mountain are now for the most part completely gone. The mines are closed, the forests have recaptured the hillsides, and Jordan Creek flows once more, unimpeded, down to the Owyhee River.

One

THE MINERS

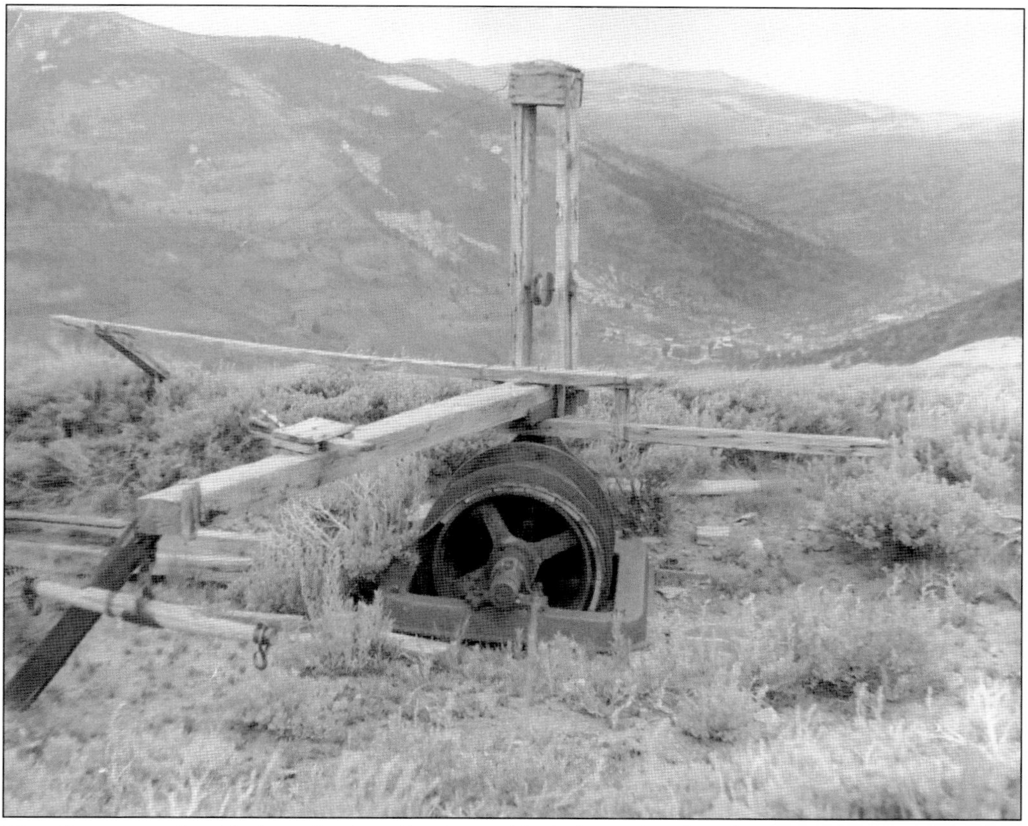

The discovery of gold along Jordan Creek quickly led to a hard-rock mining bonanza rivaling Nevada's famous Comstock Lode. Towns sprang up overnight among the mountaintops. The word went out, and the miners came. The history of Owyhee County is largely the history of these miners, who became the face of the Owyhees, shaping the towns, the people, and the land itself—some for the better, some for the worse.

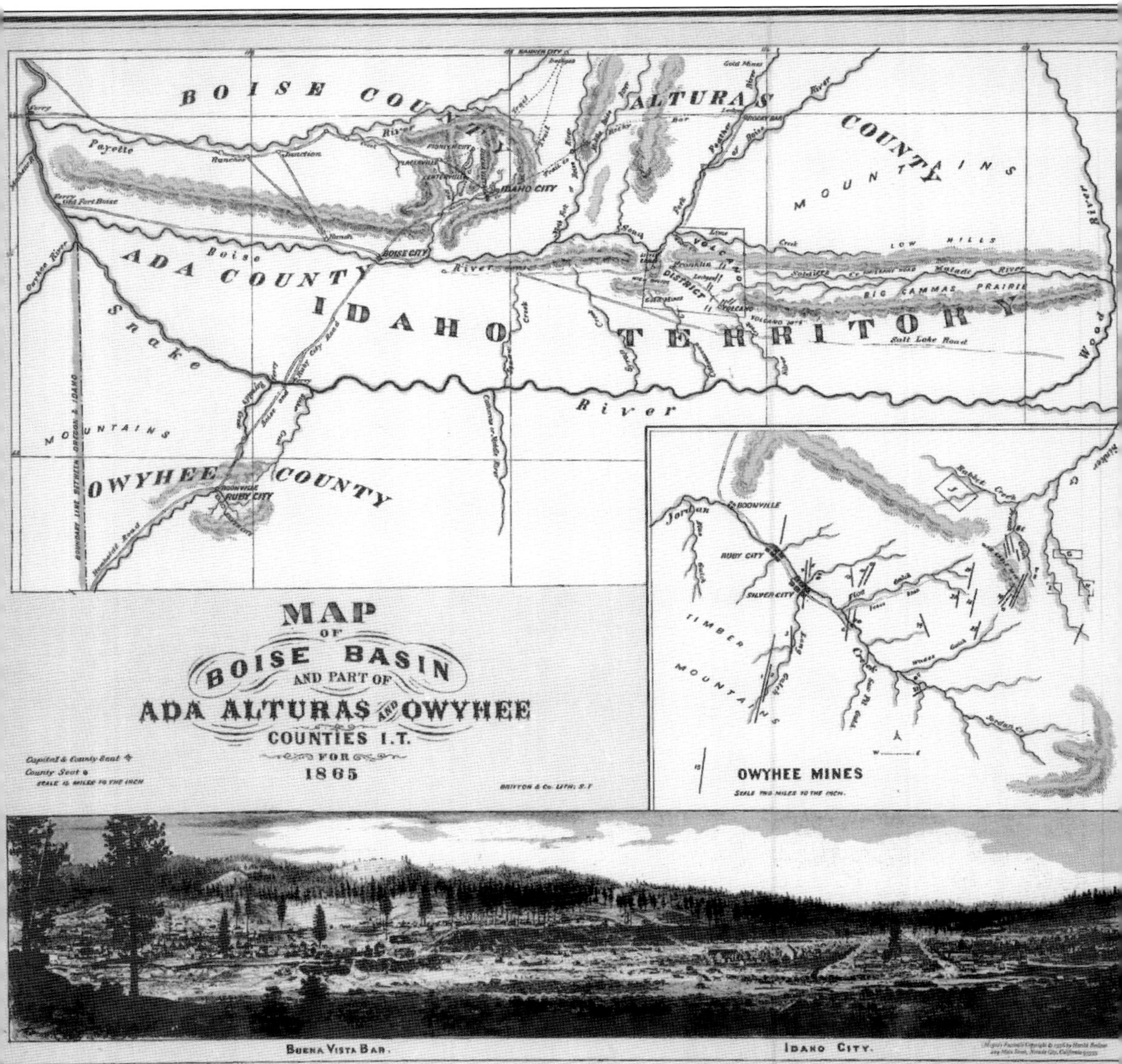

This early map of the Boise Basin, Idaho, shows the location of mining communities in the Owyhee Mountains. On December 31, 1863, Owyhee County became the first county organized by the Idaho Territorial Legislature. Owyhee County's original boundary was the portion of Idaho Territory south of the Snake River and west of the Rocky Mountains. Less than a month later, in January 1864, Oneida County was created from the eastern part of the county. Later, the formation of Cassia County in 1879 reduced it even further. The county gained its present boundaries in 1930, when land near Glens Ferry and King Hill was moved to neighboring Elmore County. Ruby City was the first county seat, and Owyhee County is comprised of 7,697 square miles. It is the second-largest county in Idaho by area. (Courtesy of the Idaho State Historical Society.)

This lithograph depicts War Eagle Mountain as it looked in the 1800s, when mining hit its stride. Mountains surrounding the mines were denuded, as trees were chopped down to furnish construction and mine materials. Forests reclaimed the hillsides after mining operations faded, and today the area is virtually unrecognizable compared to early photographs and lithographs.

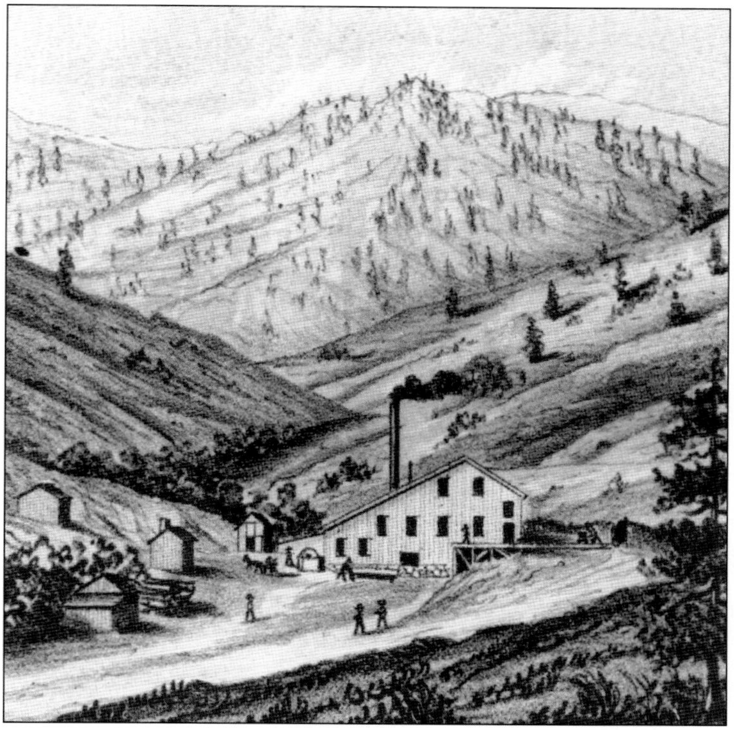

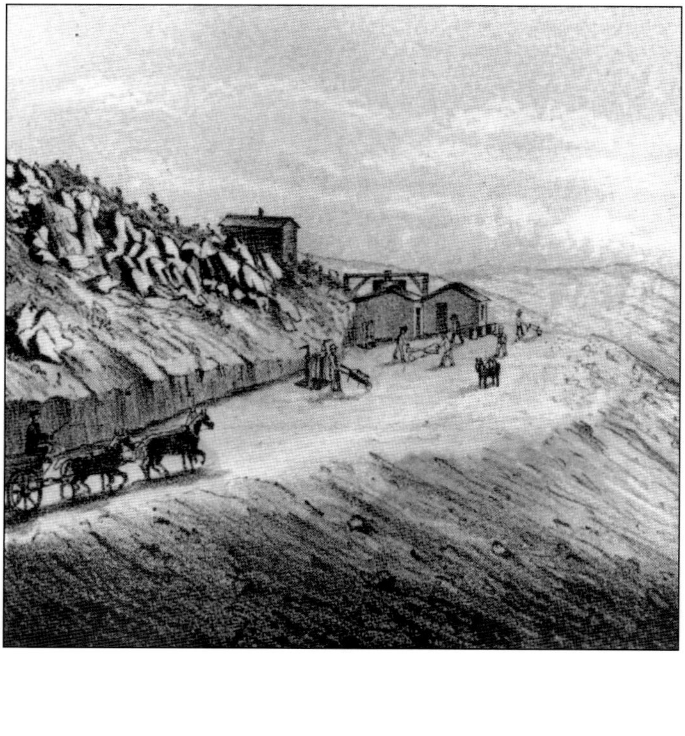

When J.M. More and D.H. Fogus developed the Orofino and Morning Star properties, rock from their mines assayed extremely high in gold and silver. By the fall of 1864, ore from their properties began to keep a number of different stamp mills busy, producing $1 million a year. In September 1865, incredibly rich ore turned up in another War Eagle Mountain mine: the Poorman. A claim war stopped work on the Poorman after a production of only six days. But, in those six days, surface operations by the hastiest methods yielded over $500,000 worth of ore.

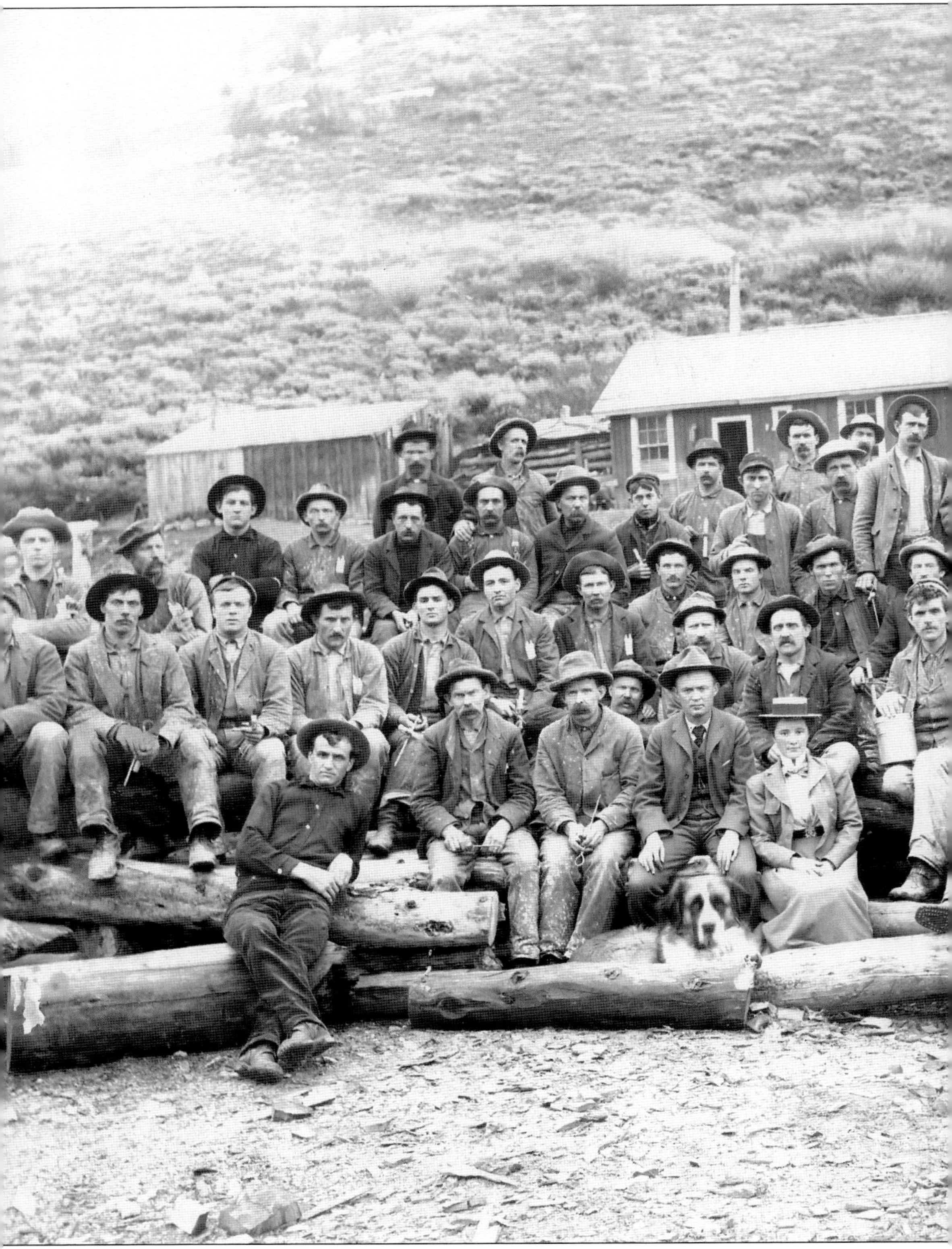

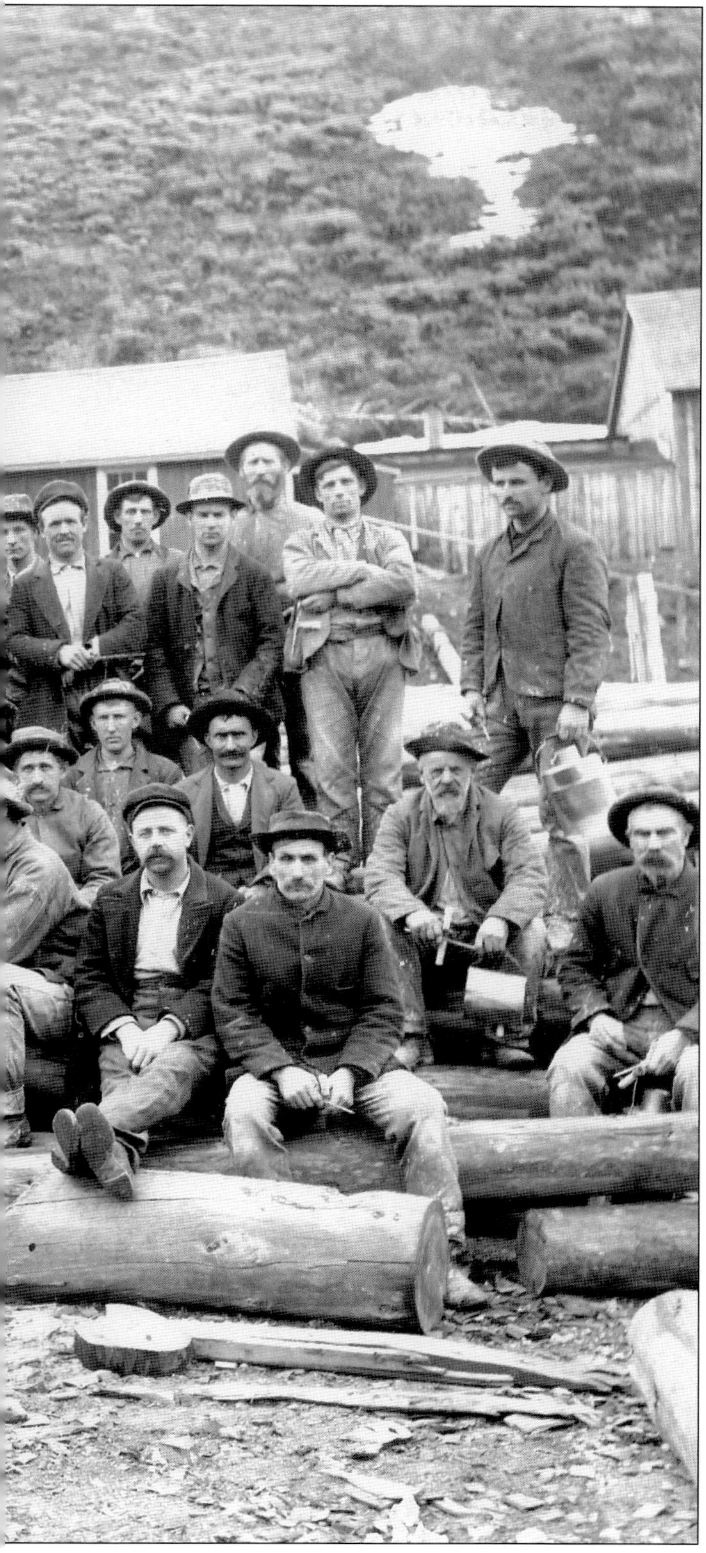

These are miners of the Trade Dollar Mine, posing on Florida Mountain. The Trade Dollar had a main tunnel 3,854 feet in length. It connected with the Blackjack Mine at its northern tunnel, having over five miles of tunnel and drifts. Eastern financier Andrew Mellon was the secretary and treasurer of the Trade Dollar Mining and Milling Company. The Trade Dollar was named after trade dollars, US coins minted to compete with other large silver dollars that were already popular in East Asia. The idea first came about in the 1860s, when the price of silver began to decline due to increased mining efforts in the West. Eventually, bullion producers such as those in the Owyhee Mountains began converting large amounts of silver into trade dollars, but they were much maligned and traded for less than $1 each. They were discontinued in 1876.

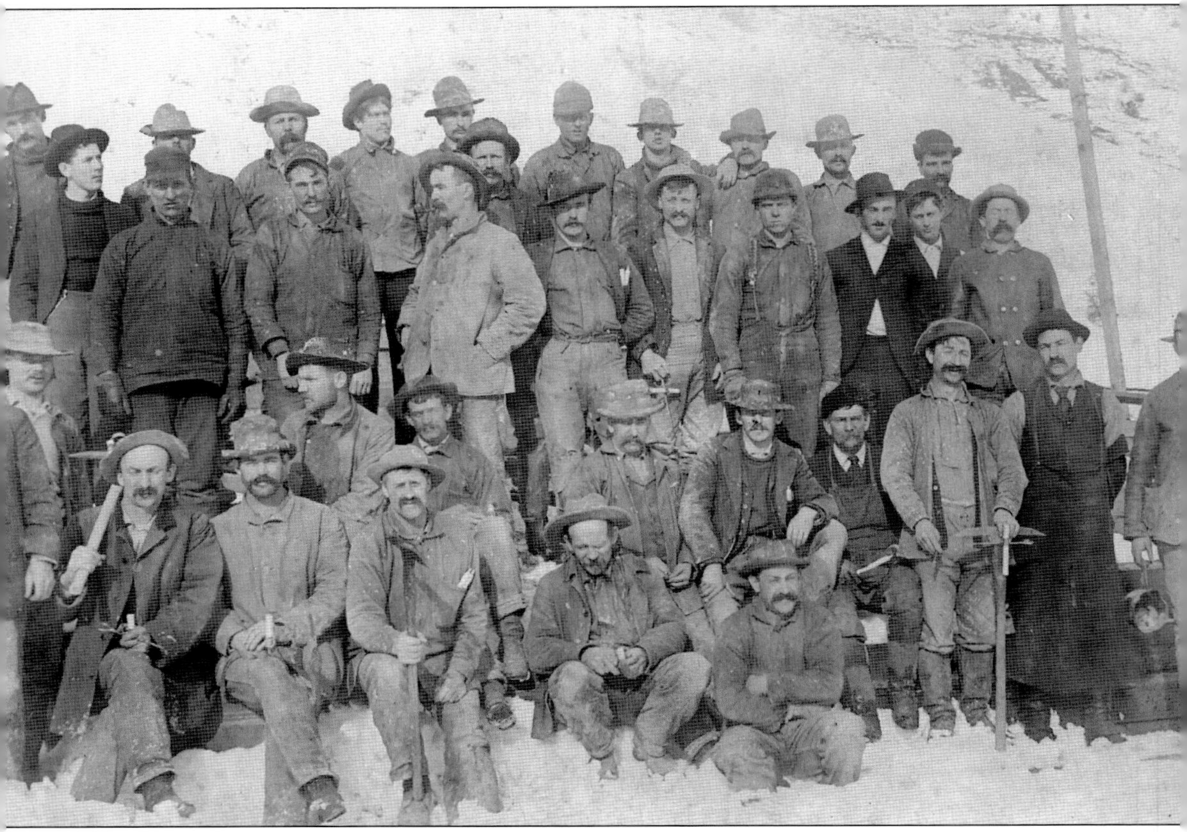

In 1896, William Dudley Haywood, better know as "Big Bill" (fourth from left, third row) got his start as secretary of the miners union in Silver City. He was a central figure in the Haywood-Pettibone trial for the assassination by bombing of Idaho governor Frank Steunenberg in 1905. He was secretary of the Western Federation of Miners at that time, which was accused of masterminding the plot. The defense hired Clarence Darrow, the most renowned lawyer of the day, and Haywood was acquitted. He was a founding member and leader of the Industrial Workers of the World (IWW) and a member of the executive committee of the Socialist Party of America. Haywood was one of 101 members of the IWW convicted of violating the Espionage Act of 1917 during the first "Red Scare" (widespread fear of Bolshevism and anarchism spurred by the Russian Revolution). While out of prison during an appeal of his conviction, Haywood fled to Russia. He died in Moscow in 1928.

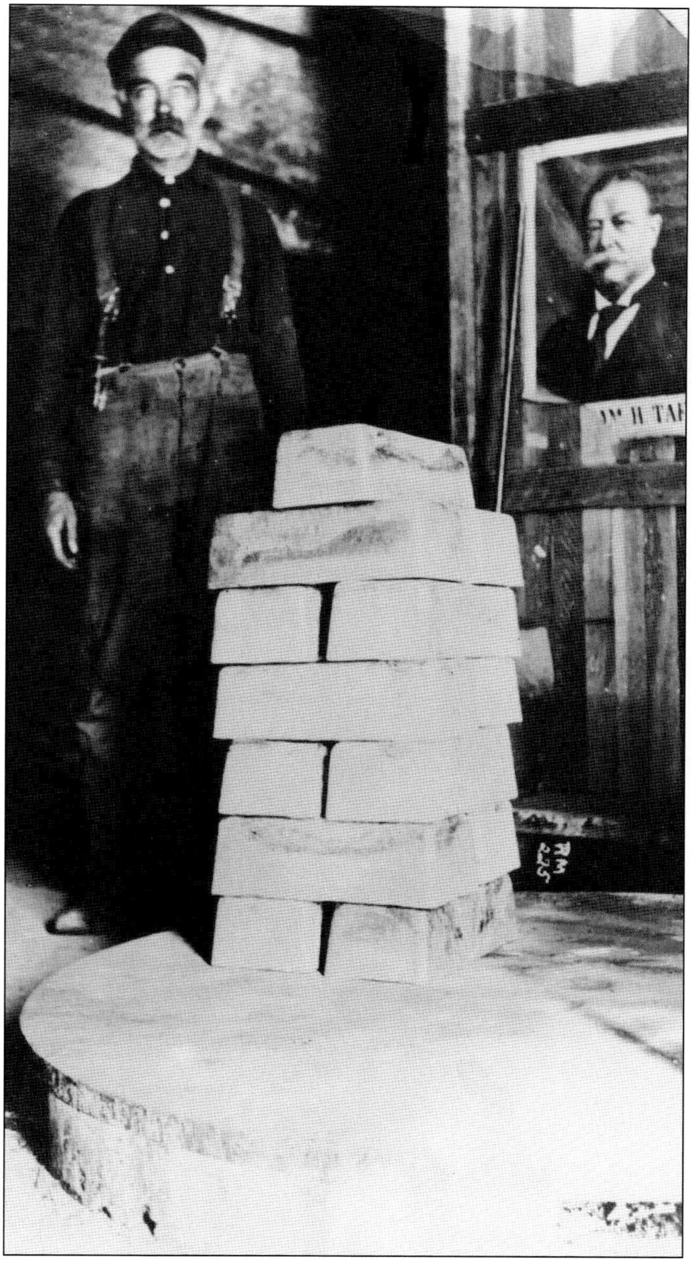

Miner Mike Rock stands with a stack of silver bars from the DeLamar mines—20,622 ounces troy in weight and valued at $31,900 at the time. During the years between the discovery of gold and silver and the financial panic of 1875, the Silver City mines alone were reported by the Idaho Department of Mines to have produced $12 million of bullion. The Silver City Mining District was the nation's second-largest silver-producing area, surpassed only by the famous Comstock Lode in Nevada (from which many of the Silver City region's miners originated). The placer and quartz vein mines largely had given out by the time Idaho became a state in 1890, although small-scale mining continued on and off until World War II. The region's remote and isolated status—it was never reached by rail or paved road—contributed to the difficulty of sustaining mining operations.

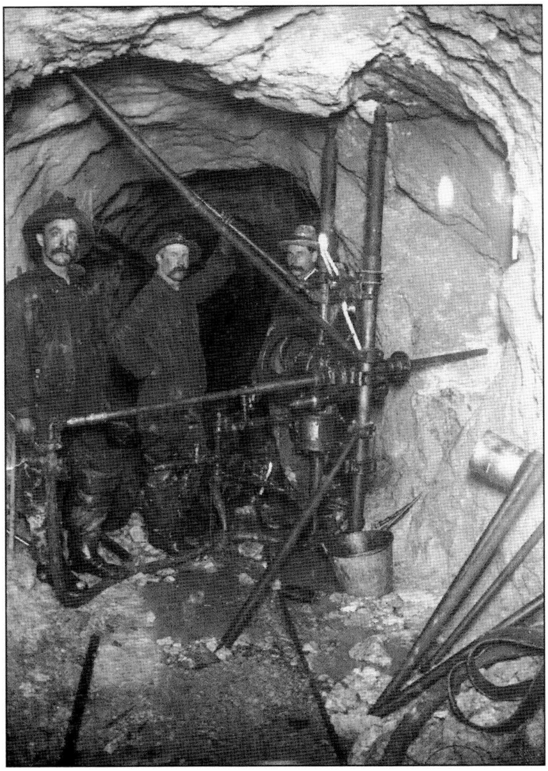

John E. McDonnell (right) and two other DeLamar miners pose with a diamond drill on January 6, 1902. The DeLamar Mine was formed in 1888 by the purchase of a number of mineral claims on DeLamar Mountain. The mine was credited with production in excess of $8 million. (Courtesy of Mildretta Adams.)

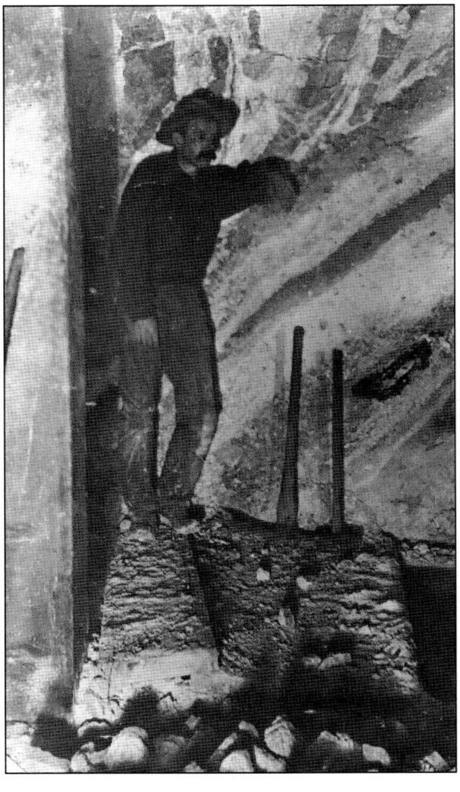

A DeLamar miner rests in a stope. Stoping is the process of extracting the desired ore or other mineral from an underground mine, leaving behind an open space known as a stope. Stoping is used when the country rock is sufficiently strong not to cave in, although, as seen in this photograph, artificial support is usually provided.

This photograph shows an Owyhee miner inspecting a cave-in. An occupational hazard of the mining industry, the possibility of a cave-in was a constant concern, particularly in the early years when mining technology was rudimentary. Speed of operations was often a far greater concern to mine owners than safety, a fact reflected in the high toll of injuries and deaths.

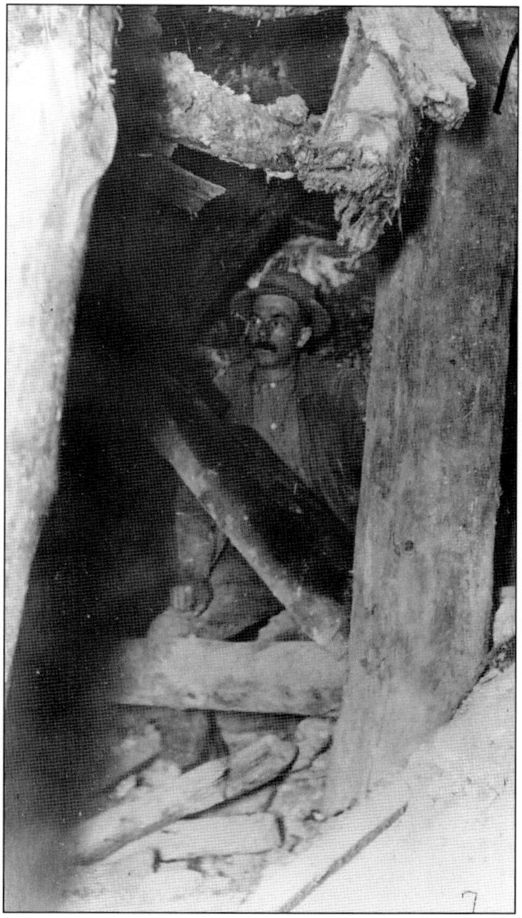

This mining engineer is using a surveying transit to chart the mine's course. By the dawn of the 20th century, mining had become an increasingly complex enterprise, requiring high levels of technical sophistication to achieve the increasingly difficult extraction of ore.

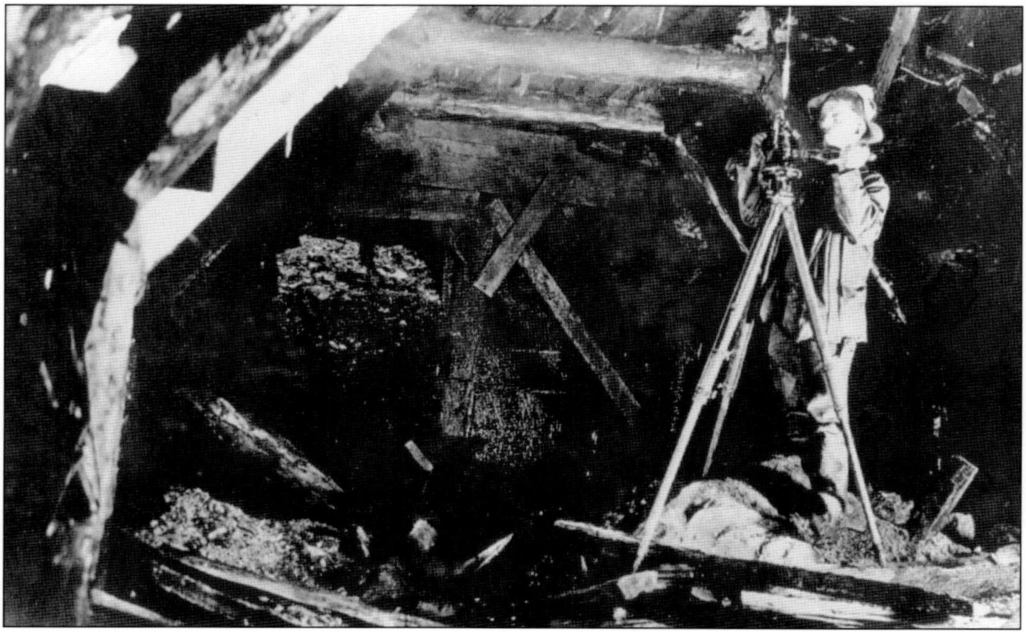

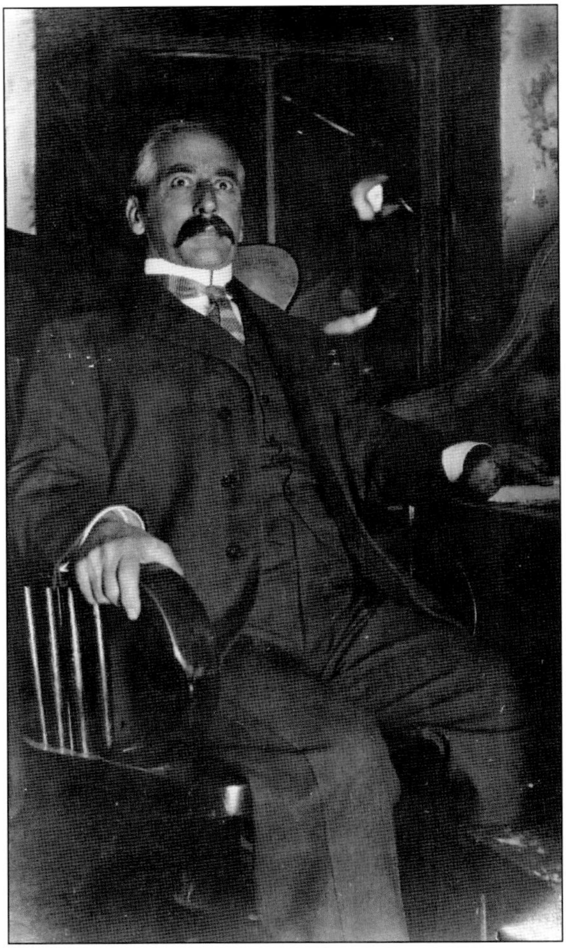

E.V. Orford was mine superintendent of the DeLamar mines in the late 19th and early 20th centuries. The DeLamar mines kept the local communities alive well into the early 1900s, long after many other operations had succumbed to dwindling production. As the ore veins played out, it took more and more effort—and money—to extract gold and silver in commercially viable quantities. Managers like Orford were tasked with maintaining profitability as a top priority.

These miners are working the filter room of the DeLamar Mine in 1910. By this time, the mines were technologically sophisticated, a far cry from their primitive forebearers of the 1800s. They were also far more expensive to operate, a factor that resulted in their ultimate demise.

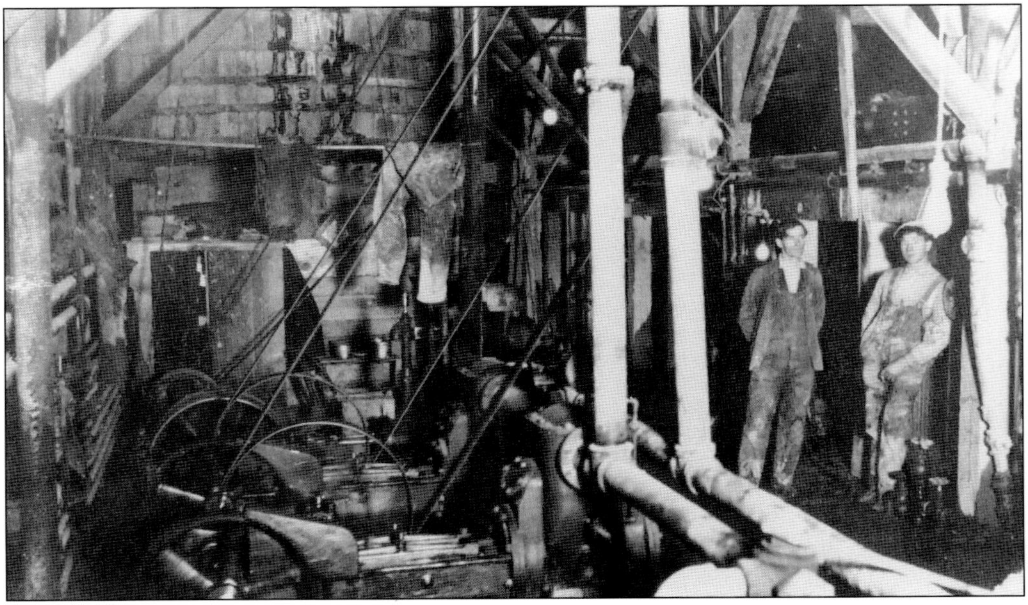

This photograph depicts a giant in operation. During hydraulic mining, pressurized water was forced through a large nozzle (called a monitor or giant) to wash away soft underground deposits. Developed during the California gold rush and highly effective at extracting gold, the process resulted in extensive environmental damage.

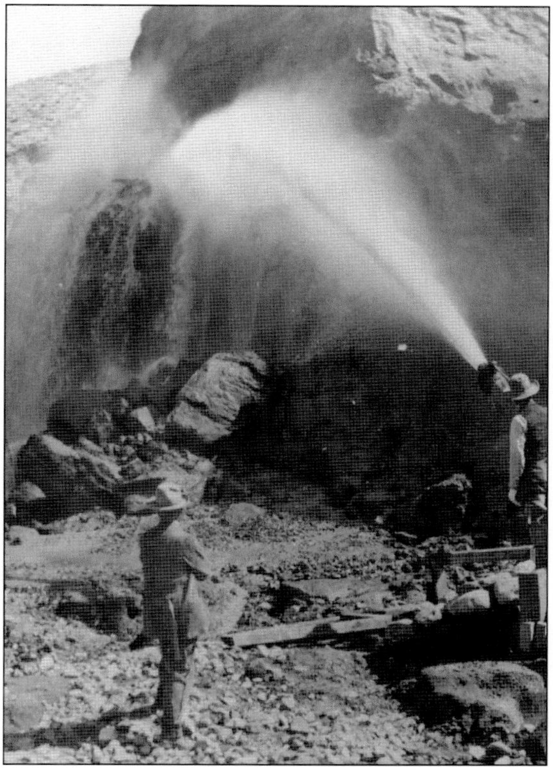

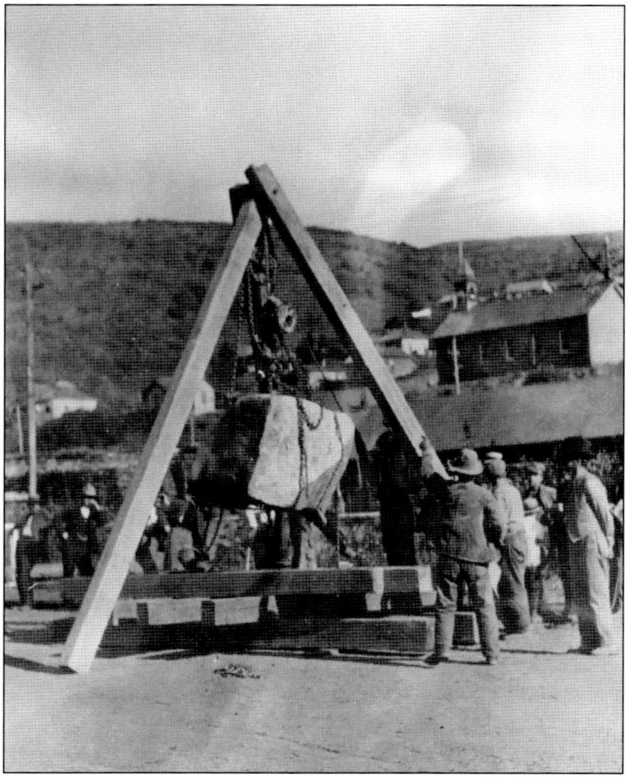

Hard-rock miners often competed with each other and displayed their skills in various ways. This photograph shows miners competing in a rock-drilling contest in DeLamar on Labor Day in 1905. (Photograph by Edith Farrer.)

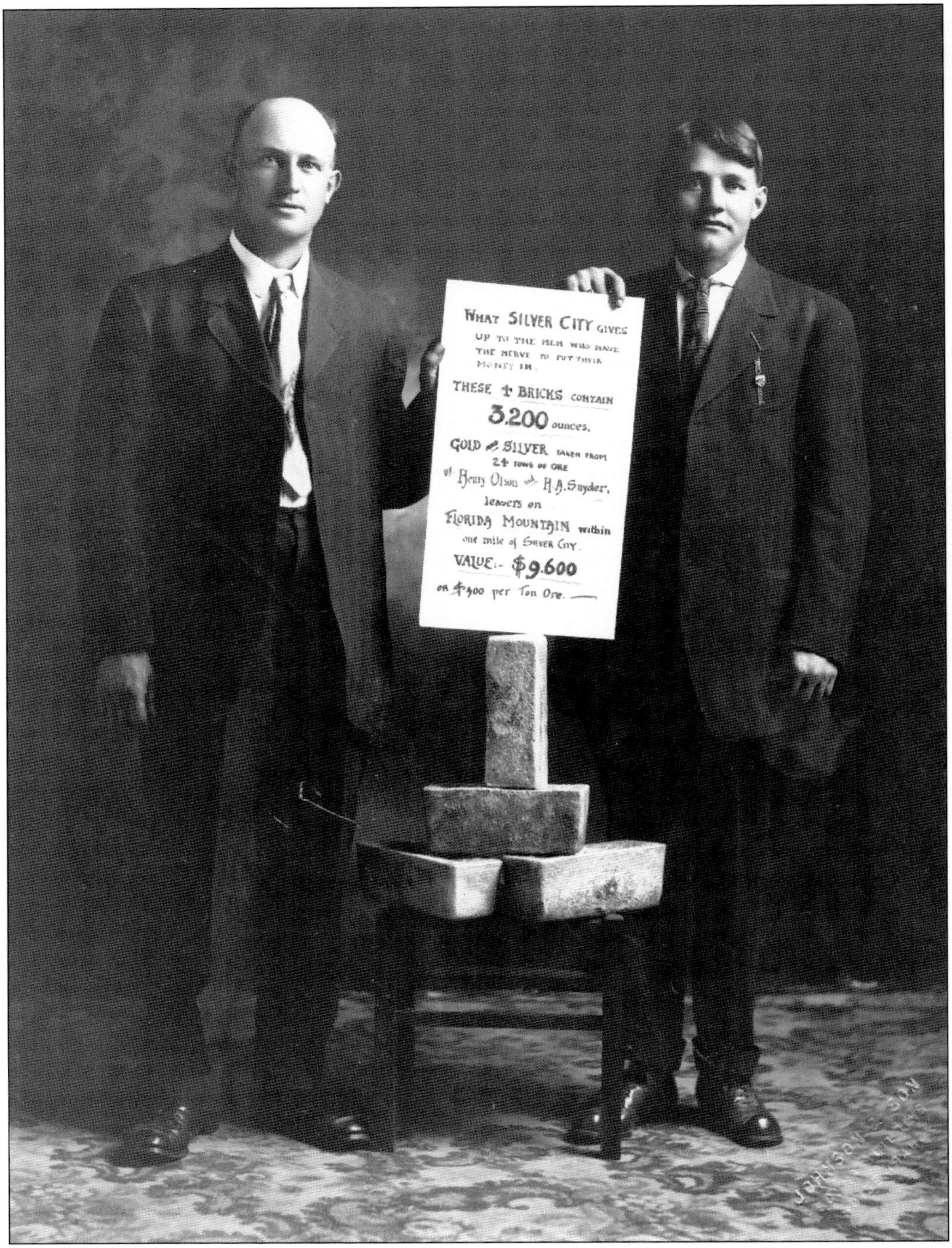

Soliciting money from investors to fund mining operations was a critical task, particularly as increasingly sophisticated mining technologies demanded higher capital investment. In addition to a large workforce of miners, capital had to be invested in bringing in a stamp mill to crush the ore and a separating and amalgamating plant (to separate gold from the rock). The remoteness of the region and poor transportation magnified the expenses involved. In this 1912 promotional photograph, Arthur (left) and Henry Olsen pose with gold bullion in hopes that its glitter would entice investors. (Courtesy of Ralph Snyder.)

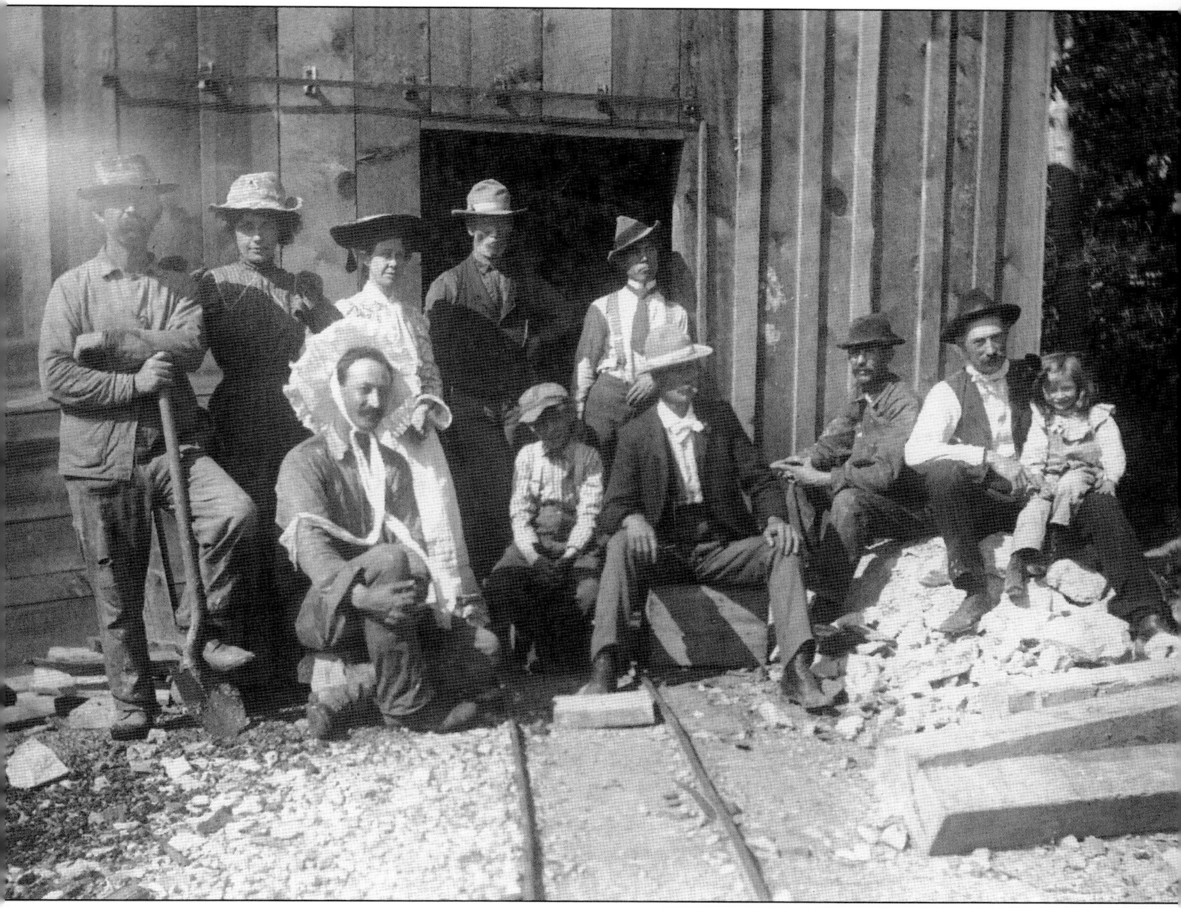

This Silver City mining family has gathered for a family photograph sometime in the late 1800s or early 1900s. As with most Western gold rushes, the original miners were almost exclusively unattached men, but as the towns developed and became more settled, families and children began to appear. Establishment of schools within each town was marked with considerable pride and celebration and noted as sign of true community. As the *Owyhee Avalanche* newspaper noted on April 8, 1866, "There is a private school being taught in Silver City by Mrs. Watson. The room is not large enough to accommodate many people. Amid the hurry and excitement of money making in new places, the education of the rising generation is often neglected." According to a school census taken in Owyhee County in 1866, there were 45 females between the ages of 4 and 21 and 61 males in that age range.

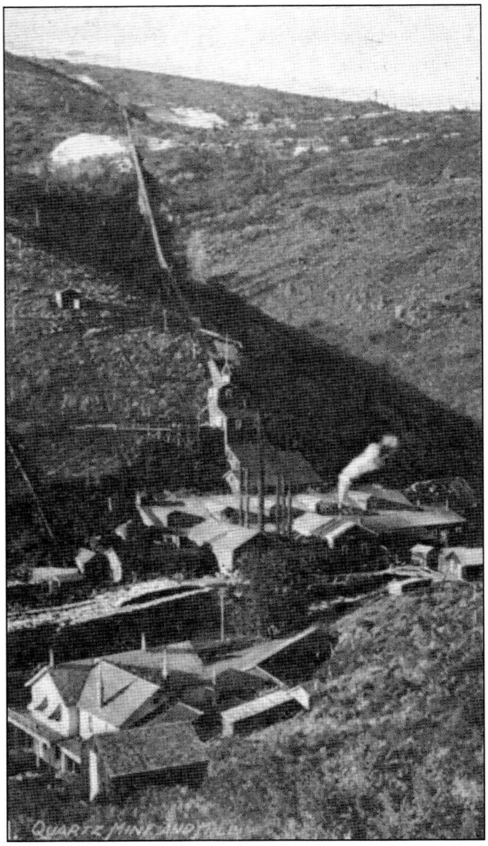

The DeLamar mines were some of the most productive and long lasting. The original claim on DeLamar Mountain was discovered by Jack Wilson, who later sold it to Captain DeLamar for $10,000. The Wilson Claim was the nucleus of what would become the famous DeLamar group of mines. Wilson went on to file a land claim along Josephine Creek. He sold the Josephine Ranch to V.F. Nettleton in 1898 for $500. (Courtesy of the Library of Congress.)

Mining magnate J.R. De Lamar established the practice of providing a boardinghouse for miners in his employ. The Trade Dollar Boarding House, pictured here, provided a comparatively inexpensive and comfortable home for single miners. On May 5, 1891, the *DeLamar Nugget* newspaper offered this description: "There are many dwellers in tents in and around this happy camp. From now until next October, tent life under the bright skies of Idaho is very pleasant." One presumes it was less pleasant when the harsh winter snows came after October, hence the popularity of the boardinghouse.

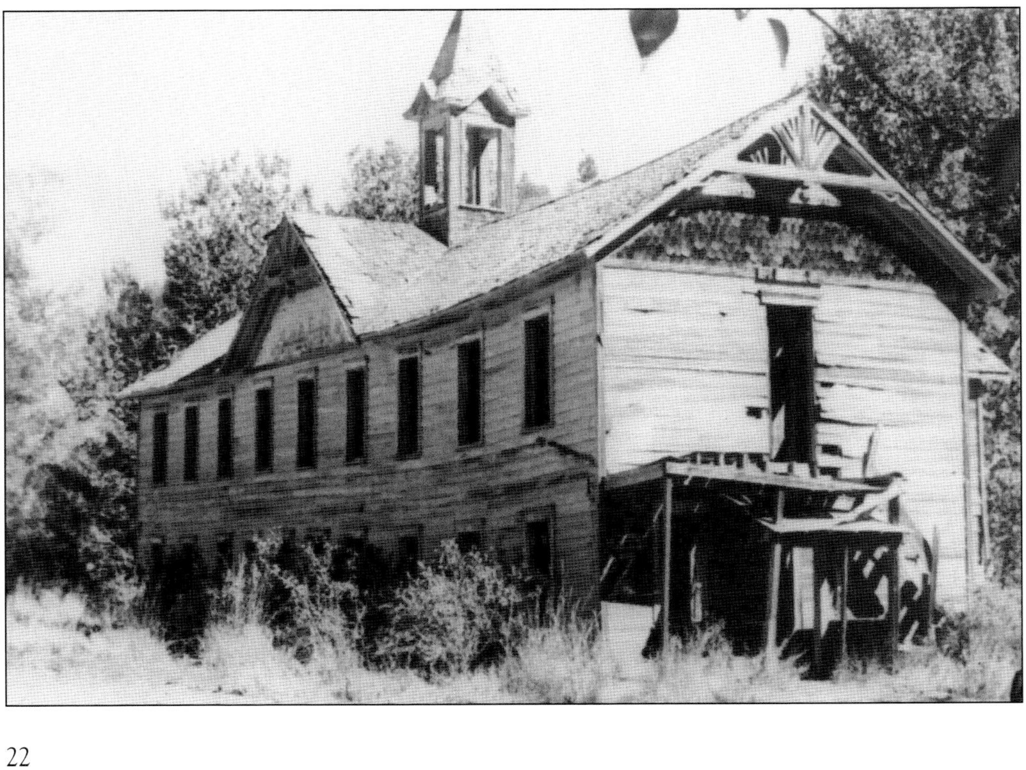

Two

Silver City

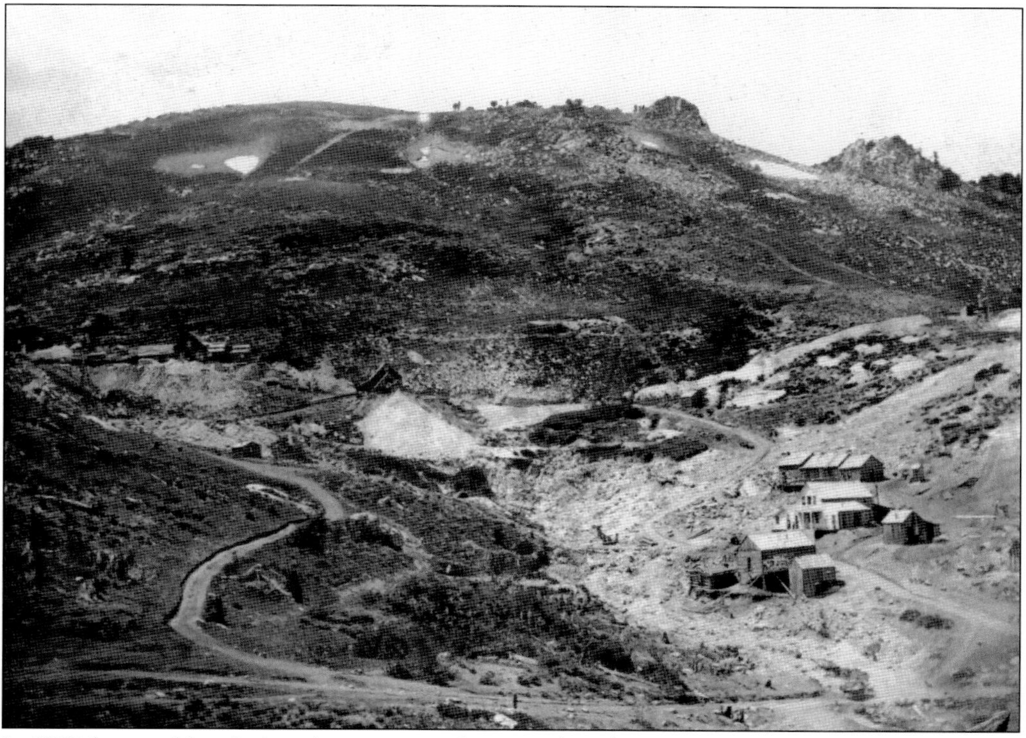

In 1863, huge gold and silver deposits were discovered in the Owyhee Mountains, and thousands of miners flocked to War Eagle Mountain. Silver City was founded in 1864 and swiftly grew into one of the major cities of the Idaho Territory. At its peak, a population of 2,500 supported nearby mines that produced millions of dollars in ore.

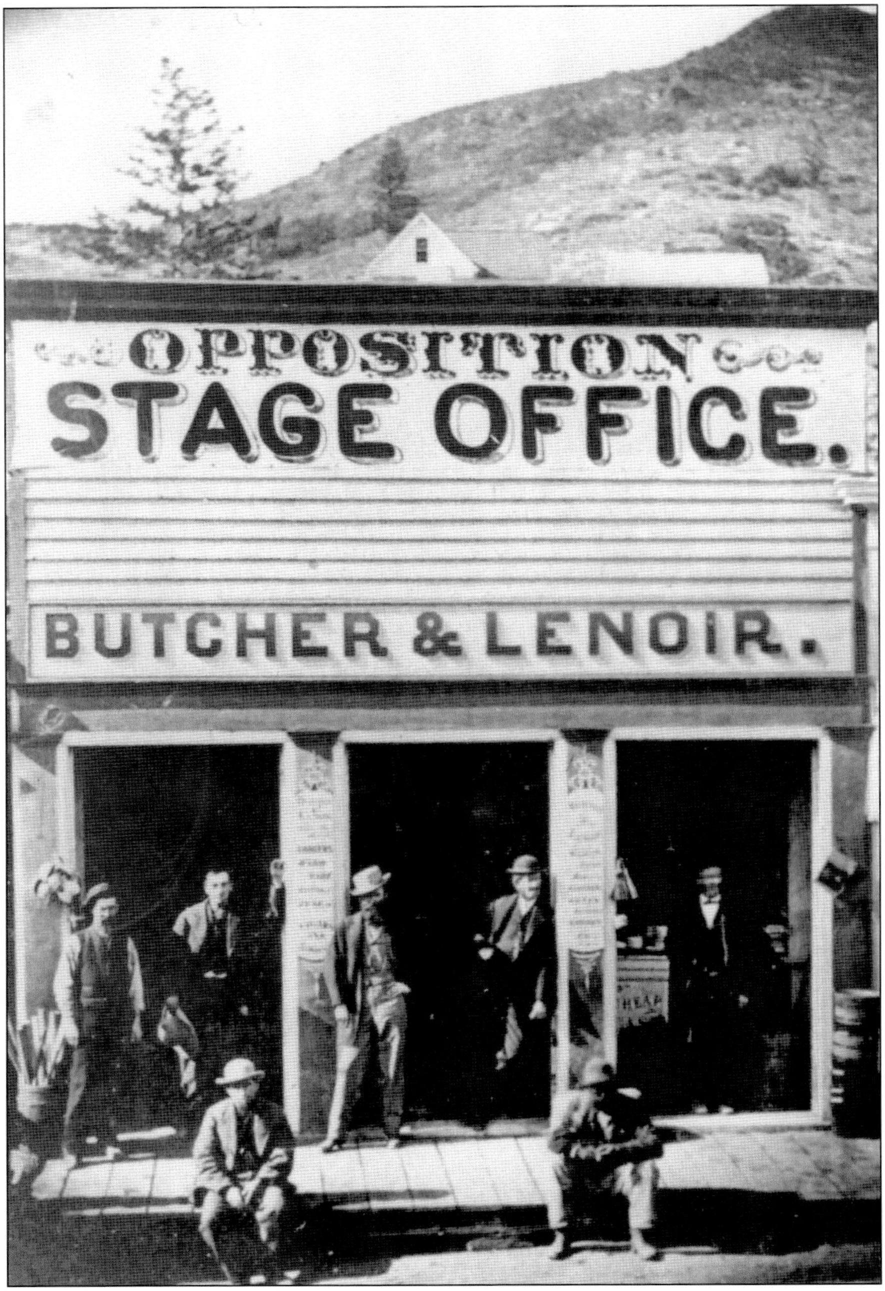

This 1868 photograph shows the Opposition Stage Line's office in Silver City. There was a struggle between Oregon and California for the Idaho mining trade in the 1860s, and stage lines vied with each other in establishing express routes to and from both states. Idahoans accused Oregonians of seizing all the mountain passes and river crossings with toll bridges and ferries. Hill Beachy, Henry Greathouse, Ish and Hailey, Samuel Kelly, and Ben Holliday were well-known names in the early transportation and staging field. Rivalry was strong among them for franchises to establish their lines. By consolidating their interests in 1866, these men became the controlling factors in stage transportation business in Idaho. The stage route to Silver City was one of the last to be operated in the western United States, making runs up until World War I.

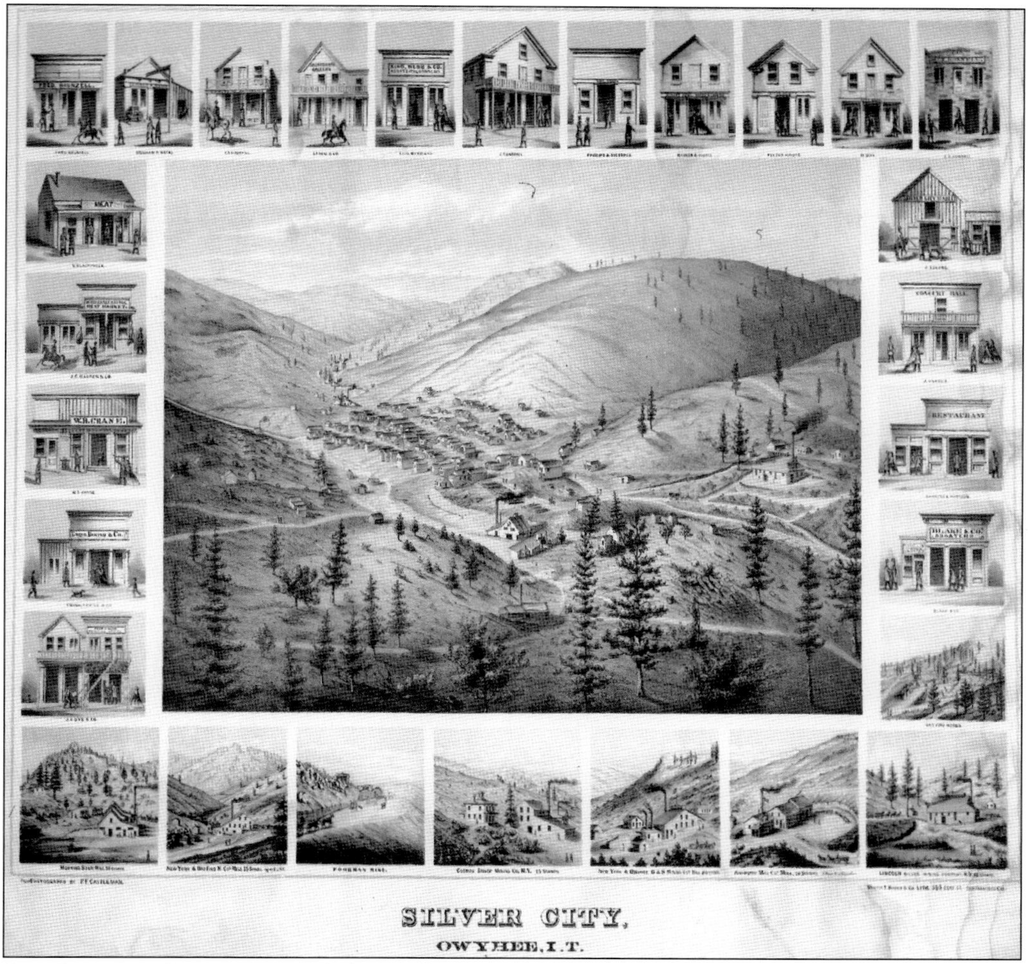

G.T. Brown, a San Francisco lithographer, visited Silver City in 1866 and later produced this lithograph. Local newspaper *Owyhee Avalanche* noted on April 18, 1866, "G.T. Brown, a San Francisco lithographer, is in town collecting the necessary data to make a true map of Silver City, its mills, principle business houses, and general surroundings. We trust that he will be met with proper encouragement as such a map would do much to show outsiders what advancement has been made in this part of Owyhee." Within a few short years, Silver City had grown into a proud and substantial community.

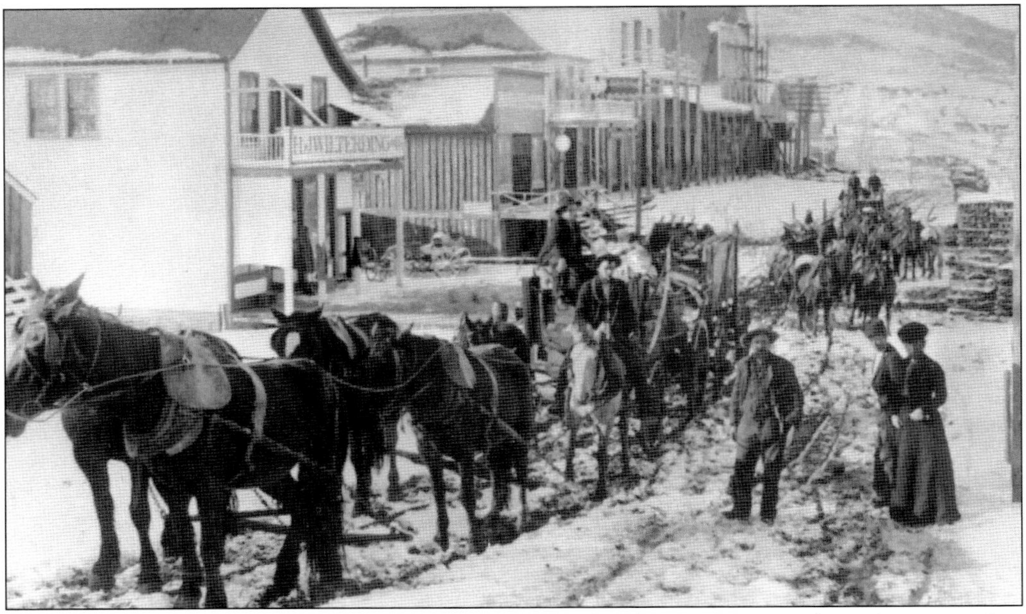

In the beginning, everything came to Silver City by freight. Horse teams brought in supplies and took out ore. Demands of the mines—and a population of more than 2,500—necessitated a constant stream of wagons. Because winter snows made access to the high mountain communities extremely difficult, in the fall pack trains bearing heavy loads were always on the road and large quantities of hay from the Jordan Creek Valley were stored. Homes and businesses were stocked with wood, and merchants stockpiled a winter's supply of goods. The women pictured here are Maggie Jorce Nettleton (left) and Myrtle Shea.

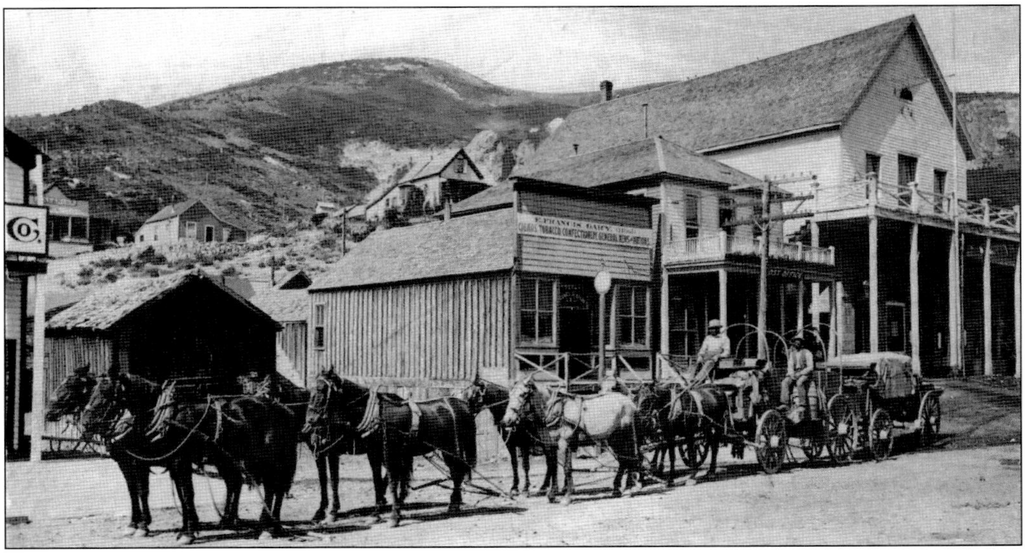

Billy Mills (left) drove freight teams with check lines. The box on the wagon seat contained rocks to throw at horses. On the right is the courthouse, Jack Nelson sits on the trail wagon, and the Avalanche Building is on the hill at left. The *Owyhee Avalanche* reported, "Mr. Streshly brought in sixteen ox teams, loaded with 35,000 pounds of flour and 45,000 pounds of barley. He came through from Susanville, California in thirty odd days. He would willing contract to bring freight through to Owyhee from Chico next season for ten cents per pound."

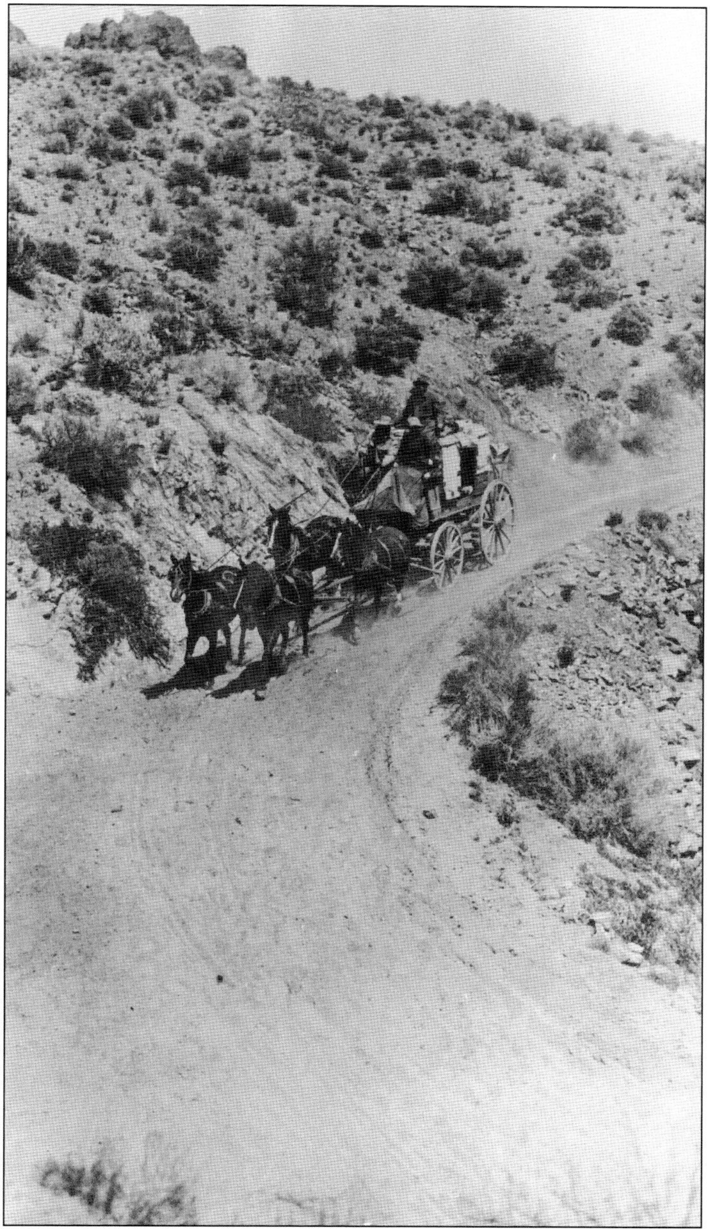

The Silver City stage, pictured here in 1910 topping Whiskey Hill, was one of the last operating stage coaches in the West. Stage travel could be exciting, as one newspaper account details in the 1902 *History of Grant, Baker, Malheur and Harney Counties*: "The Silver City stage, with Nathan Dixon driving, was surrounded by a band of howling Indians near Summit Springs. The stage was loaded to capacity that day with 15 men and one woman. All the men had small arms, and some had rifles. One man had a brace of bulldogs. The savage yells of the Indians struck terror to every man's heart and they fled to the sagebrush for cover. The woman passenger seized a rifle from a frightened male companion and calling the bulldog, jumped from the stage. She rested her rifle on the wagon wheel and began firing. Soon the Indians were routed, and the retreating men came silently forward from their cover. It is said that when they reached Silver City that night they registered at the hotel under assumed names." (Courtesy of the.)

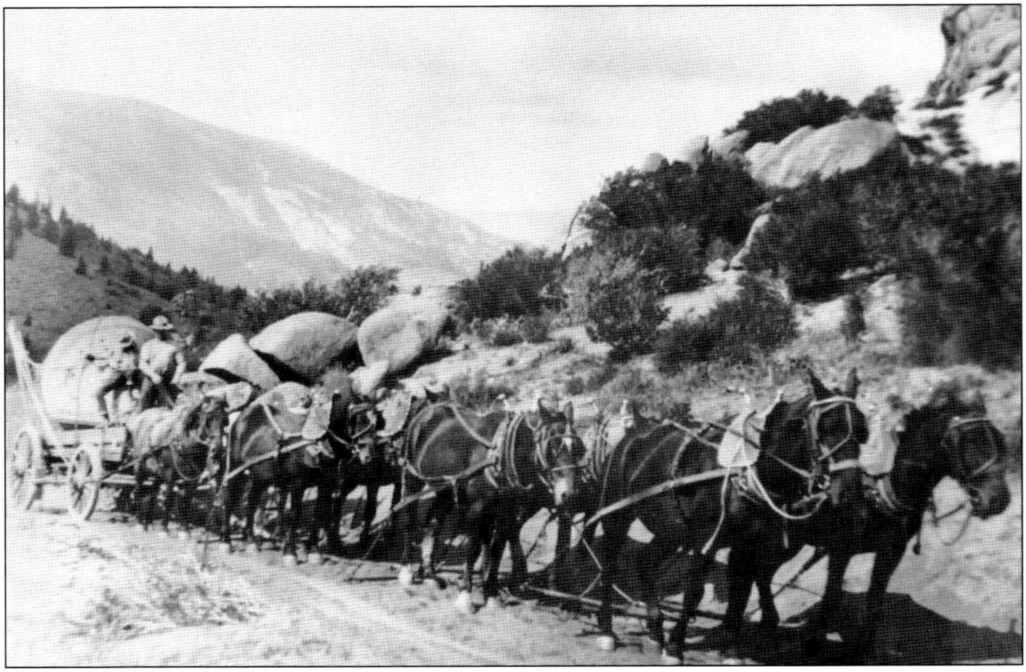

All supplies were laboriously brought in by wagon up the steep trail to War Eagle Mountain. Silver City's remote location was always a logistical challenge, and maintaining adequate roads was a constant struggle. Deep snows required the use of sleds in the winter; an attempt to reach the city with a railroad was never completed. The town's remoteness has been a key factor in its remarkable preservation to this day. It may still be visited by adventurous travelers at the end of 15 miles of dirt road.

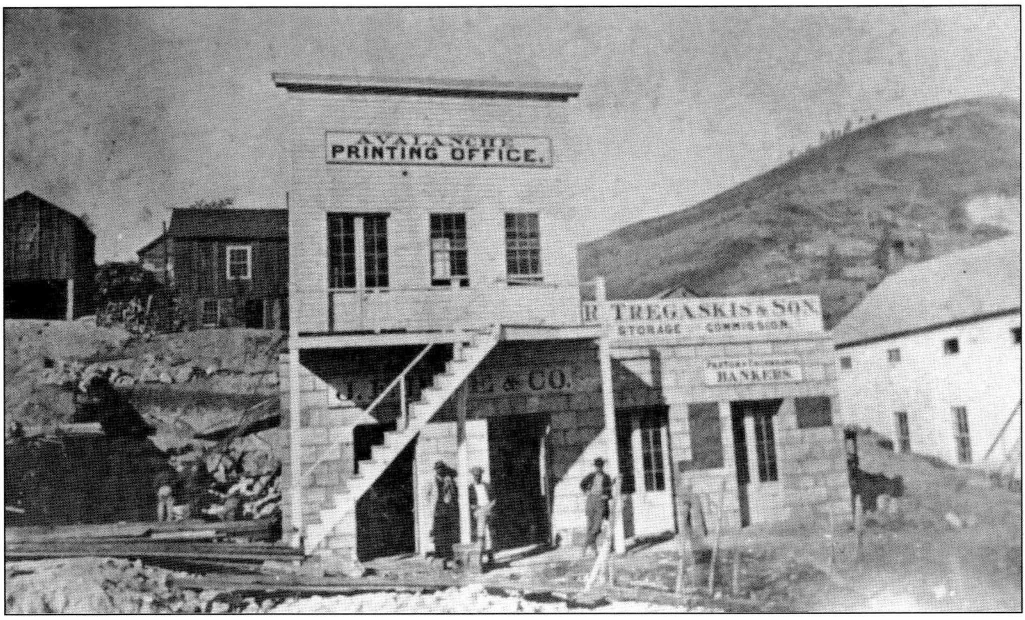

The *Owyhee Avalanche* was an early chronicler of the life and times of Silver City, and it is one of the best sources of information about the community's early years. This photograph shows the newspaper's offices on Washington Street around 1865.

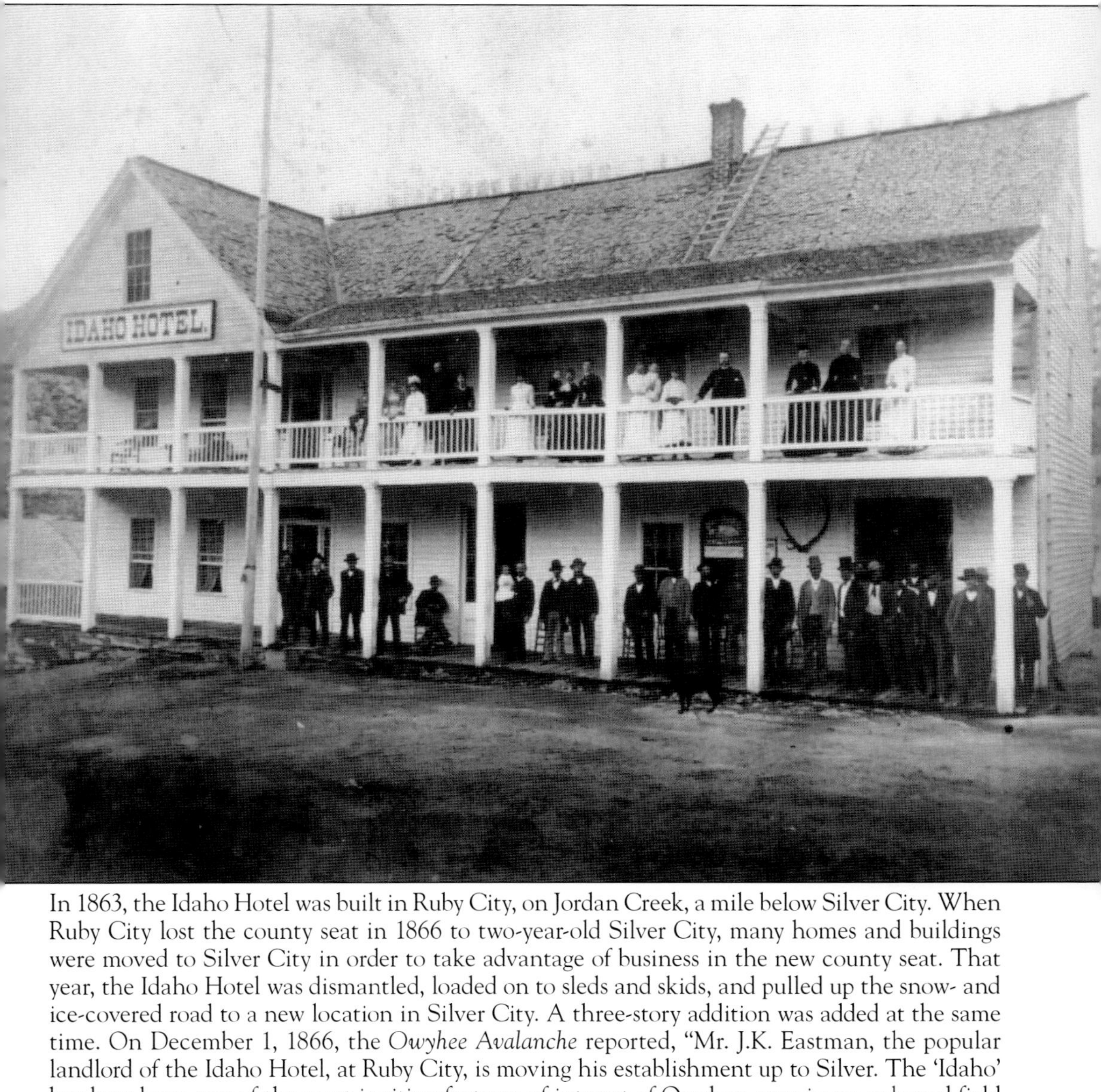

In 1863, the Idaho Hotel was built in Ruby City, on Jordan Creek, a mile below Silver City. When Ruby City lost the county seat in 1866 to two-year-old Silver City, many homes and buildings were moved to Silver City in order to take advantage of business in the new county seat. That year, the Idaho Hotel was dismantled, loaded on to sleds and skids, and pulled up the snow- and ice-covered road to a new location in Silver City. A three-story addition was added at the same time. On December 1, 1866, the *Owyhee Avalanche* reported, "Mr. J.K. Eastman, the popular landlord of the Idaho Hotel, at Ruby City, is moving his establishment up to Silver. The 'Idaho' has long been one of the most inviting features of interest of Owyhee, now in an enlarged field of usefulness, in the way of home comforts to those contemplating a visit to our mines. The new hotel is situated near the banking house of King, Webb and Co. on Jordan Street."

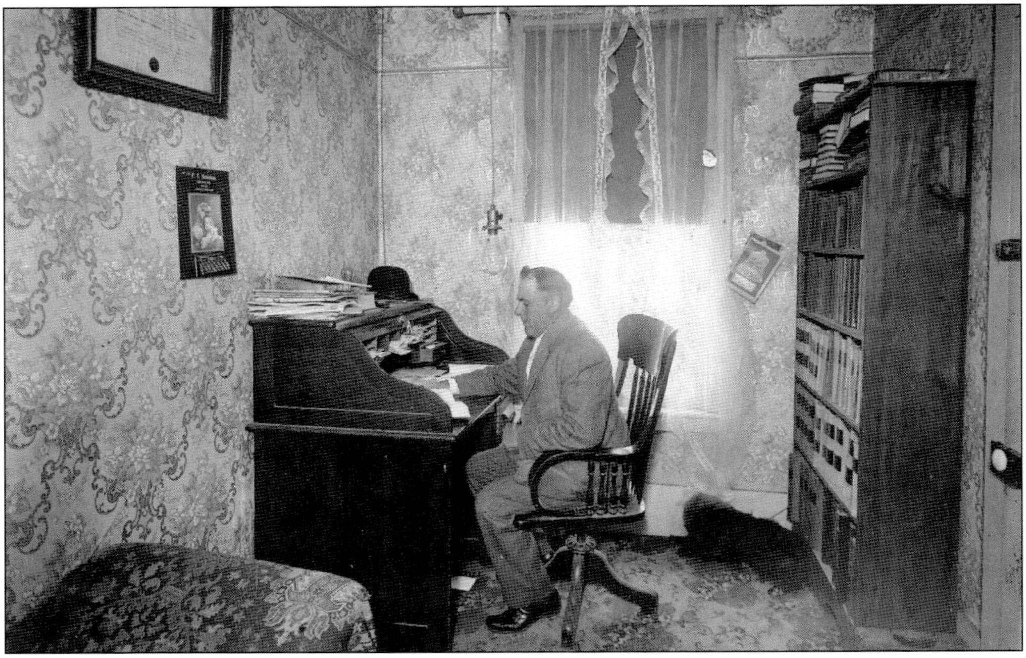

Dr. Hamilton located his office in the hotel annex north of the Idaho Hotel in 1902. There are eight rooms in this building, four on the ground level and four on the top level, which are reached by an extension of the boardwalk from the hotel. This photograph was given to Tom Rack by Dorothy Hamilton Black—daughter of Dr. Hamilton—at Murphy, Idaho, on April 25, 1952.

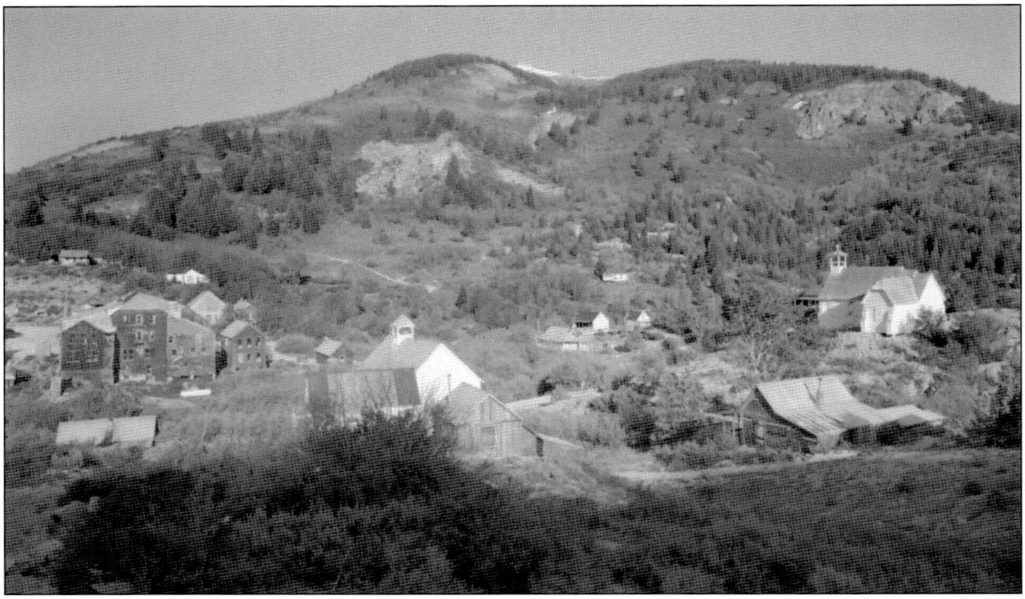

This view of Silver City shows Florida Mountain in background. This is a relatively recent photograph, as the area has reforested itself after being essentially denuded during the peak of the mining era in the 1800s. As the *Owyhee Avalanche* cheerfully noted in 1865, "Timber for fuel, building and mining purposes is plenty and close at hand in Owyhee County now, and will be for ten years to come." Unfortunately, those 10 years did come, and then some, and nearby forests completely disappeared. (Courtesy of the Library of Congress.)

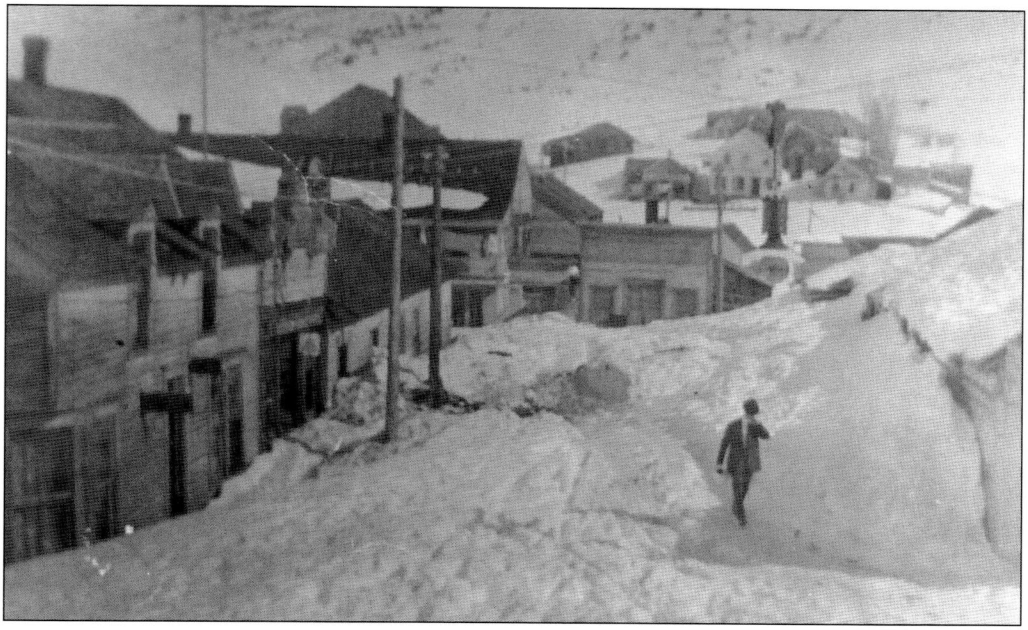

Heavy snows were part of winter life in Silver City, as evidenced by this 1911 photograph. Winter caused sanitation problems, as trash and other filth accumulated near buildings. Each spring, the county health office placed a notice in the local newspaper instructing property owners to clean up their premises. Garbage was to be picked up, privies cleaned out, and the contents thrown into Jordan Creek while the water was high.

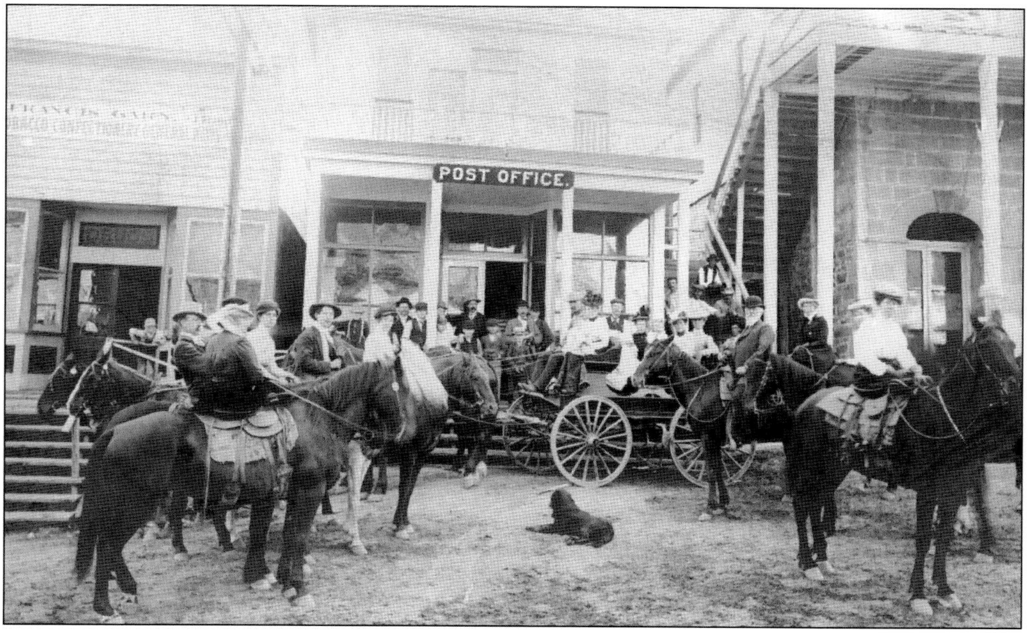

The Silver City Post Office in the center of town was a popular gathering place. A post office for Silver City was approved on February 5, 1867. William Clemens moved the post office from Ruby City to Silver City on May 16, locating it (along with his book and confectionery store) on Washington Street. David Willman became postmaster in 1868, and when Idaho gained statehood in 1890, Richard Euler was serving as postmaster.

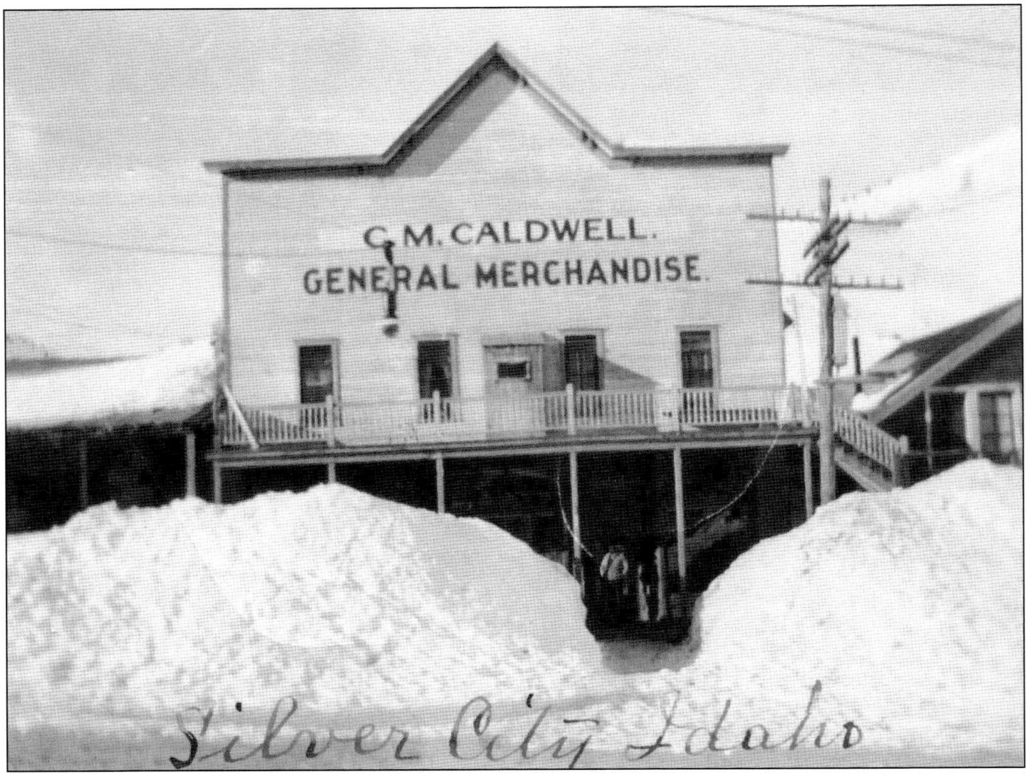

The C.M. Caldwell General Merchandise store prospered in Silver City. Charlie Caldwell operated his store in four different locations. The first was in the old city drugstore building. Caught in the path of a fire sweeping up the block on the east side of Washington Street in December 1908, it was dynamited to prevent the fire from spreading further. Caldwell moved into the Golden Rule Store building next to Long Gulch, then later purchased the "Big Store" in the Granite Block.

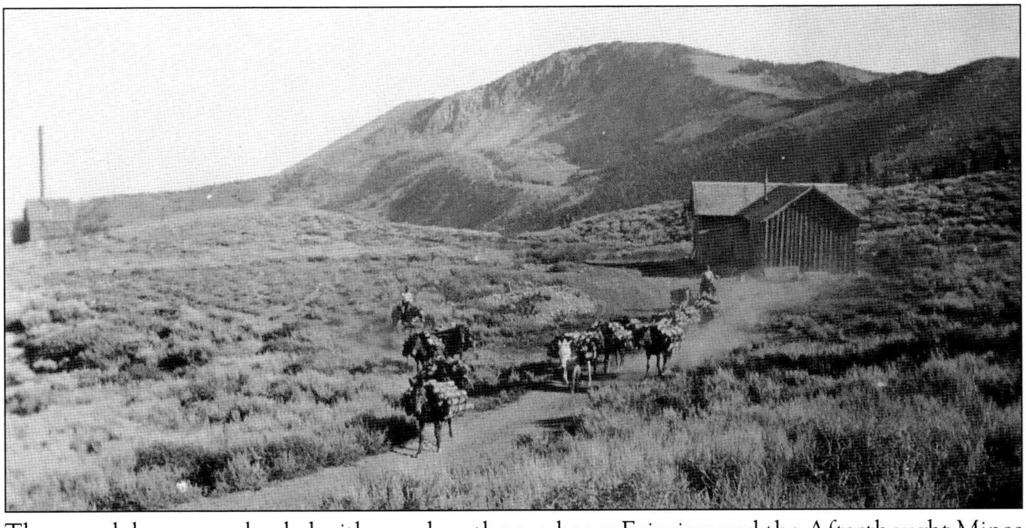

These pack burros are loaded with wood on the road near Fairview and the Afterthought Mines with Quicksilver Mountain looming in the background. Seven burros were required to pack a single cord of mahogany wood, which went for $3. Tremendous quantities of wood needed to be cut, transported, and stored in order for the fuel needs of the long, snowbound winters to be met.

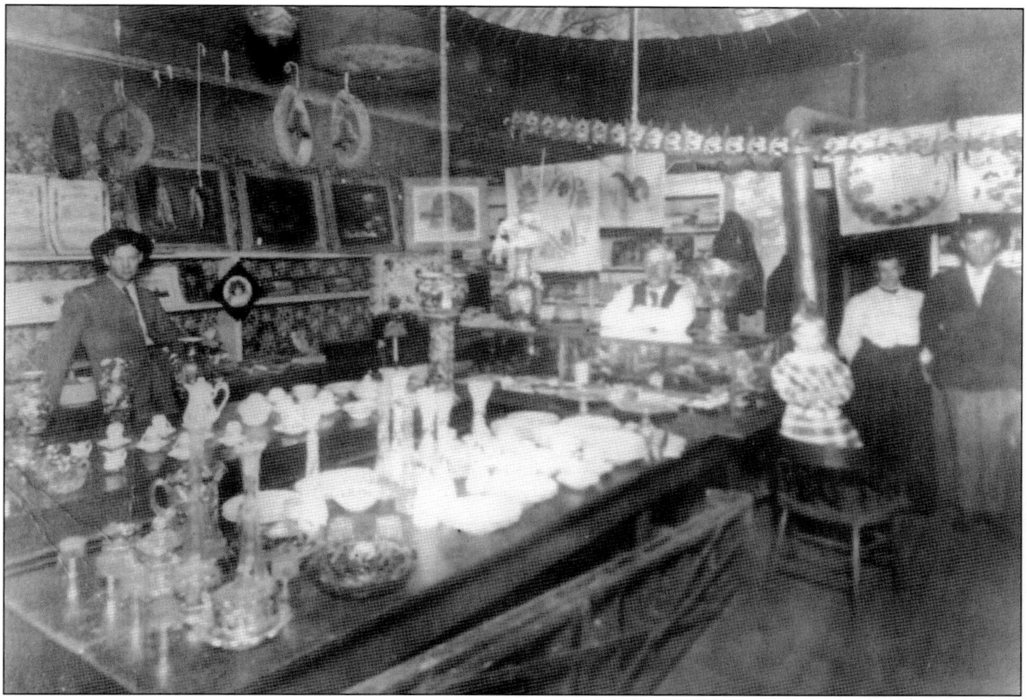

Pictured here is the Silver City General Store sometime before 1908, when Charlie Caldwell's general store was destroyed in a disastrous fire on December 29. The store was dynamited in an effort to prevent the fire from spreading even farther into the town. The buildings on Washington Street were mostly of flammable frame construction and either attached to each other or so close as to have the same effect in a fire.

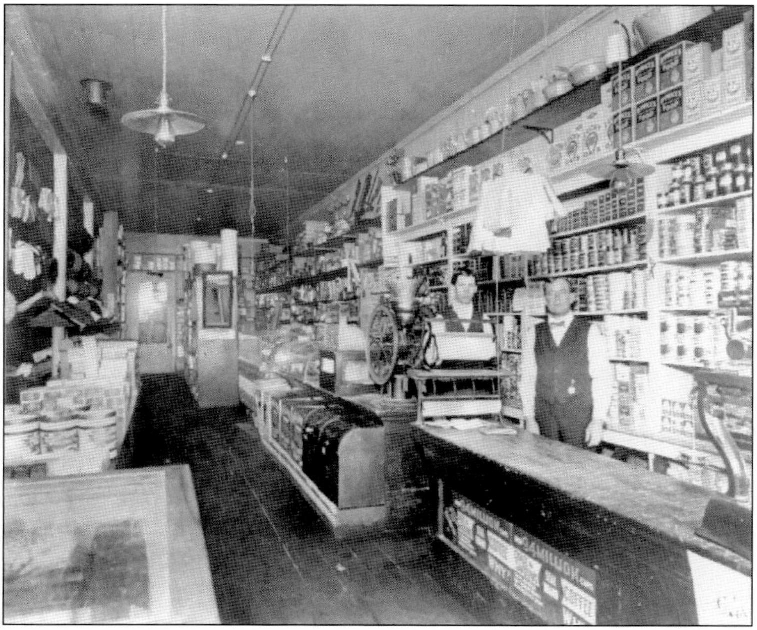

For many years, Charlie Grete and his family ran a general store in Silver City. Pictured here are clerks Charles Grete (right) and Ernest Ronett. Members of the Grete family were prominent local businessmen from the town's founding. Frederick Grete Sr. and his brother John Grete Sr. moved to the United States in the 1800s, marrying women from New York before coming to Silver City around 1863.

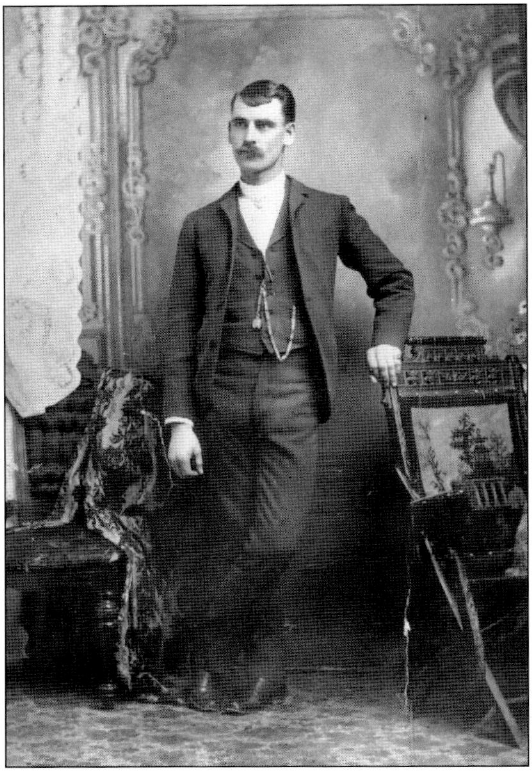

Fred Grete Jr., at left, was a leading Silver City businessman of the prominent Grete family. He married Charlotte Townsend, whose mother, Nellie, had come to the United States from Ireland. The pair had four daughters: Gwen in 1900, Edna in 1893, and then Nelle and Alta. "Grandpa though, all he wanted to do was mine," his granddaughter Pat Hinton recalled. The Gretes also ran a bakery. On March 1, 1890, the *Owyhee Avalanche* published a notice of the wedding of Minnie Grete to Dr. J.N. Weston at the Masonic hall: "The groom is a worthy young physician who is attaining an enviable reputation by reason of his knowledge of medicine. The bride is known to all our citizens as one of the loveliest and most charming young daughters of the estimable couple, Mr. and Mrs. John Grete." Below is the Silver City home of Fred Grete Jr.

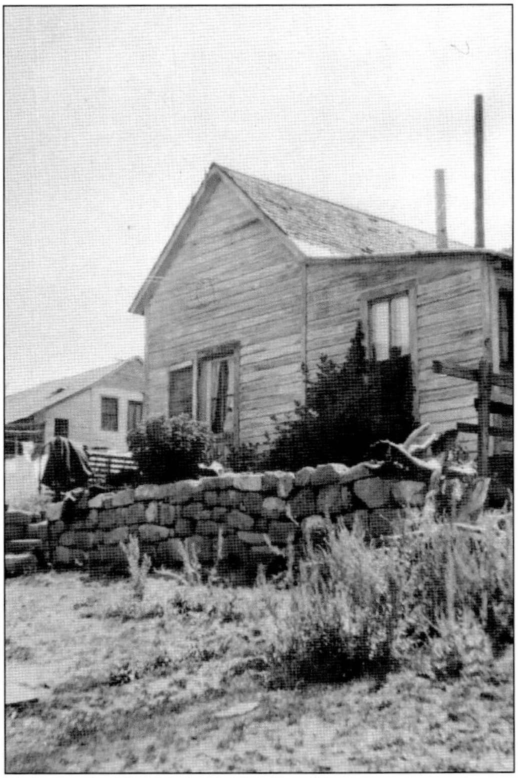

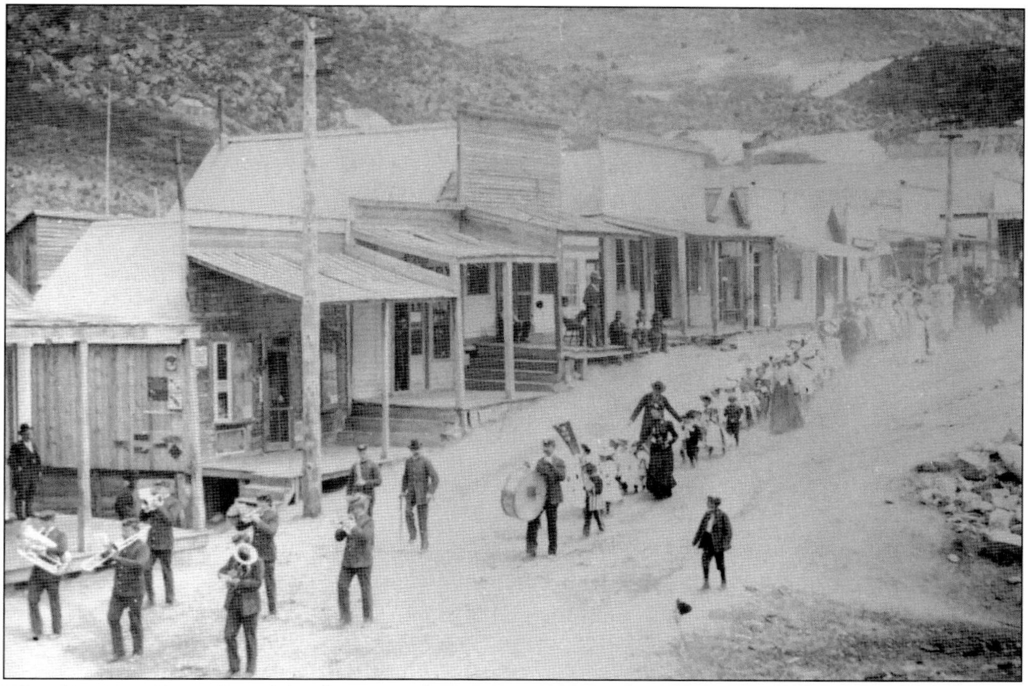

The Owyhee Brass Band leads a parade down Washington Street. According to the *Owyhee Avalanche*, on November 10, 1866, "The outside world may not be aware that Owyhee has an organized brass band of twelve or more instruments." The Owyhee Brass Band was organized May 12, 1866, and enlivened Silver City with its music, often performing from the balcony on the corner of Washington and Second Streets.

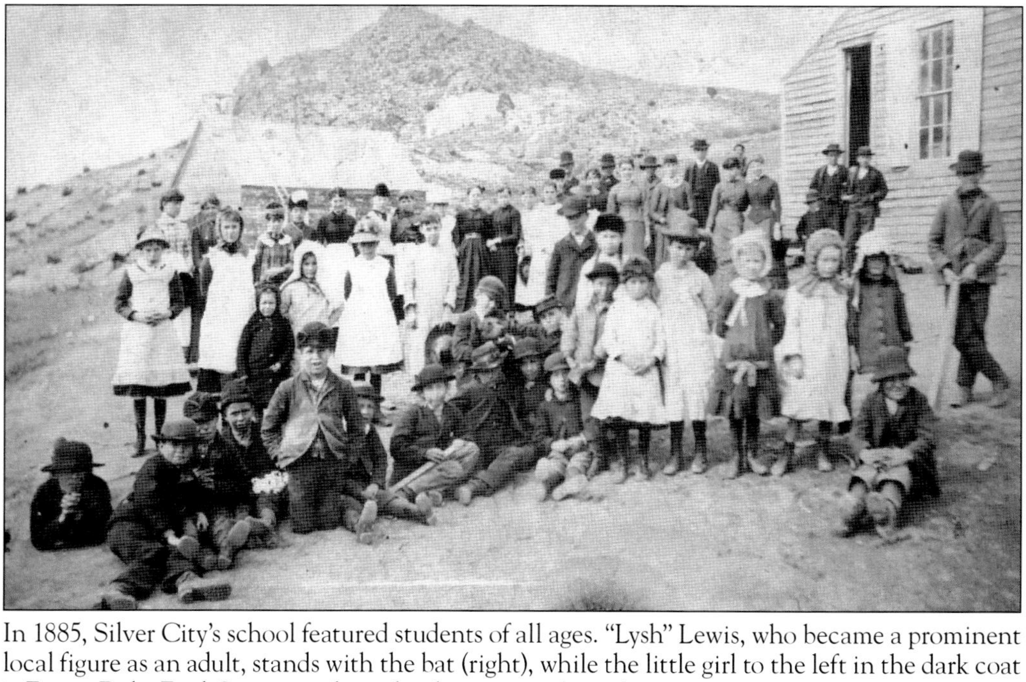

In 1885, Silver City's school featured students of all ages. "Lysh" Lewis, who became a prominent local figure as an adult, stands with the bat (right), while the little girl to the left in the dark coat is Fanny Daly. Fred Grete stands in the doorway at the right.

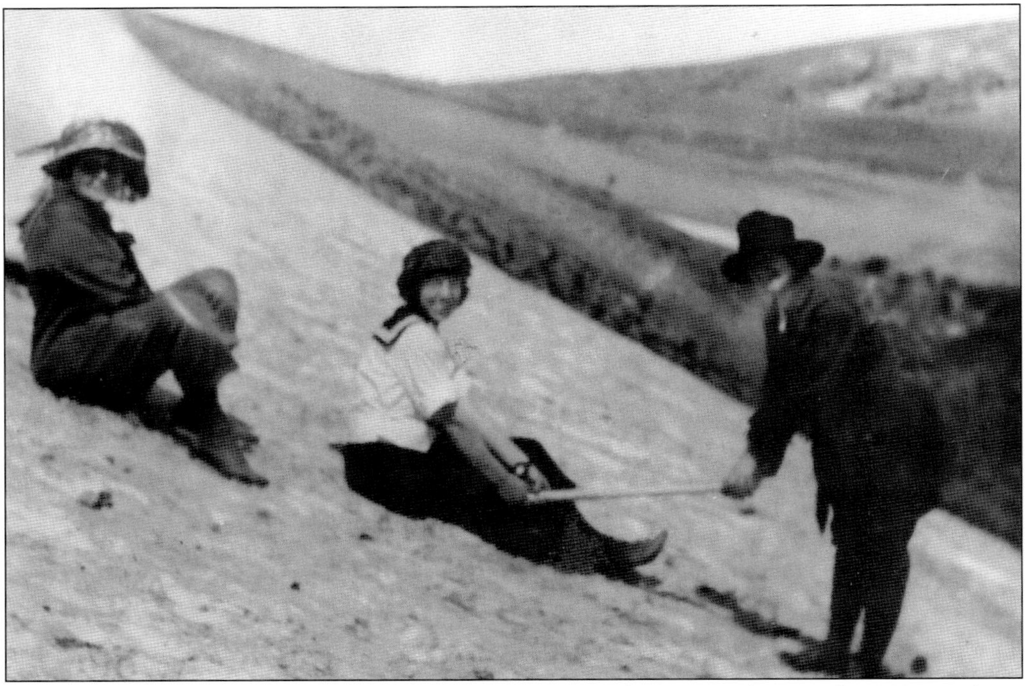

Snow was a prominent feature for much of the year in Silver City. These early-1900s residents appear to be enjoying a slide. A 10-foot-deep accumulation of snow during winter was not unusual, and homes and businesses were often equipped to offer access from second-floor doorways and stairways. Supplies, food, firewood, and medicine—essentially every need—had to be stocked up and stored away to last through the winter. The town and its residents had to fend for themselves during the winter with no expectation of outside help.

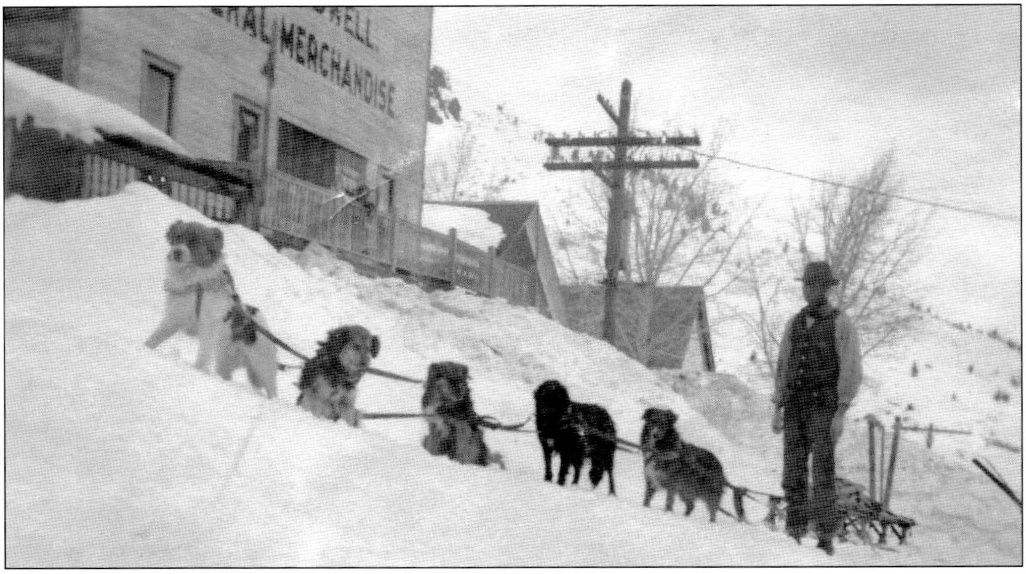

Snow was also an obstacle, as roads were regularly impassable during the winter months and often much of the fall and spring as well. Sled dogs delivered the mail. Today, there is no winter access to Silver City, although local property owners often arrange for a caretaker to spend a lonely and isolated winter keeping an eye on the area.

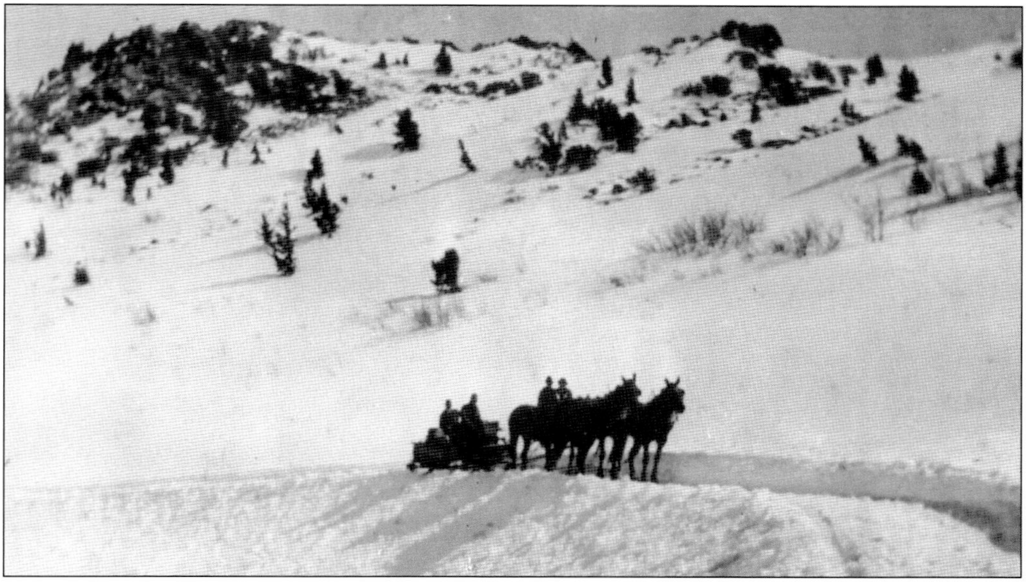

During the winter and spring, if roads were passable at all, it was usually by sleigh. The sleigh in this photograph is on the road to Silver City in the spring of 1927 at the Cottonwood turn near the New York Summit.

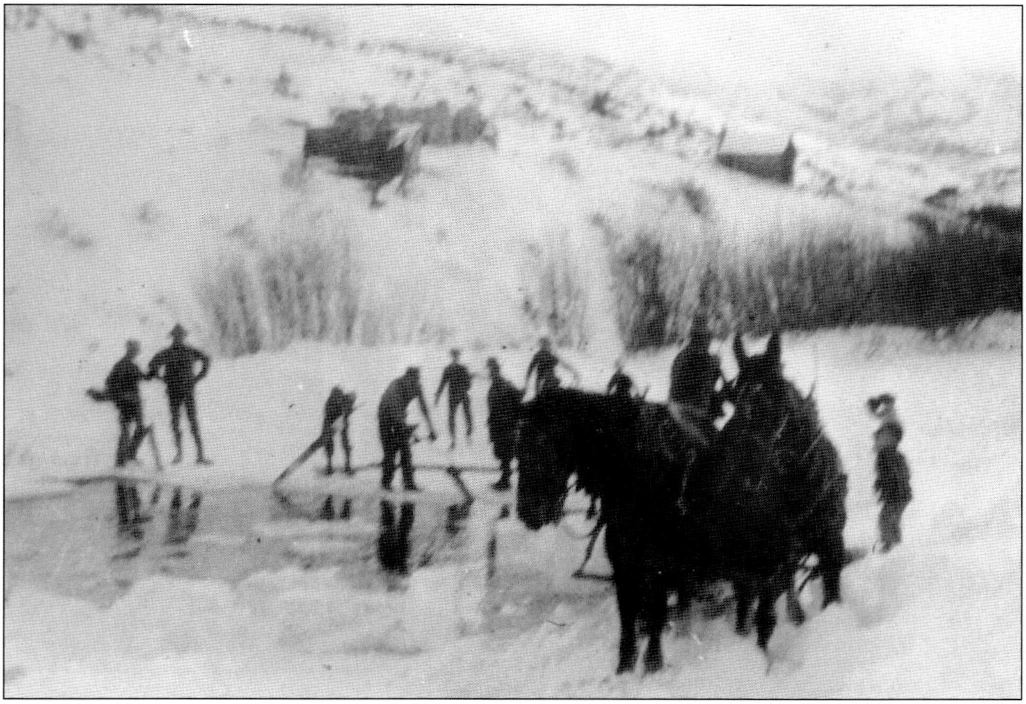

There were two dams above Silver City, on Jordan Creek, used for milling purposes and also as ice ponds in the winter. All of the saloons, hotels, restaurants, and butcher shops had icehouses that were filled each winter. The October 3, 1868, *Owyhee Avalanche* reported, "George Gans & Co. are making preparations to put up an unlimited amount of ice this winter. We also learn that John Cassady is preparing to put up a large quantity for his own use next summer." The ice was cut into 14-inch square blocks and packed in sawdust.

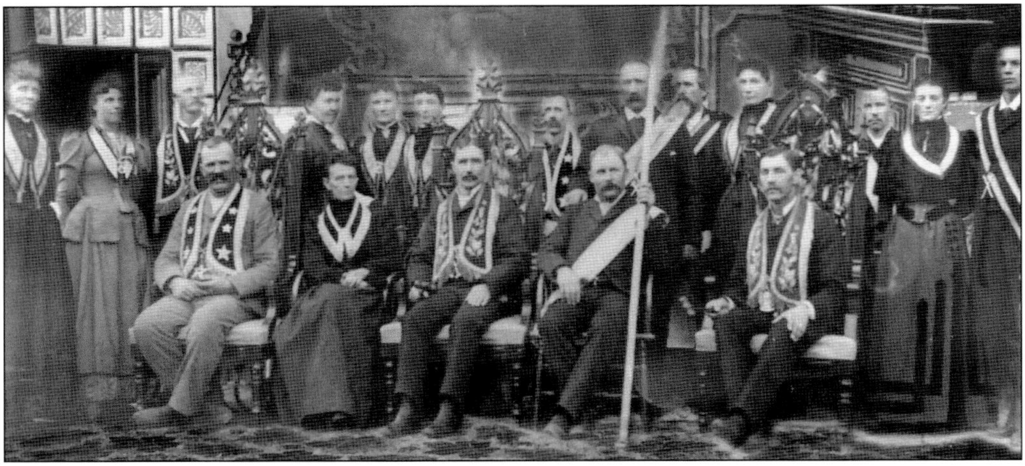

In 1865, a Masonic lodge was formed in Silver City. A large Masonic hall, one of the oldest in Idaho, spans Jordan Creek in Silver City, and the Masons still hold meetings there during the summer. For most of the city's history, the hall was a social gathering place and the scene of many a lively dance. The city also featured a cemetery for Masons. J. Marion More, a Mason and owner of the Ida-Elmore Mine, was murdered in the street in front of the Idaho Hotel during the War under the Mountain in 1866. A committee of Masons took his body to Idaho City for burial, and an oil painting of him hangs in the Idaho City Masonic Lodge to this day.

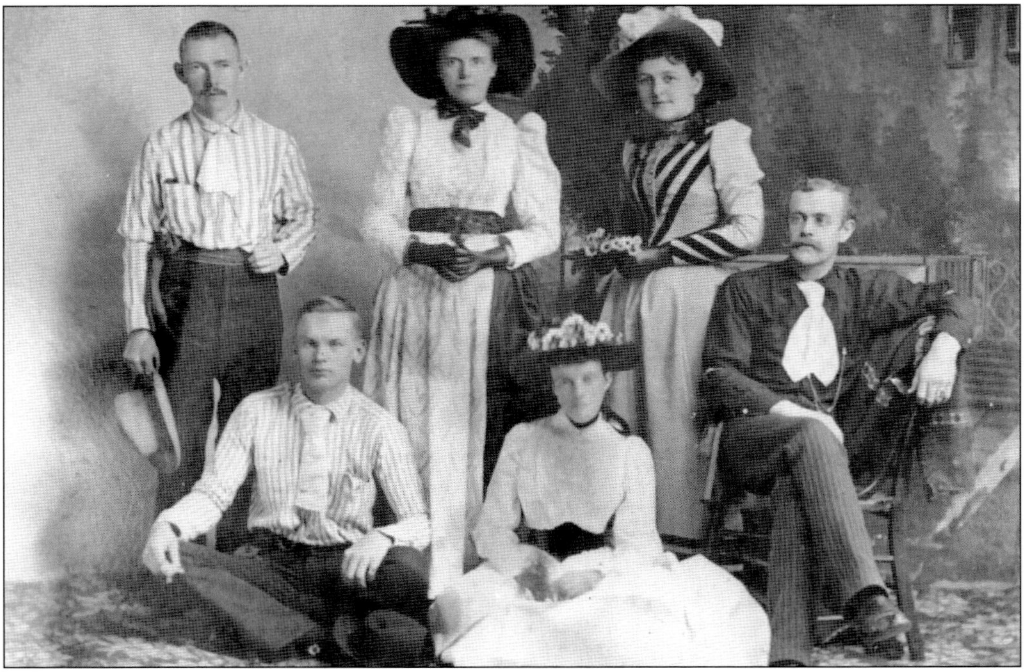

These Silver City residents are posing for a formal photograph. Pictured from left to right are (first row) Meserve Getchell and Maude Hays; (second row) Lem York, Lottie Townsend (Grete), May Stucker, and Charlie Grete. About this time, Silver City was on the decline, and local residents were sensitive about their diminishing importance relative to nearby cities such as Nampa and Boise. On April 7, 1904, the *Owyhee Avalanche* felt compelled to point out that "Boise, the Capital City, and Nampa would hardly be on the map, let alone be the progressive cities that they are, had not the mines of Silver City furnished the motive power for their construction."

Three

The Lost Towns

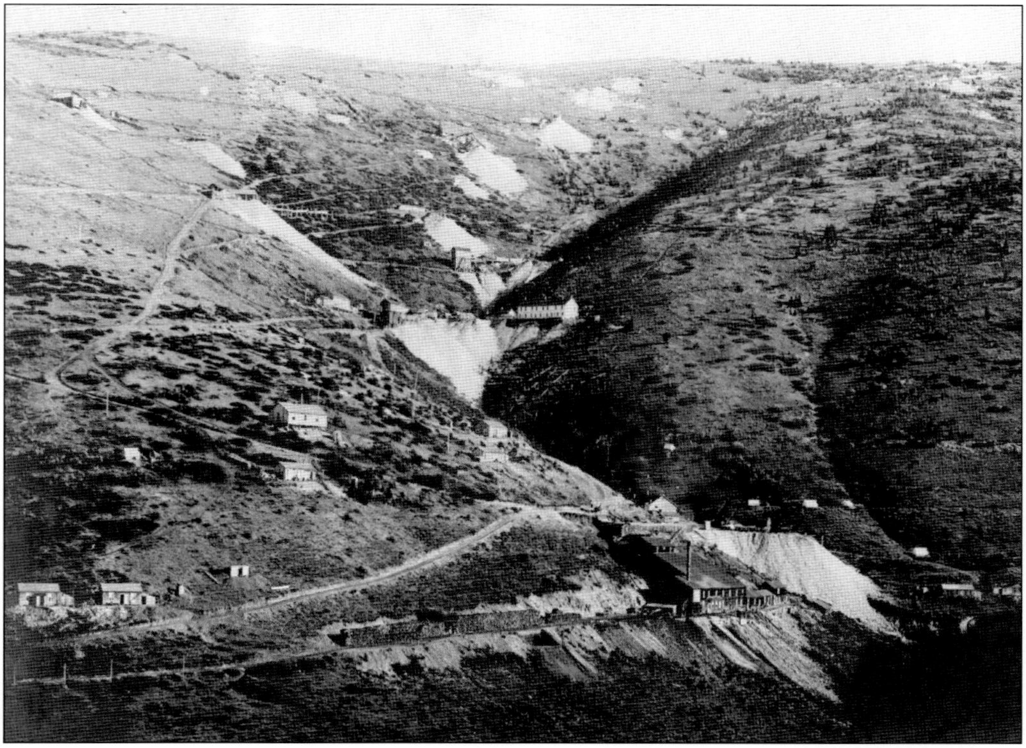

Mining towns of the 1800s sprang up where the gold was—in the rough terrain of the Owyhee Mountains. This photograph shows Blue Gulch of War Eagle Mountain. When the gold and silver ran dry, the people left and the towns died. Today, one can walk through the valleys and draws of the mountains and never guess that thriving communities once covered the landscape. The towns of DeLamar and Dewey (pictured) were the most prominent. Dewey was built five miles, and DeLamar nine miles, down Jordan Creek from War Eagle Mountain.

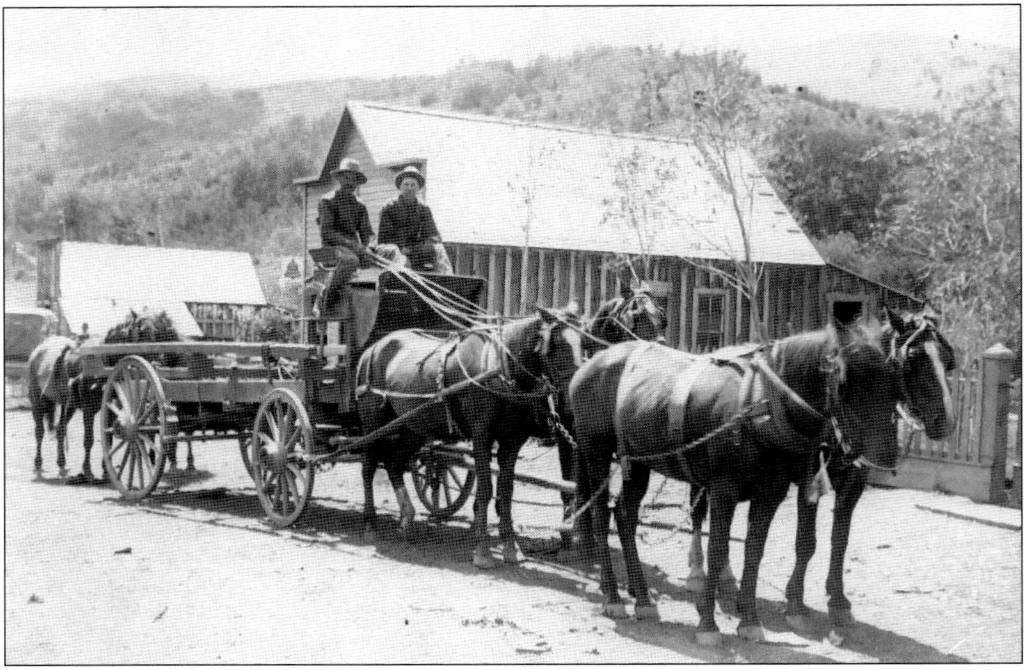

Freight brought virtually everything to DeLamar, which began its growth in 1889 with the start of Charles Knapp's residence and a boardinghouse, spurred by construction of a new ore mill. A telephone line had been completed by July 1889, and electricity followed soon. By the summer of 1890, M.B. Gwinn's mercantile house, several saloons, a barbershop, and a drugstore were added. By 1895, average daily attendance at the town's brick schoolhouse (donated by Captain DeLamar) was 65 students.

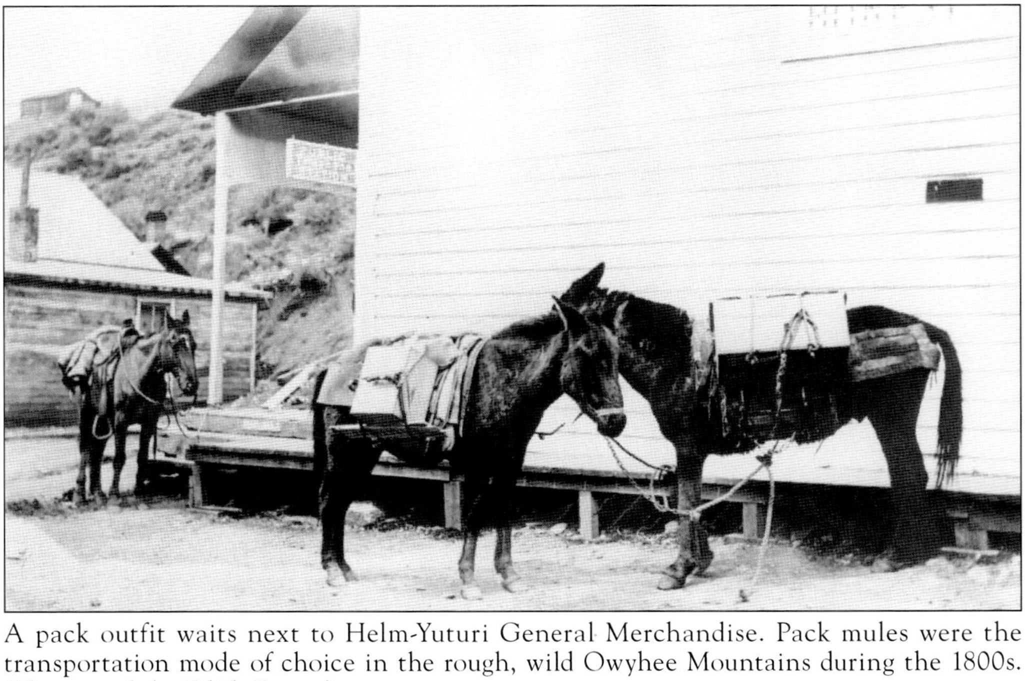

A pack outfit waits next to Helm-Yuturi General Merchandise. Pack mules were the transportation mode of choice in the rough, wild Owyhee Mountains during the 1800s. (Photograph by Edith Farrer.)

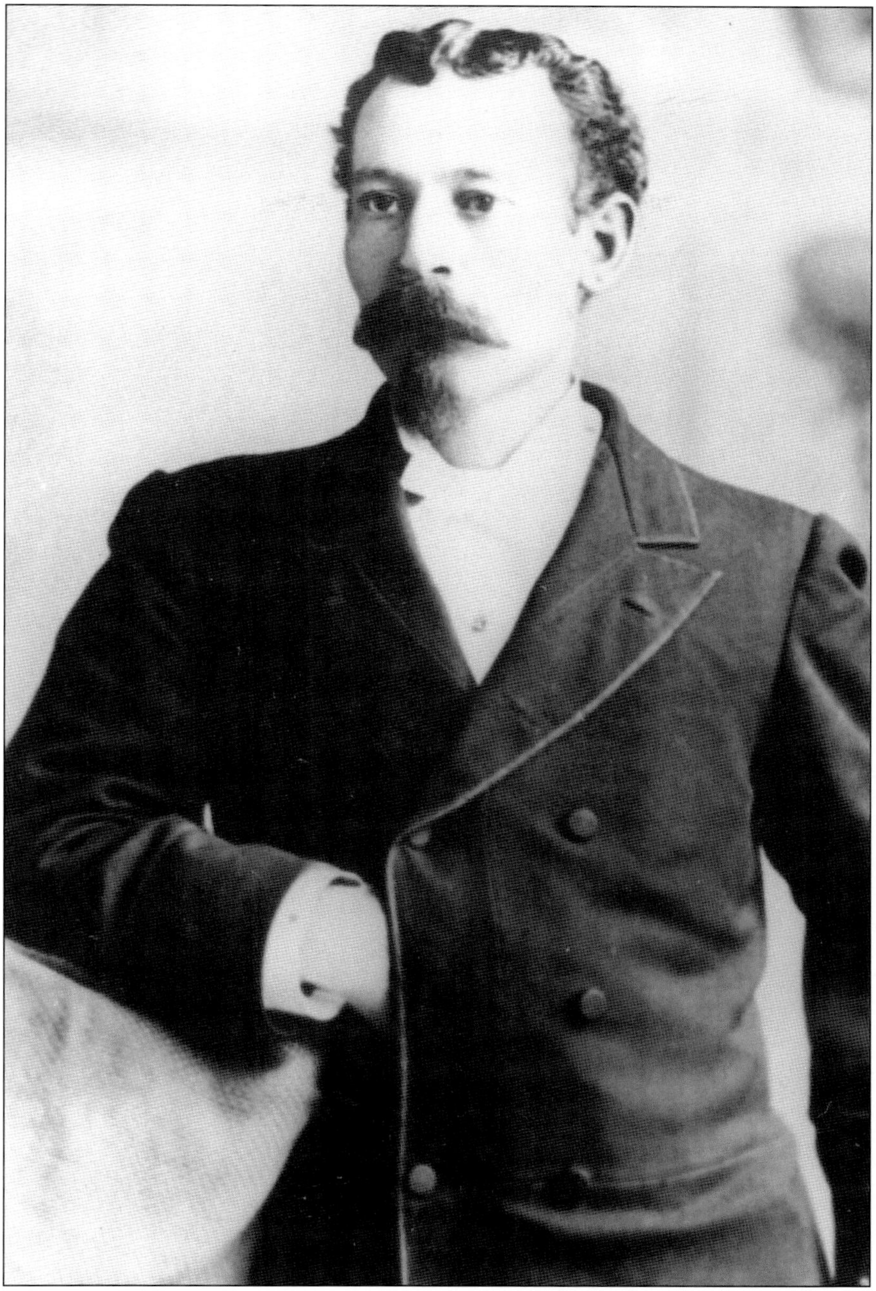

Known as the "Monte Cristo of Idaho," Capt. Joseph Rafael DeLamar founded the mining town of DeLamar in 1886. He was born in Holland in 1843 and began a successful sea career by stowing away as a young boy on a Dutch ship bound for the West Indies. He entered the salvage business and was a boat captain by 23. He became incredibly rich in the mining industry. Three former mining cities were named after him: DeLamar, Nevada, DeLamar, Idaho, and DeLamar, California (the latter is now under the waters of Shasta Lake). He served as a state senator in Idaho's first legislature. He later moved to New York, where he was known on Wall Street as the "man of mystery." His New York mansion was thought to be one of the inspirations for Jay Gatsby's amazing abode in *The Great Gatsby*.

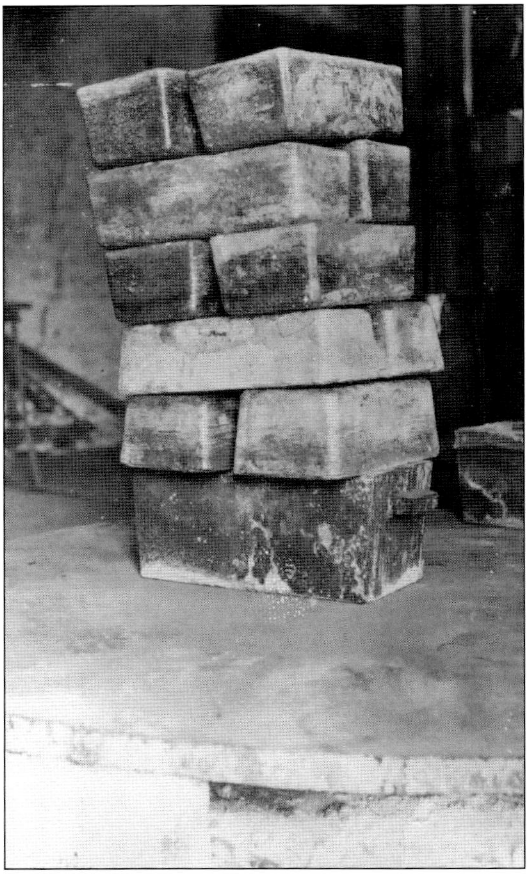

Silver bullion flowed from the DeLamar mines, which produced millions of dollars worth of gold and silver before their closure in 1913, after which the town quickly faded. DeLamar's miners worked 10 hours a day, six days a week. They were given half a day off on payday, which fell on the 10th day of each month. (Photograph by Edith Farrer.)

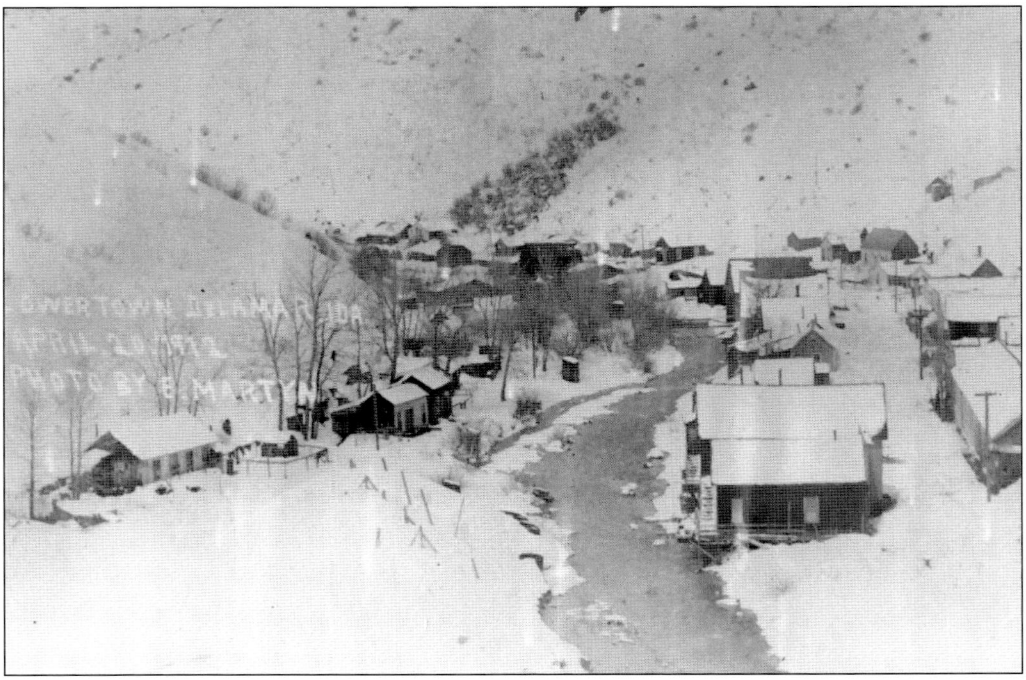

This photograph shows DeLamar below Silver City on Jordan Creek. A sharp end in the creek separated Upper Town from Lower, or "Tough Town," and was known as the Point. Most of DeLamar's 13 saloons were in Tough Town. When DeLamar was booming, Jennie Mitchell brought her girls from Hailey, Idaho, to set up one of the more popular houses of ill repute in Tough Town. One of her most popular girls was "Long-Toed Liz." The July 13, 1913, *Owyhee Avalanche* ran an obituary for Jennie Mitchell, stating that she was "a well-known character of the underworld, who died in DeLamar on July 10." After Mitchell's death, Long-Toed Liz moved to Silver City, where she eventually committed suicide.

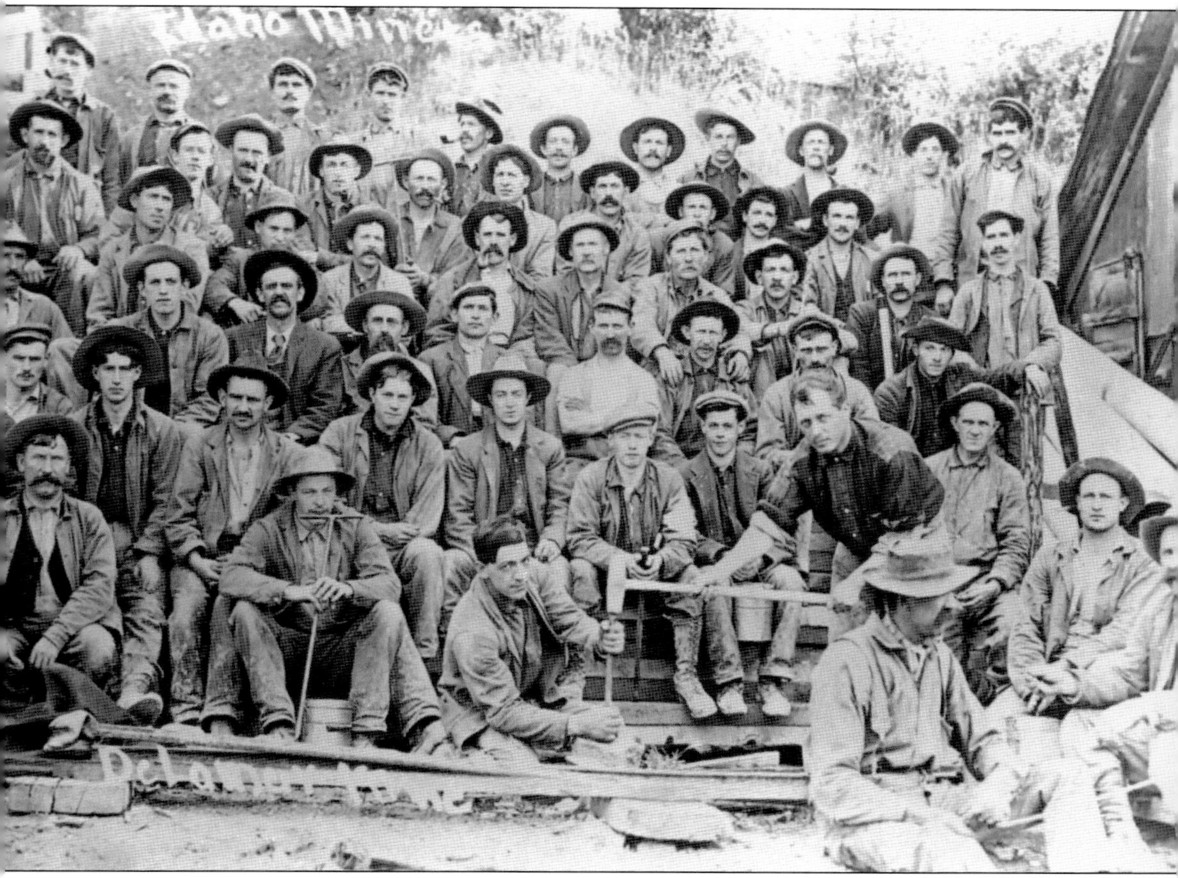

According to the 1894 *DeLamar Nugget*, "The DeLamar Mines are situated on a mountain rising little more than 1,000 feet above the creek level, where the town and mill are located. The value of the production from the DeLamar Mining Company's ground is about one million dollars per year. The ores of this district predominate in gold, containing 60 percent in gold and 40 percent in silver."

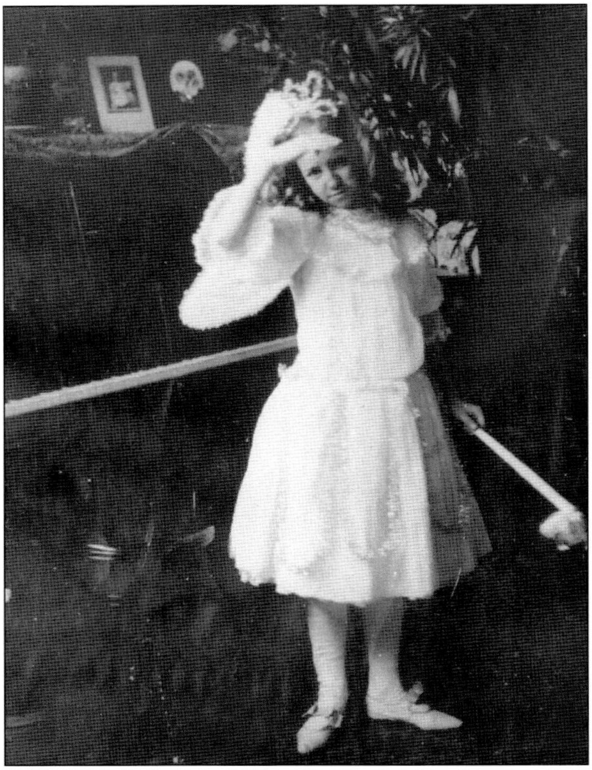

These photographs show two young girls from DeLamar. Captain DeLamar had a brick schoolhouse build on the south side of town. Average daily attendance in 1895 was 65 pupils. In 1915, as DeLamar declined, the school bell was removed from the school's belfry and taken by wagon by Don McDonnell to nearby Jordan Valley, where it was installed in the new Catholic church. (Both courtesy of the Alida Brunzell Lawson Bird collection.)

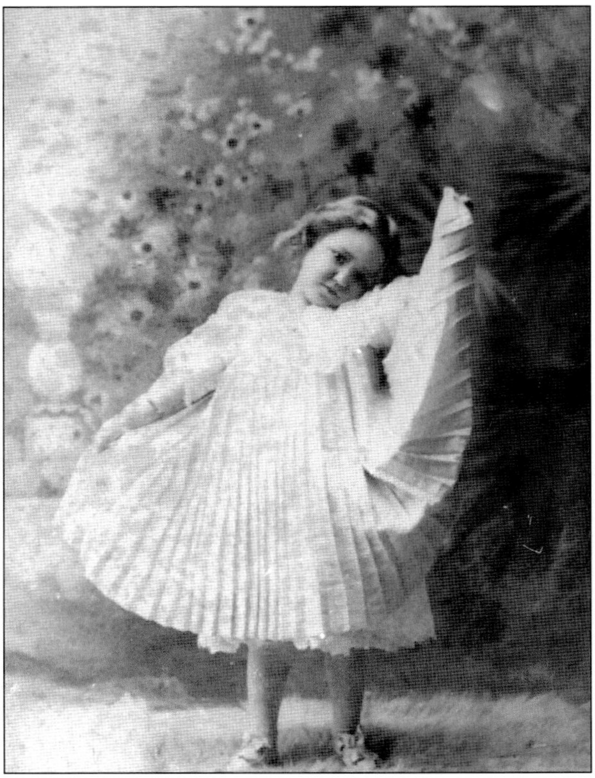

This photograph by Edith Farrer captures DeLamar children amusing themselves on a porch. The May 1891 *DeLamar Nugget* described the community, "DeLamar now has some of the best mines in the state, a fine brick schoolhouse, a good water works system and fire protection, a large general merchandise store, two drug stores, fruit and news stands, two livery stables, a meat market, a barber shop, five saloons, telephone connection to Silver City, Nampa and Boise and all immediate points, a dentist, two restaurants, a fine large hotel, two doctors, fine residences, a boot and shoe shop, two blacksmith shops, a deer park, a large mill working night and day on rich ore, about 300 industrious and enterprising inhabitants. All the symptoms of making a booming mining camp."

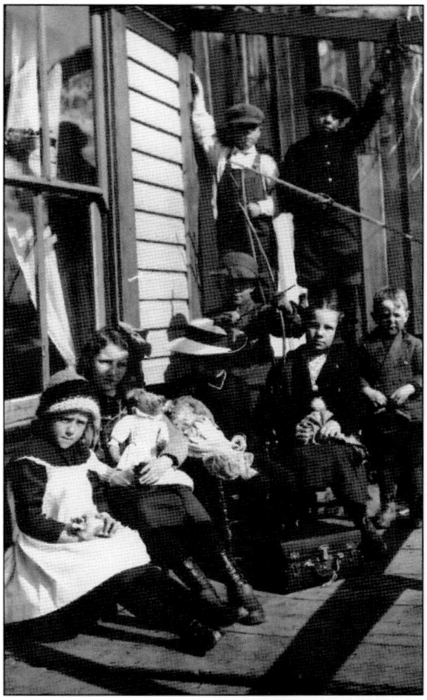

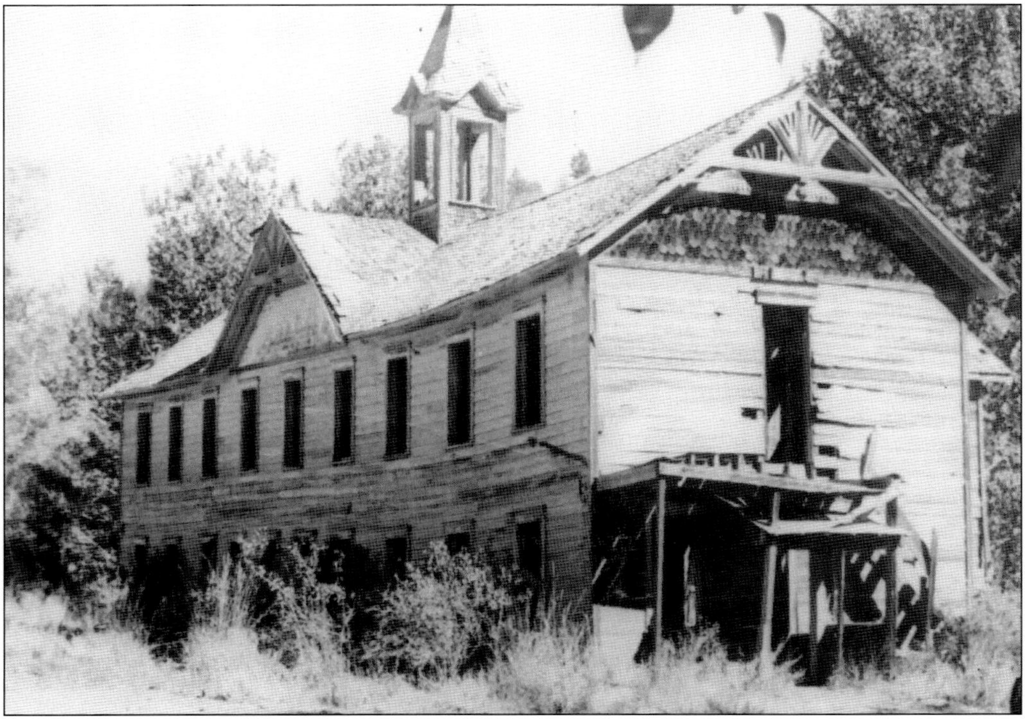

The DeLamar Hotel Annex, across the street from the site of the DeLamar Hotel, was built as dormitory-style housing for miners at a lower cost than the individual rooms of the hotel itself. The square cupola centered on the intersection of the roof gables and served as a skylight for the second-floor hallway. This photograph was obviously taken in the town's declining years, and the annex burned in the 1970s.

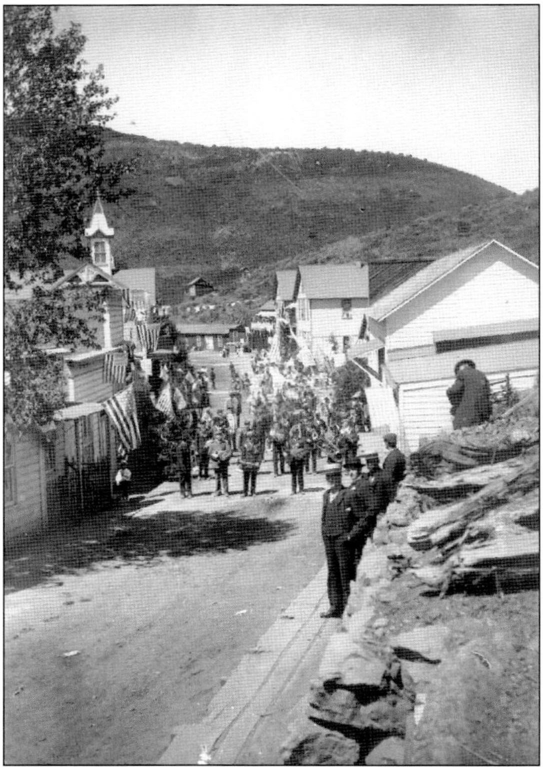

These two photographs show a Fourth of July parade in DeLamar during its heyday in the late 19th century. The hardworking mining communities seized every opportunity to let off steam and enjoy time away from the mines. Celebrations often included races, ball games, and competition among the miners that demonstrated their various skills, especially hand drilling. A surprising number of the mountain mining towns proudly featured their own brass bands. DeLamar's band was rated the best in southeastern Idaho in the 1890s.

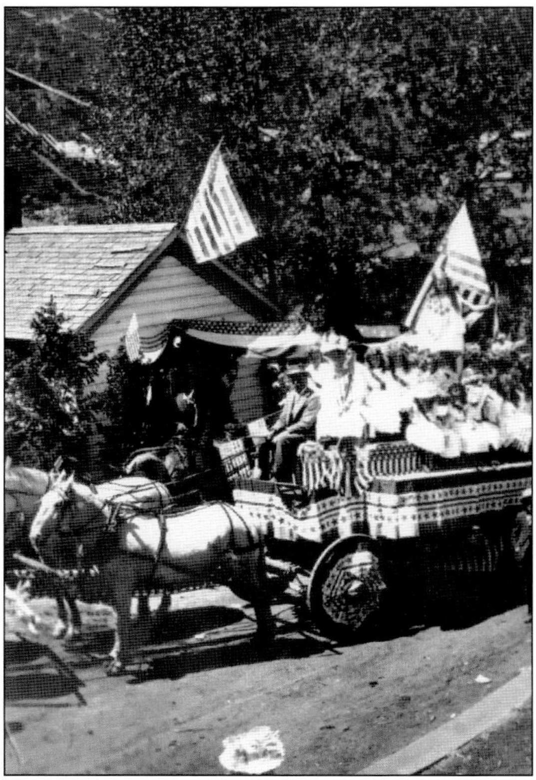

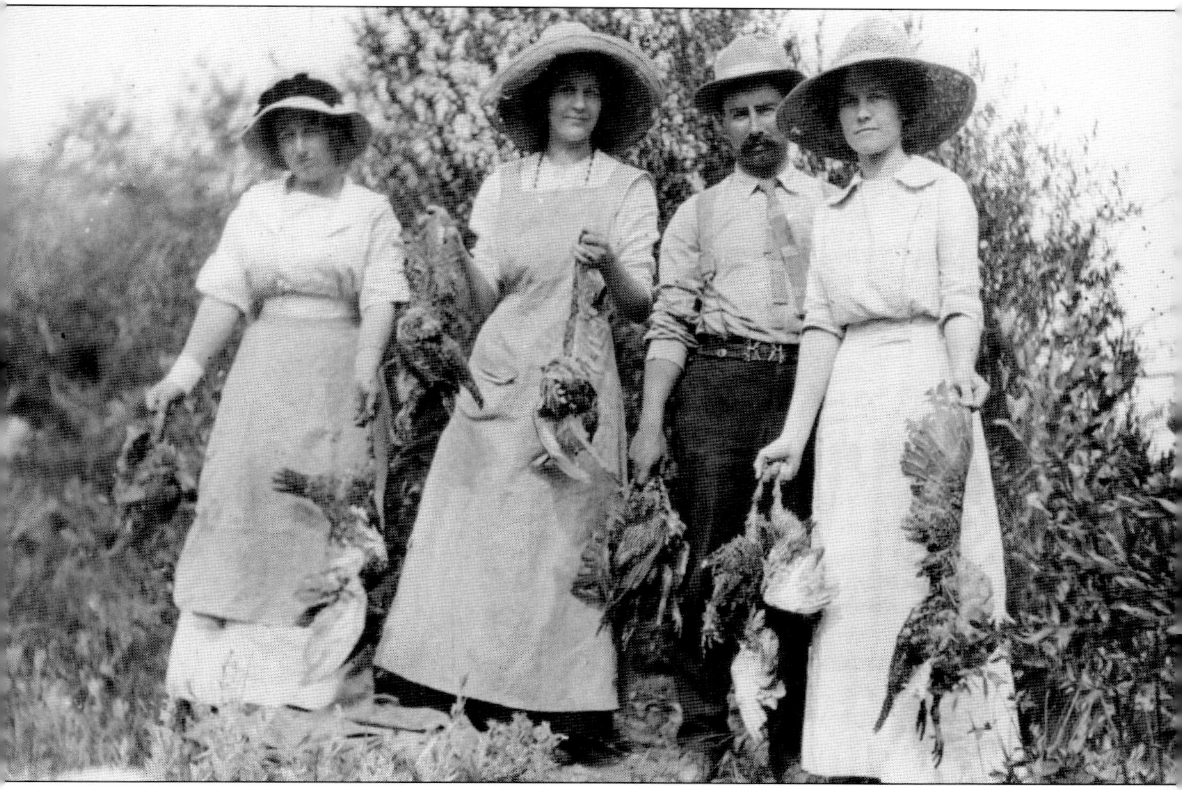

DeLamar citizens proudly display sage hens from a local hunting expedition. Game was plentiful in the high desert and mountains. Before the arrival of the white man, the area was a frequent hunting ground of Native Americans, who visited to hunt but preferred to live in the valley regions to the north and east. Pictured here are, from left to right, Dorothy Oxford, Beth Bergh, Colin Oxford, and Charlotte Bergh. (Photograph by Edith Farrer.)

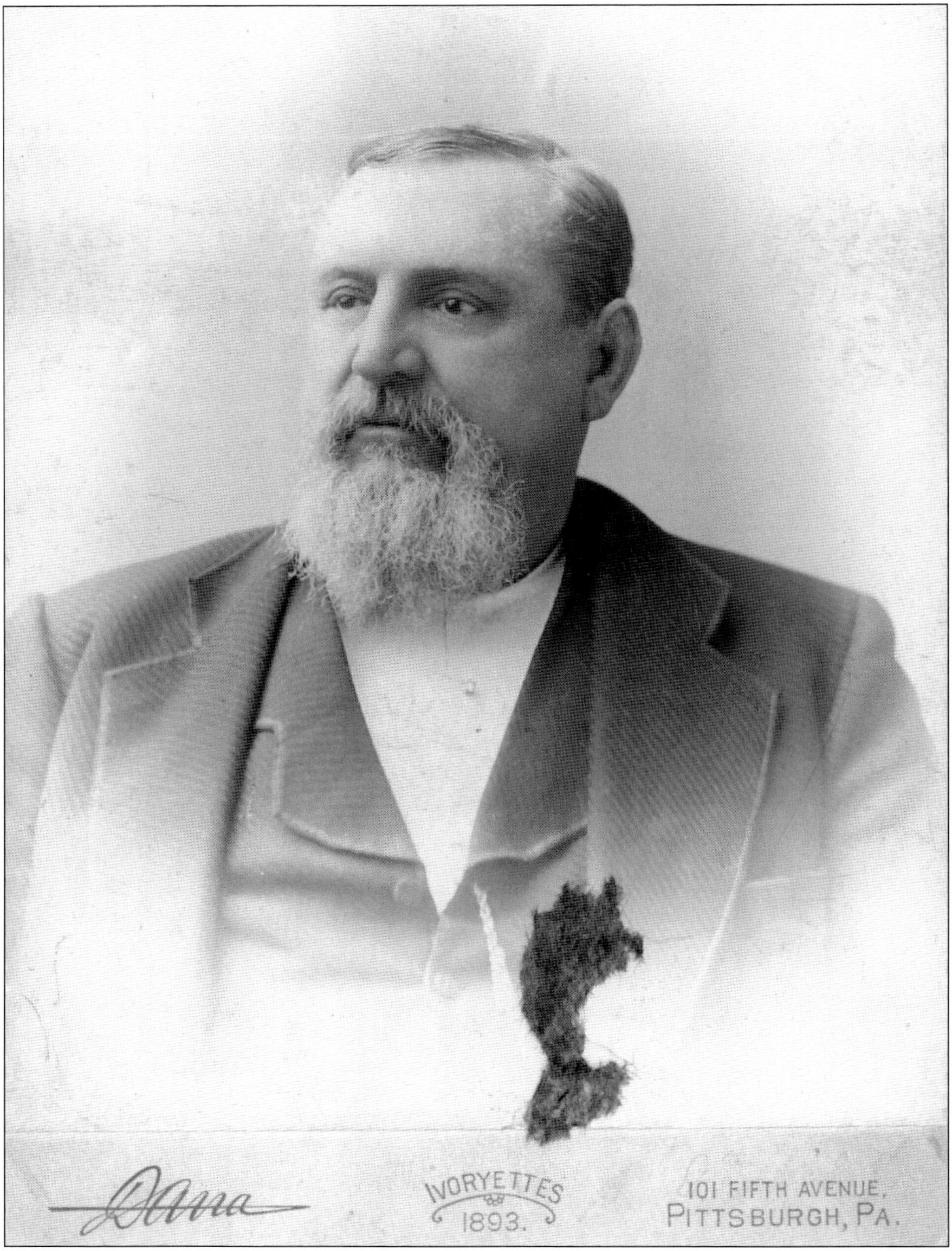

In the spring of 1896, the old Booneville Hotel and surrounding property was purchased by Colonel Dewey, and the building of a new town was soon underway. The town of Dewey was located about four miles northwest of Silver City at the base of Florida Mountain on Jordan Creek. As a young man in 1863, Dewey had walked all the way to the Owyhee Mountains from Virginia City, Nevada. He never served in the military, but in his later years he adopted the title "colonel" as befitting a man of his stature. An authority on whiskey, it was said that he could tell the age of whiskey by pouring it over the back of his hand.

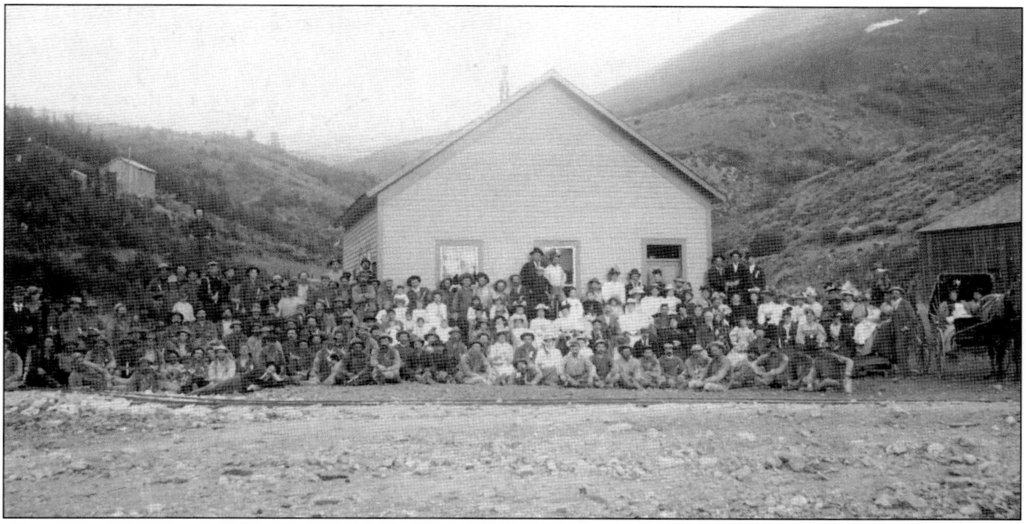

This photograph of Blue Gulch, between Dewey and Silver City, shows the roughness of the mountain terrain upon which the mining communities were perched. Society was rough, too. In 1888, Colonel Dewey shot Joseph Koenig, a bartender, in the entrance of the Sommercamp Saloon, owned by a former partner with whom he had quarreled. Dewey claimed self-defense, but he served a short term in prison. Exonerated in a second trial, his supporters claimed he had been set up as a means of taking over his Florida Mountain mines.

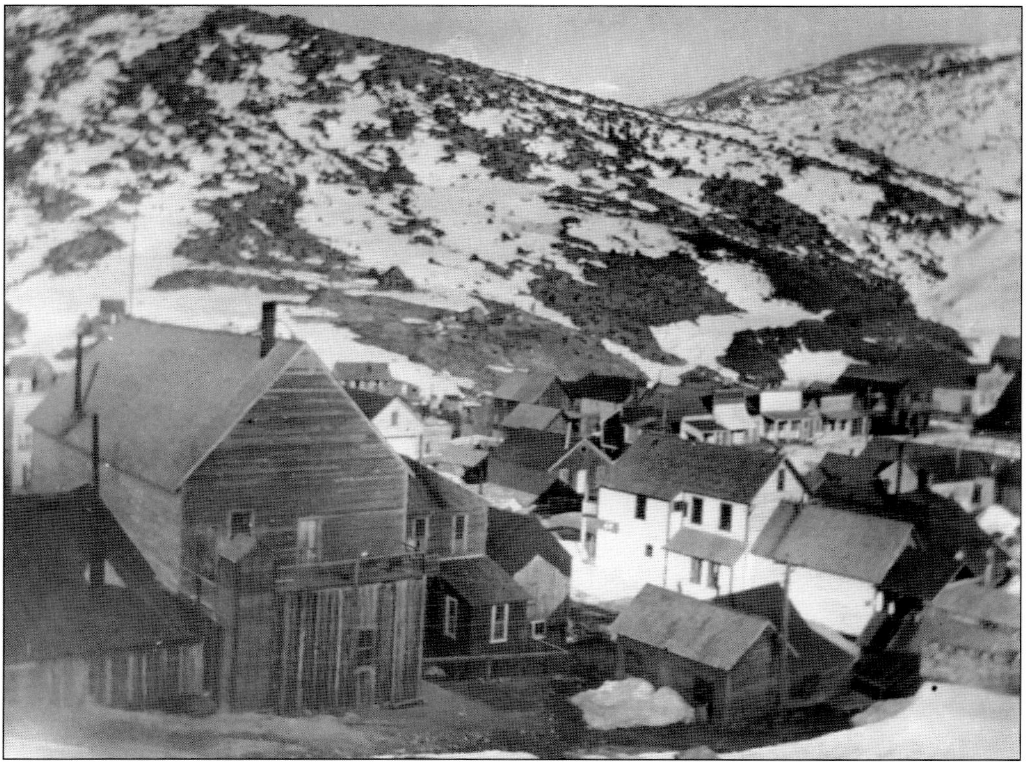

Dewey was intended to be the terminal point of the Boise, Nampa, & Owyhee Railroad. Colonel Dewey had aspirations—unfortunately never realized—of continuing the railroad to Winnemucca, Nevada, connecting with the Central Pacific line.

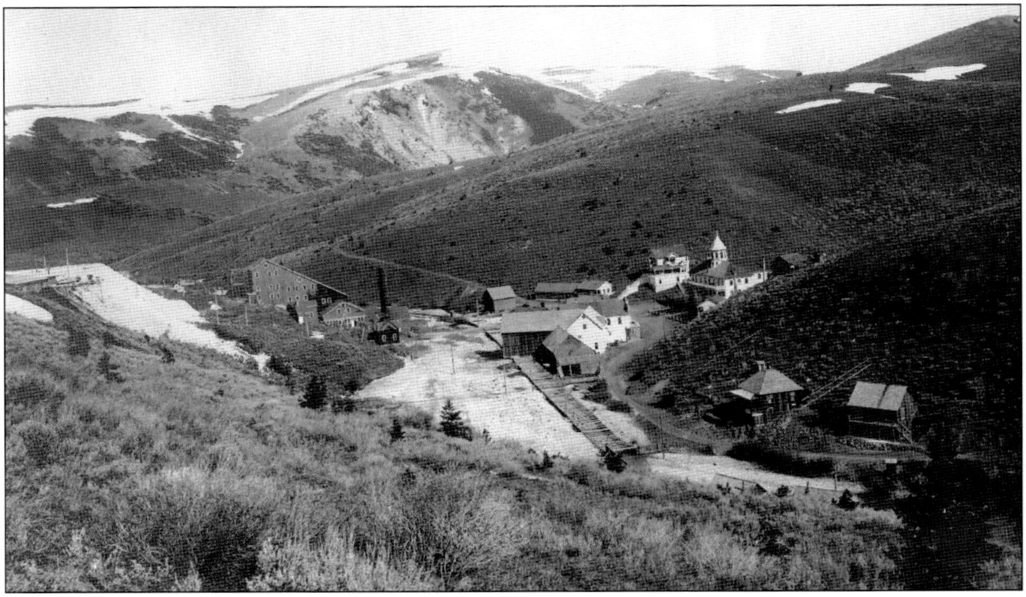

The Dewey Mill dominated the town, and mining was a dangerous business. New drilling machines earned the nickname "widow makers," dynamite was routinely employed, and poor ventilation and drainage systems were the norm. Fires were a serious danger, as tunnel shoring contained millions of board feet of flammable timber. Cave-ins were also a constant possibility.

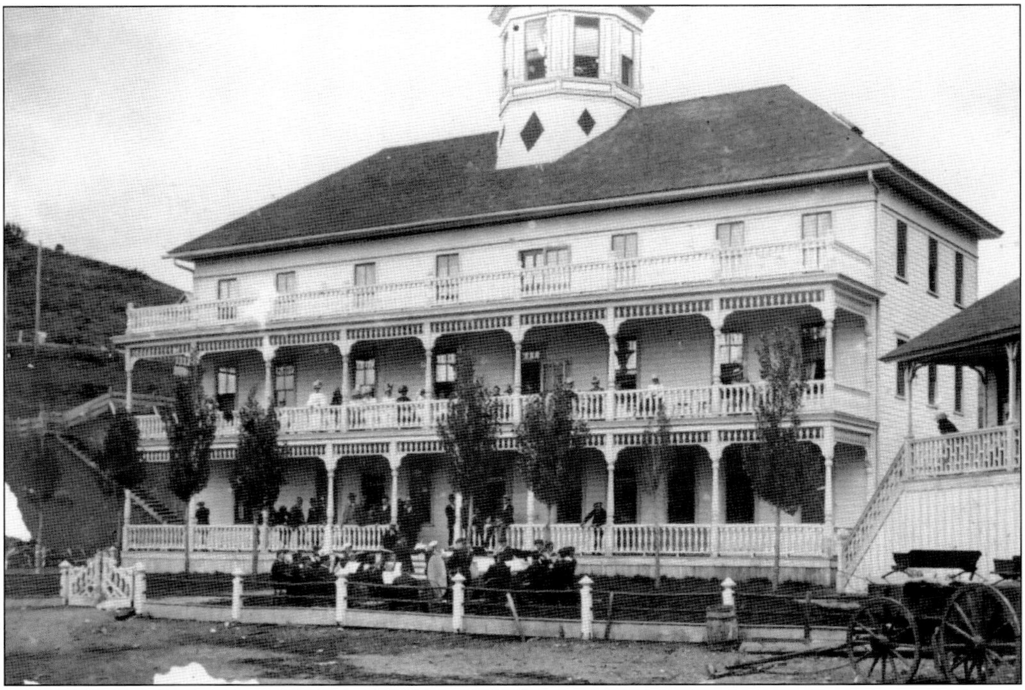

The Dewey Palace Hotel was considered one of Colonel Dewey's finest accomplishments; however, it was located in Nampa, Idaho, not the town of Dewey. The hotel was torn down in the 1960s. Colonel Dewey put his efforts behind constructing the BN & O Railroad from Nampa, first to Guffey in 1897 and on to Murphy in 1899. He was a major developer of Nampa, which is a sizable city today located in Canyon County, Idaho.

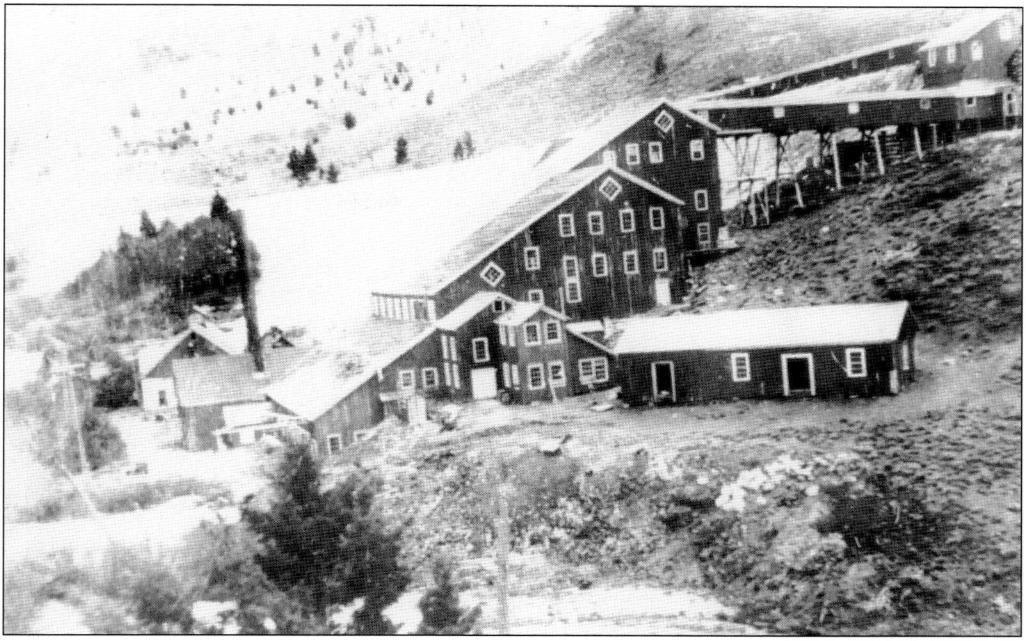

Colonel Dewey founded the Trade Dollar Mining and Milling Company. Its largest mill was commissioned in 1903. Dewey purchased the Humboldt and the 79 Mines on the north end of Florida Mountain, and after a fundraising trip back East he formed the Florida Mountain Mining and Milling Co. After managing his Florida Mountain properties to a high stage of production and establishing Owyhee County as a top-of-the-line producer, he sold his interests to the Pittsburg Mining and Milling Company. A tireless promoter, no one did more to revive flagging interest in the region's mining industry.

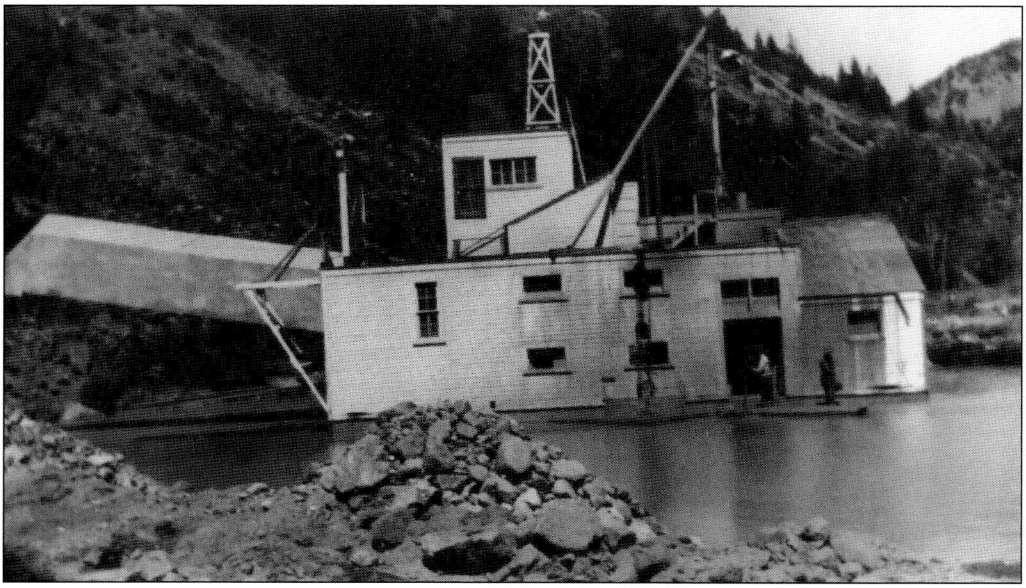

A gold dredge operated on Jordan Creek at Wagontown, one of the smaller mining communities that has since disappeared. Wagontown was also a stage station for the Ruby City-Chico stage and later the Silver City-Winnemucca line. One of its most favorable attributes was a large, open, level area that was ideal for horse racing, a favorite pastime with large bets routinely placed.

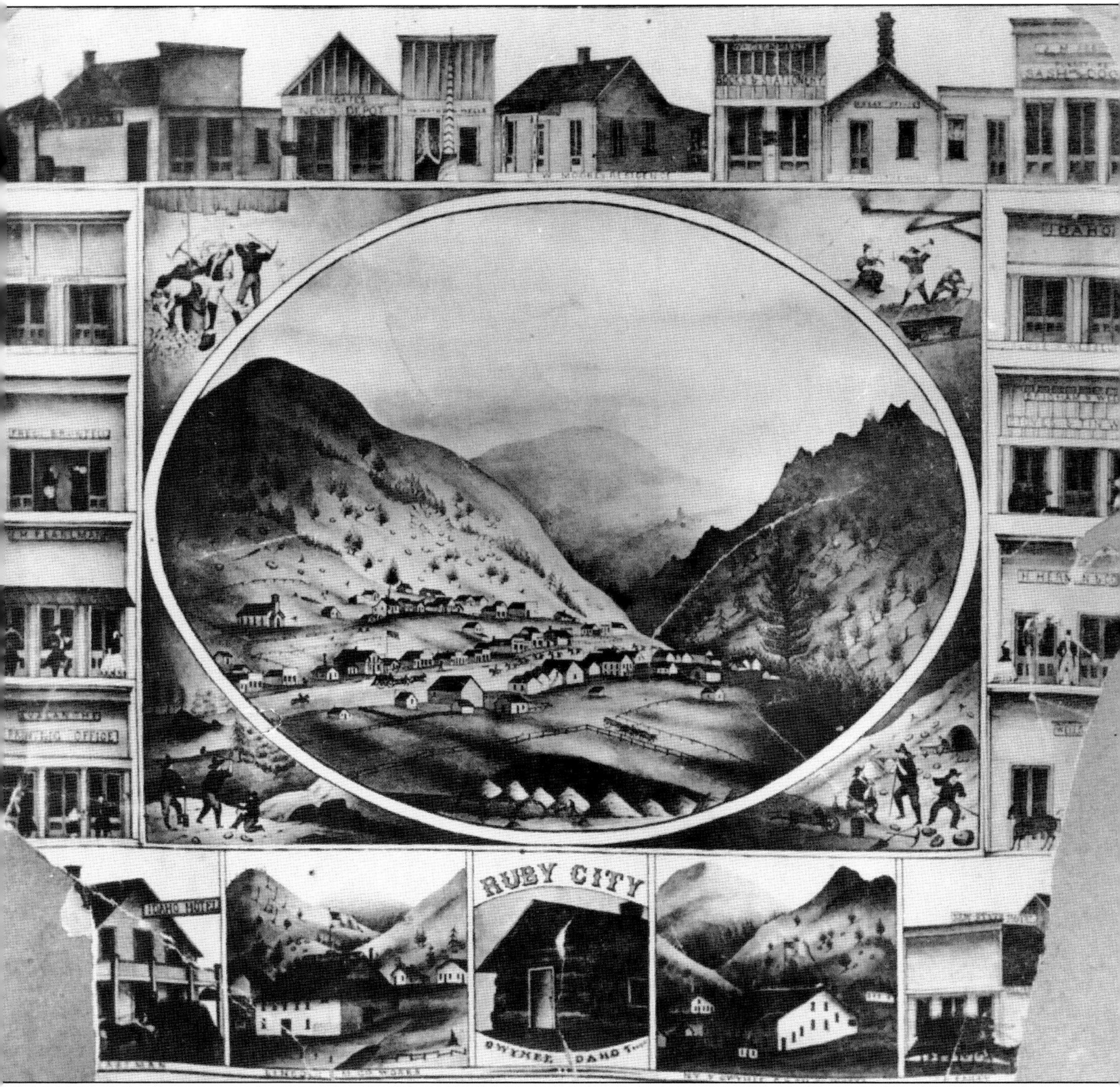

Thomas H. Smith made this sketch of Ruby City in 1866. An attorney, Smith displayed the sketch in his Ruby City office, later sending it to San Francisco, California, to be lithographed. Ruby City was Owyhee County's first official city, with a post office established on June 22, 1864. The town was later almost completely erased by hydraulic placer mining (some foundations are still visible).

Four

The Native Americans

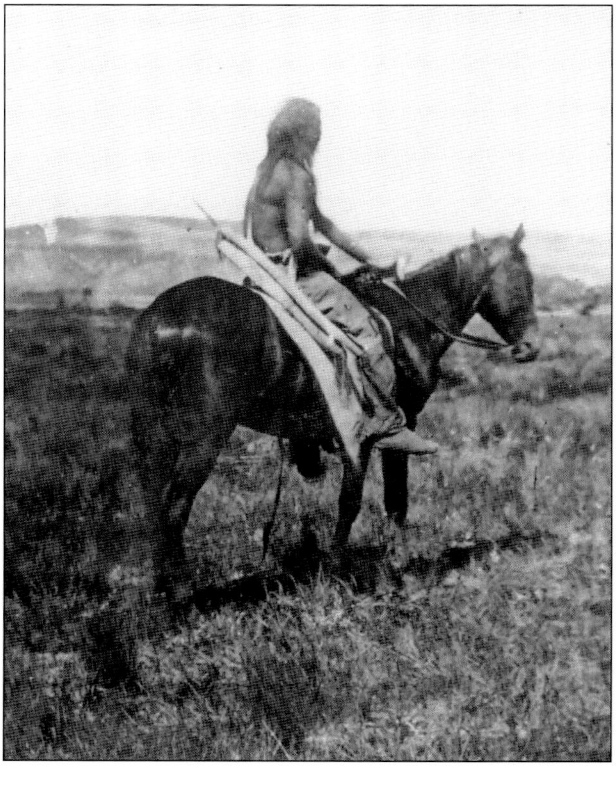

Native Americans populated the Owyhee high desert thousands of years before Europeans arrived. Early explorers encountered the Bannocks, a subdivision of the Shoshoni tribe, and the Paiutes. Nomadic in nature, the Bannocks occupied a large swath of territory that included what is now Owyhee County. Though centered in the more fertile regions to the east, all of southern Idaho was their range. Today, most descendants of Native Americans in Owyhee County live in the Duck Valley area and describe themselves as Shoshoni or Paiute. The most famous battle of the Bannock War of 1878 was fought on the slopes of South Mountain in Owyhee County, between white settlers and a Bannock raiding party from Fort Hall to the east. (Image published with permission of the Idaho State Historical Society.)

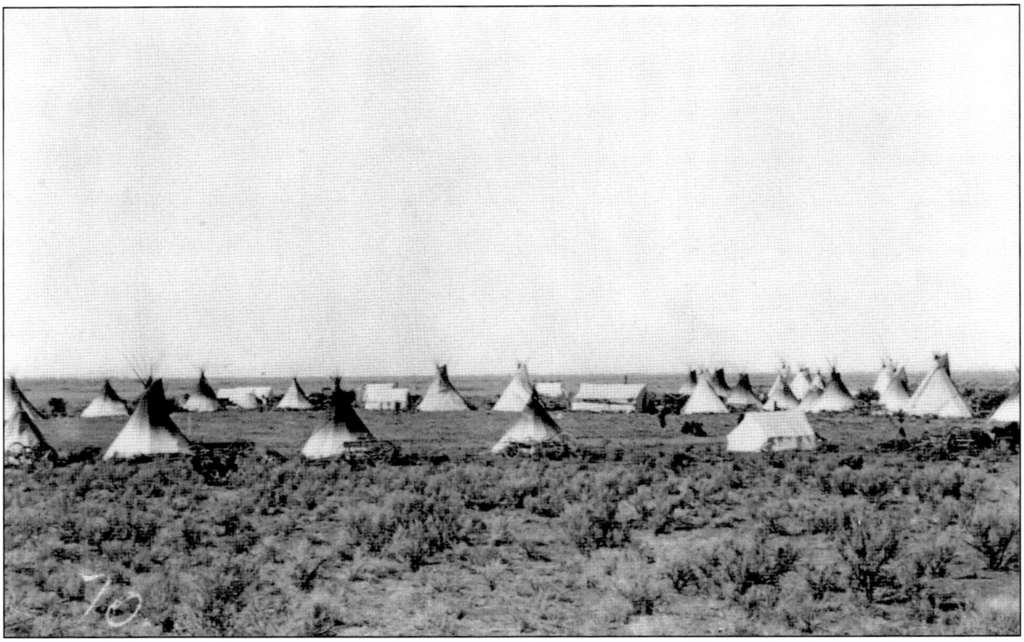

The Bannocks used teepees in the traditional style of the plains Indians. Pres. Andrew Jackson signed the Fort Bridger Treaty of 1868, forcing Bannocks and Shoshoni tribes to settle on the Fort Hall Reservation, where this photograph was taken. (Image published with permission of the Idaho State Historical Society.)

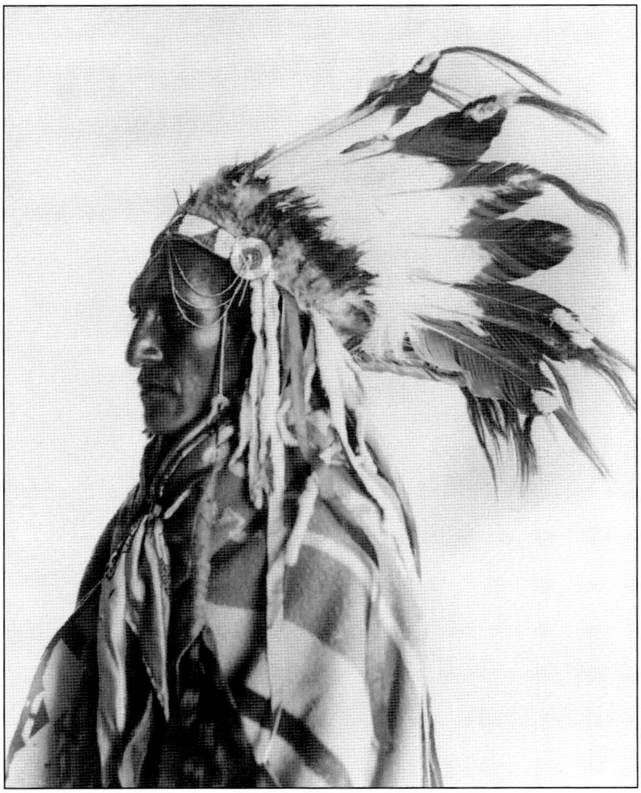

Pictured here is a Shoshone chief wearing the traditional feather bonnet. The Bannocks were a subdivision of the Shoshoni tribe. The Shoshone Indians occupied territory in California, Idaho, Nevada, Utah, and Wyoming, but they were nowhere more prevalent than in the Snake River area in Idaho. Despite the huge land area they roamed, the total population probably never exceeded 8,000. Historical documents from the Lewis and Clark expedition refer to them as the Snake Indians. In fact, the name Shoshone means "the Valley People," and the term translates as "inland' or "in the valley." (Image published with permission of the Idaho State Historical Society.)

This is a studio portrait of a Bannock woman with her child taken at the Fort Hall Indian Reservation. The reservation was established by the Fort Bridger Treaty of 1868 between the United States and the Shoshone and Bannock tribes in the wake of the Bear River Massacre in 1863. Located on the Snake River Plain, it was poorly suited for the traditional native way of life, and the government often failed to provide the food and goods promised by the treaty. The resulting dissatisfaction contributed significantly to unrest that ultimately played itself out in the Bannock War of 1878.

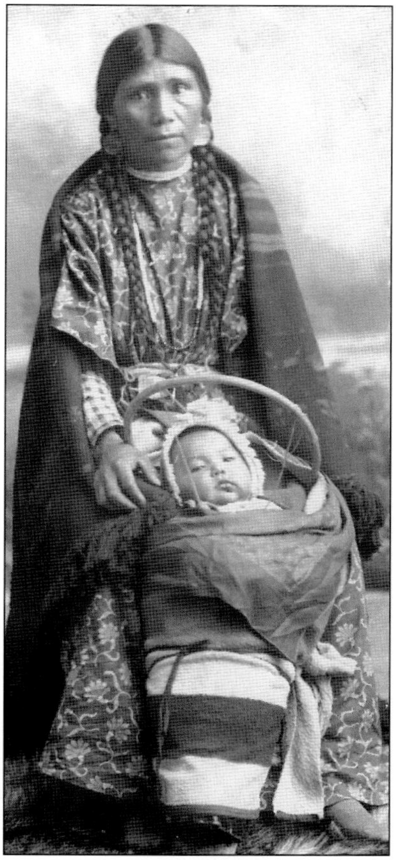

The name Bannock derives from the tribe's word *bampnack*, meaning "to throw backwards," which referred to the custom of the braves to wear their hair in a lock thrown back from the forehead. (Image published with permission of the Idaho State Historical Society.)

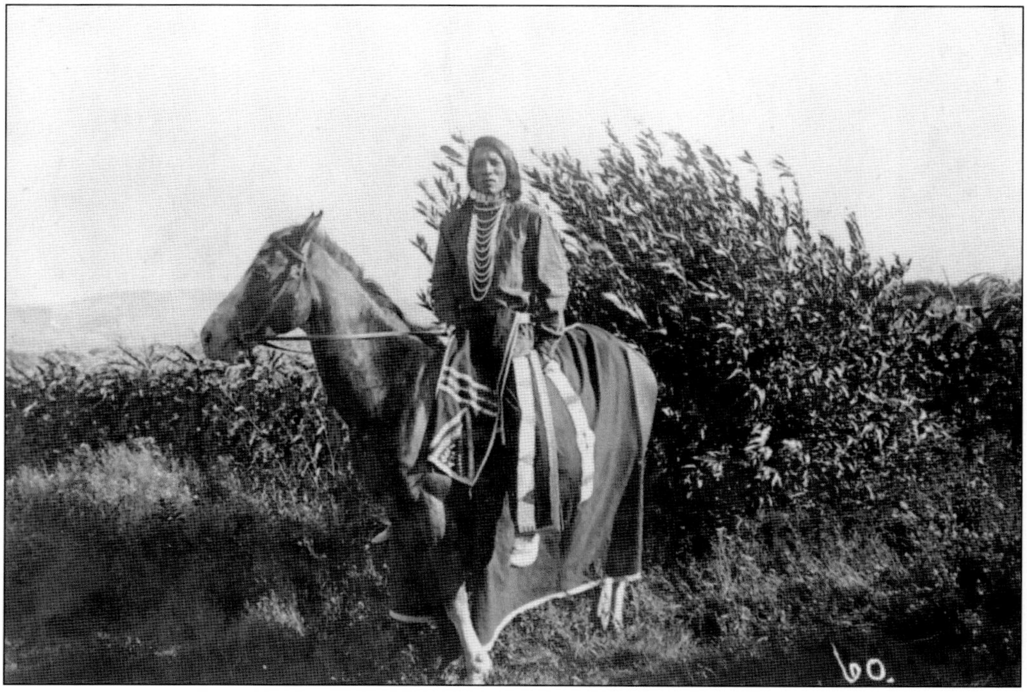

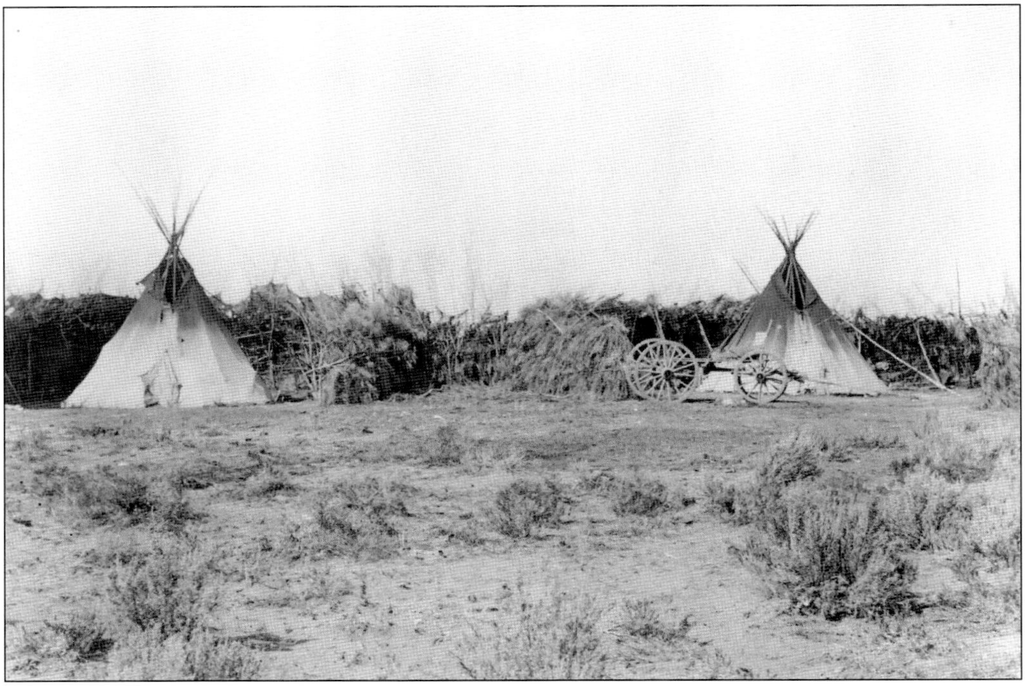

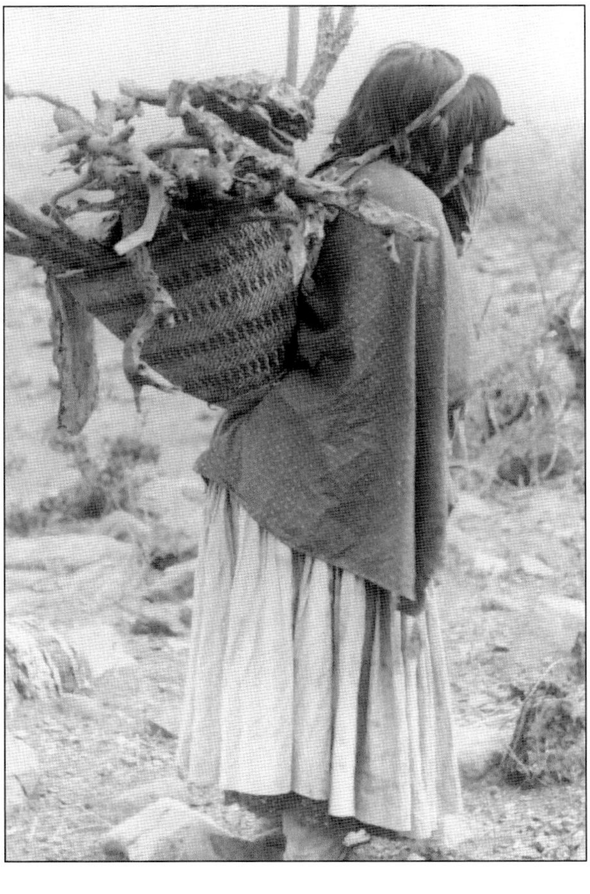

Bannock Indians wintered at Fort Hall. Note the sagebrush windbreak in the background. Founded in 1868, the reservation was named for Fort Hall, a trading post and important stop along the Oregon and California Trails in the mid-1800s. Today, the reservation is located in southeastern Idaho on the Snake River Plain northwest of Pocatello, Idaho, and is comprised of 814 square miles of land area spread over four Idaho counties: Bingham, Power, Bannock, and Caribou. (Image published with permission from the Idaho State Historical Society.)

A Shoshone-Bannock woman gathers wood on the Fort Hall Reservation in the late 1800s. Fort Hall was not in Owyhee County, but the Bannocks traveled frequently from there into the high desert. (Image published with permission from the Idaho State Historical Society.)

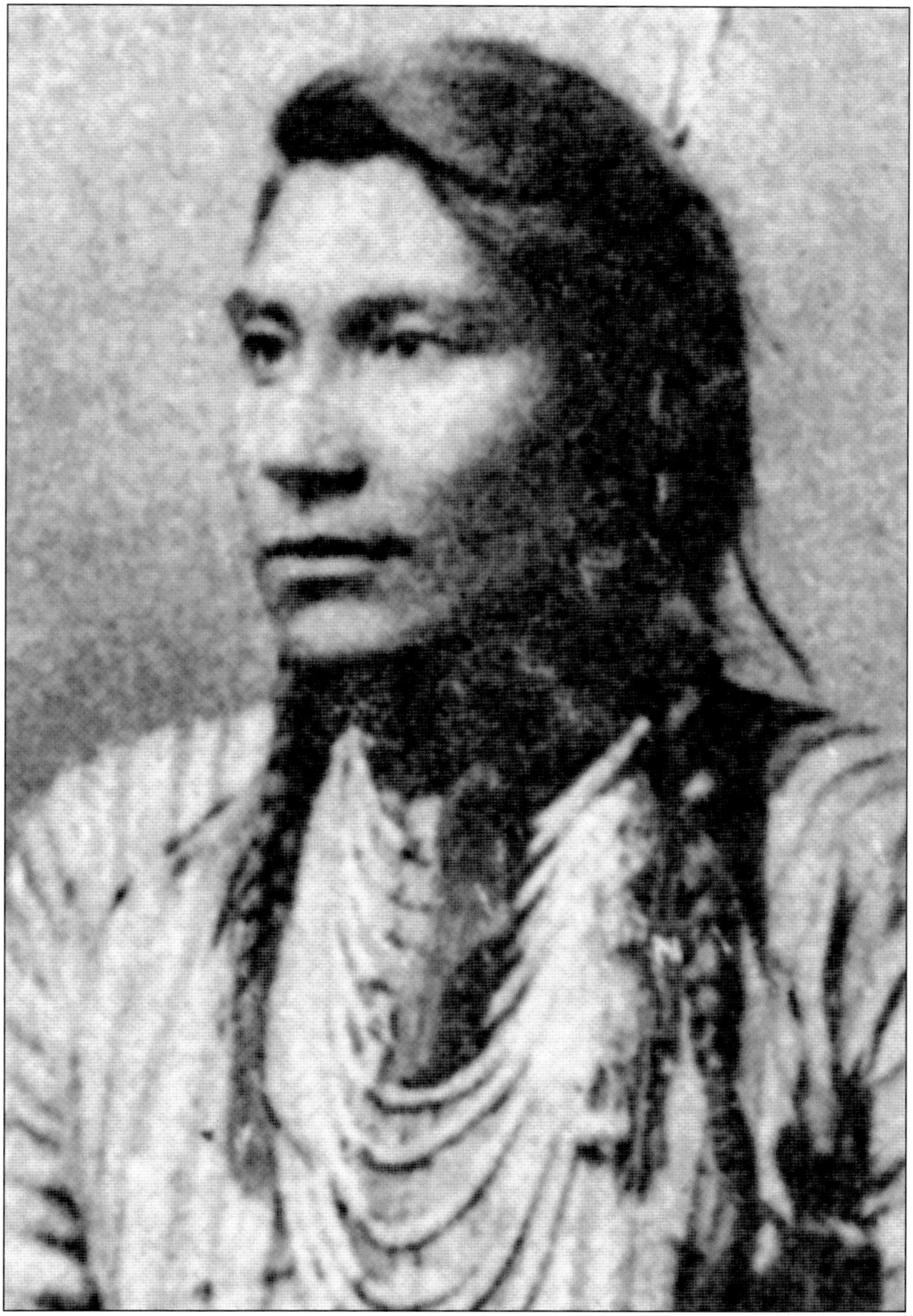

The charismatic Chief Buffalo Horn led his tribe in the Bannock War of 1878. Bannocks from the Fort Hall area east of the Owyhees were angered by treaty violations and an incident where white settlers released hogs that destroyed the camas bulbs upon which the tribe depended upon for food. His raiding band cut a swath across southern Idaho and through Owyhee County, killing some 40 whites (only three in Owyhee County). Chief Buffalo Horn was mortally wounded in a pitched battle with local volunteers from Silver City. His remaining fighters moved south to join the Paiute, who continued hostilities in Oregon until suppressed by federal troops. (Image published with permission of the Idaho State Historical Society.)

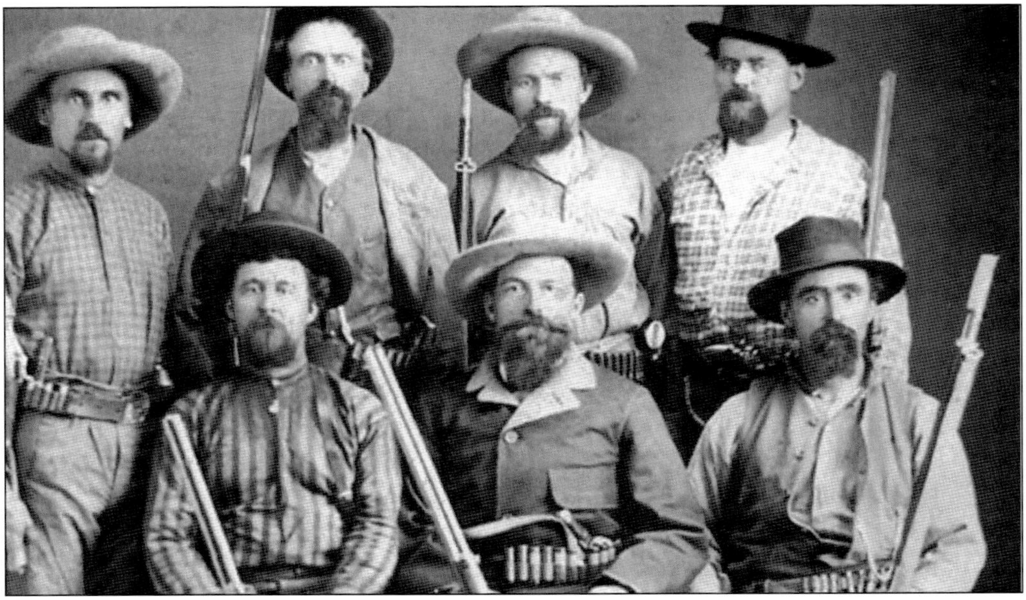

A local home guard militia was raised during the Bannock War. Pictured here from left to right are (first row) Charles Adams, Rube Robbins, and Henry Pierce; (second row) Ameleen McQuaid, George Banks, F.J. Parker, and Jack Campbell. Militia member O.H. Purdy (not pictured) was killed by the Bannocks in the Battle of South Mountain. A militia member recalled, "He fought so bravely that the Indians in their admiration of his courage did not mutilate his body by scalping as is their usual custom. They hung his spurs in a tree." (Image published with the permission of the Idaho State Historical Society.)

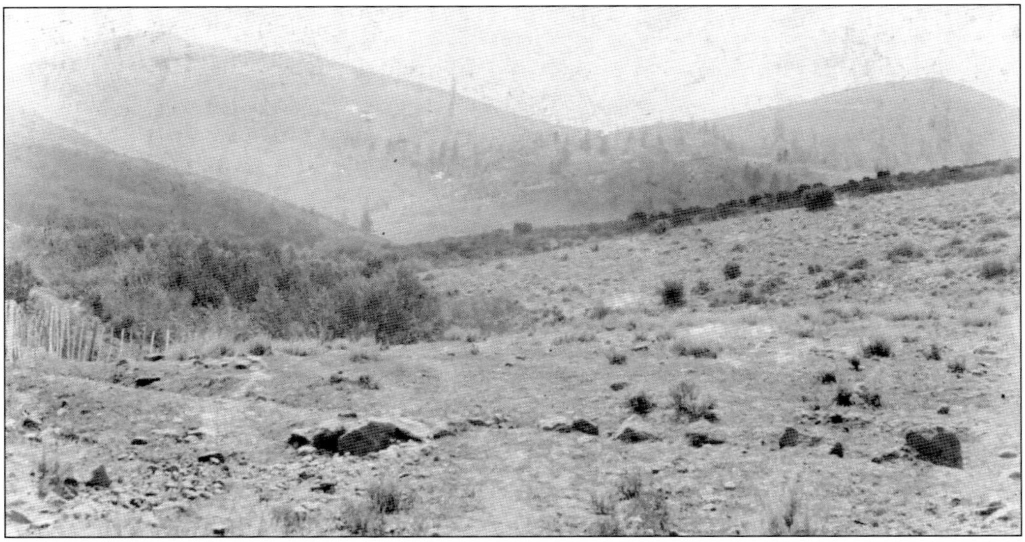

Pictured here is South Mountain, near where Chief Buffalo Horn was fatally wounded. The Silver City volunteers ran into Chief Buffalo Horn and more than 40 warriors near a small mining camp at South Mountain, about 20 miles southwest of Silver City. The Bannocks were in a good defensive position, but the volunteers charged anyway. Although the volunteers lost two men and three were wounded, they succeeded in mortally wounding Buffalo Horn and wounding a few other Bannocks. The Indians headed towards Oregon with their chief, who ordered them to leave him in the underbrush to die, which occurred two days later.

A Paiute woman stands with her children. The Paiute were closely related to the Bannocks their allies. After Buffalo Horn's death, the new leader, Chief Egan, headed to Juniper Mountain in Idaho and Steens Mountain in southeastern Oregon to meet with the Paiute. They continued the conflict in Oregon until suppressed by federal troops.

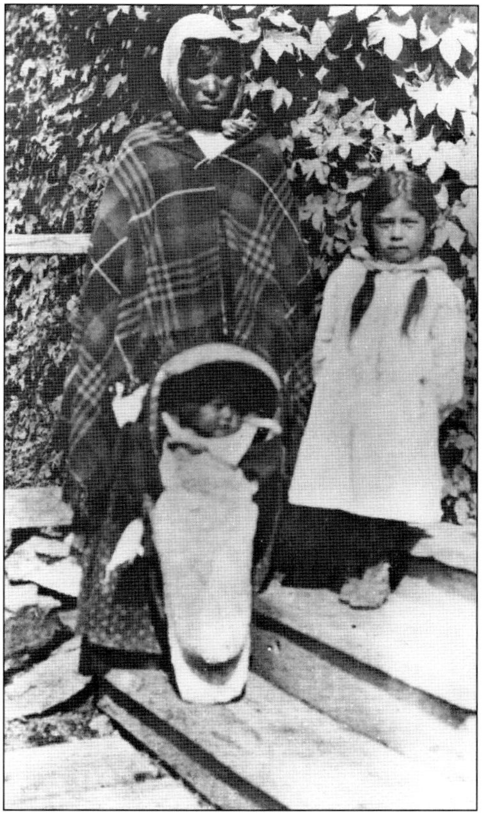

By the 20th century, many Bannocks had integrated into the new ranching communities that replaced the mining economy as the ores played out. Ira Purjue was a well-known cowboy from the Bruneau area.

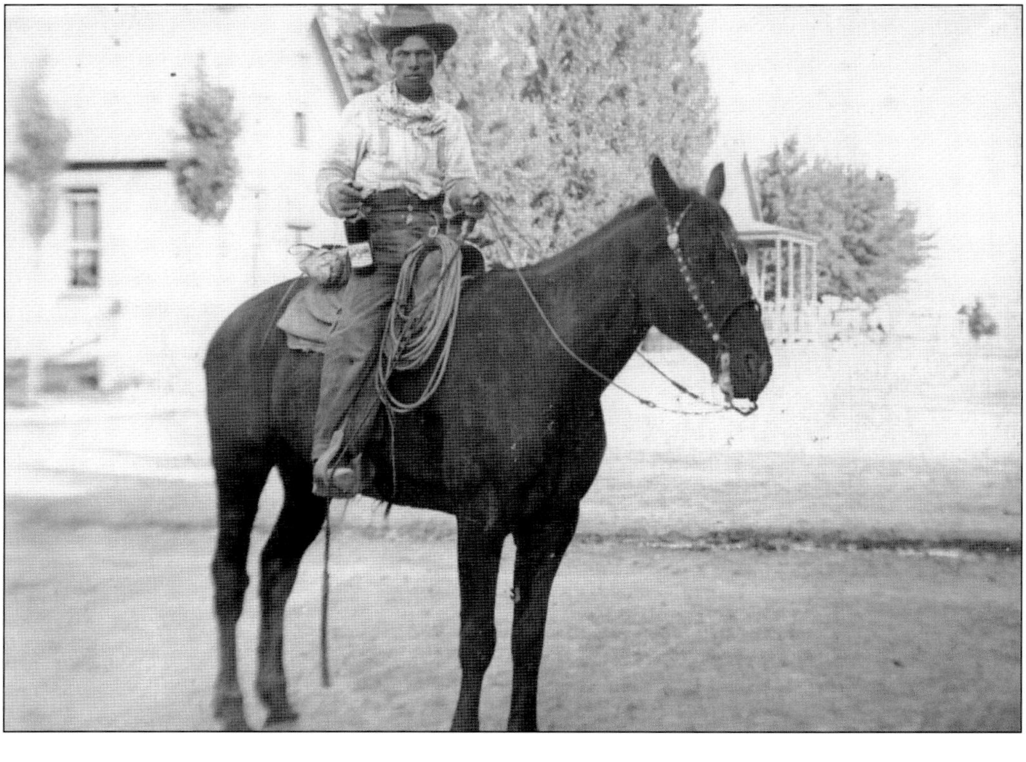

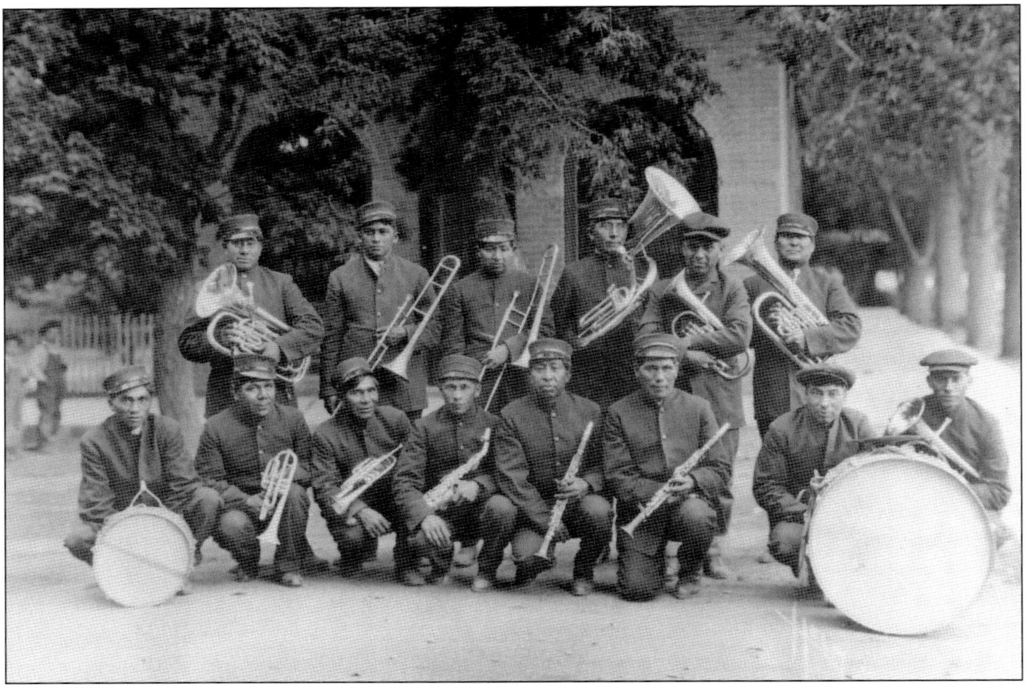

Bruneau featured its own Indian Band, shown here in 1914. Pictured are, from left to right, (first row) Sam Charles, John Para Dice, Wesley DeHall, Harry Thaccher, Fritz Smith, Charley McGee, Johnny Adams, and Thomas Joyce; (second row) John Teller, Dick Hoky, John Harney, Charles Francis, Pete Jackson, and Charley Kasky. (Courtesy of the Ruth Randall collection and the OCHS.)

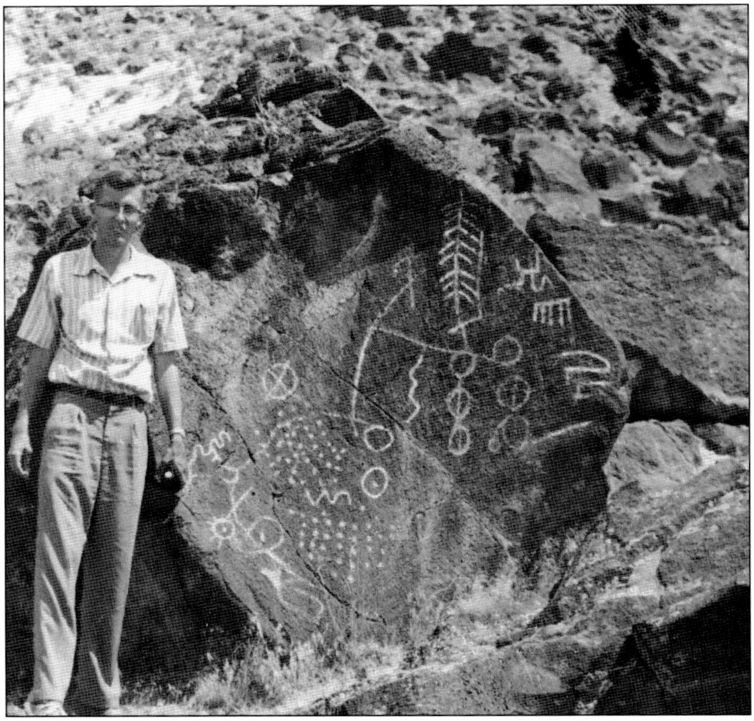

Petroglyphs are a common feature along the Snake River and in the high desert mountains. This is the locally renowned Map Rock, on the bank of the Snake River just across from Owyhee County's northern border. Crossing the face of the rock is a line corresponding to the course of the Snake River joined by other lines depicting tributaries. Images of deer, antelope, and mountain sheep seem to align with roughly the Silver City area.

Five

The Cowboys and Ranchers

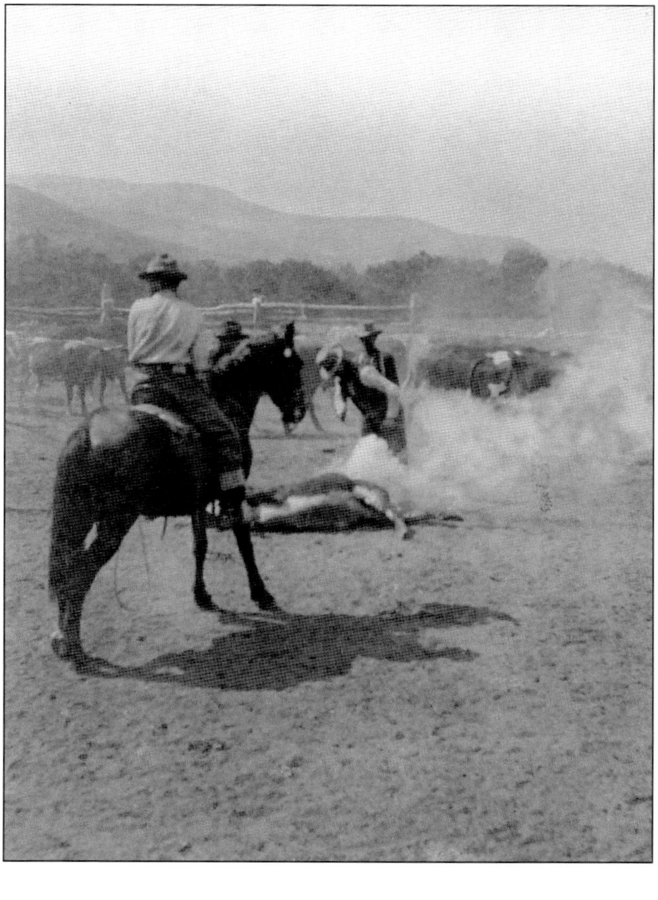

After the mines dwindled in the early 1900s, ranching became a more important component of the Owyhee County economy. Reynolds Creek, dropping down from the mountains into the plain of the Snake River, was a significant cattle area.

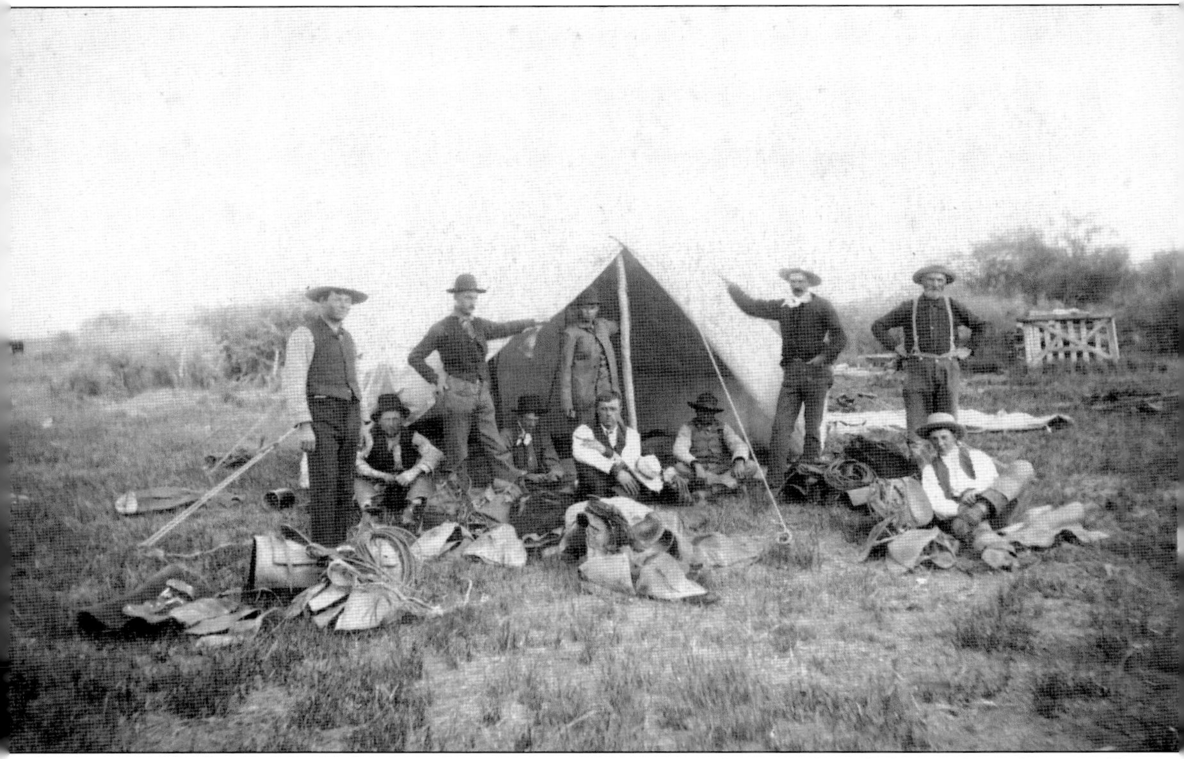

Pictured here are "Castle Creek Cowboys" at Silver City. They are, from left to right, John Percell, Fred Graves, Eugene Howe, Rose Slack, Thad Parter, Rufus Fletcher, William Hearst, Thomas Beggs, Bill Davis, and Frank McMahon. Owyhee County's cattle industry originally provided food to the swelling mining populations. Later, as mining faded, ranching became an important industry in and of itself, and the cowboy rather than the miner became the hero of the local economy. (Image published with permission of the Idaho State Historical Society.)

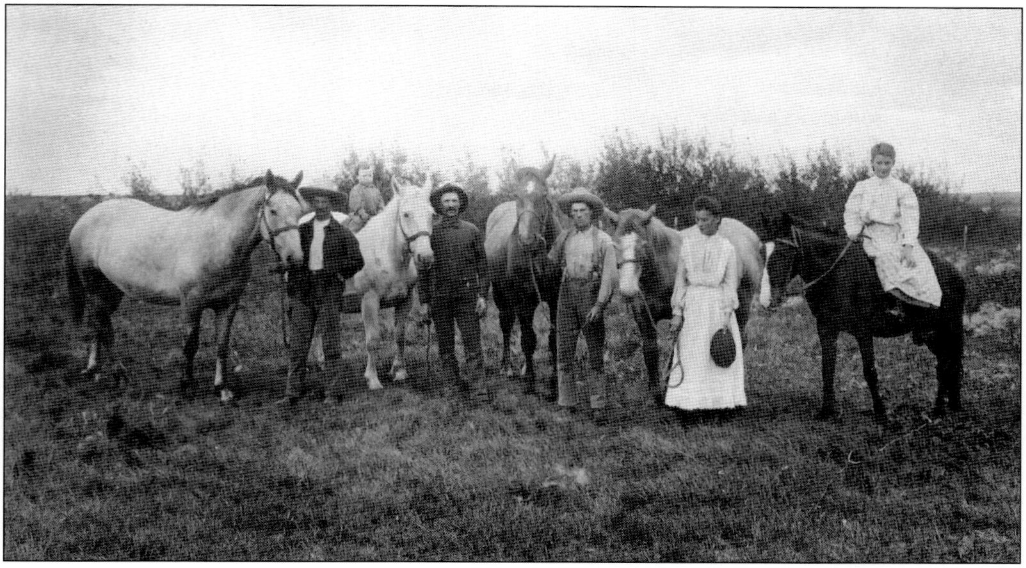

An early ranching family turns out in their Sunday best for a portrait. Having a photograph taken was an event in the early days when cameras were few and far between. By 1869, a series of annual cattle drives from Texas helped to diversify cattle stock in Owyhee County. By 1870, a number of Owyhee cattle growers who had begun operations as destitute immigrants had become prosperous ranchers. By 1874, they were opening large export markets in Arizona and California for cattle and horses.

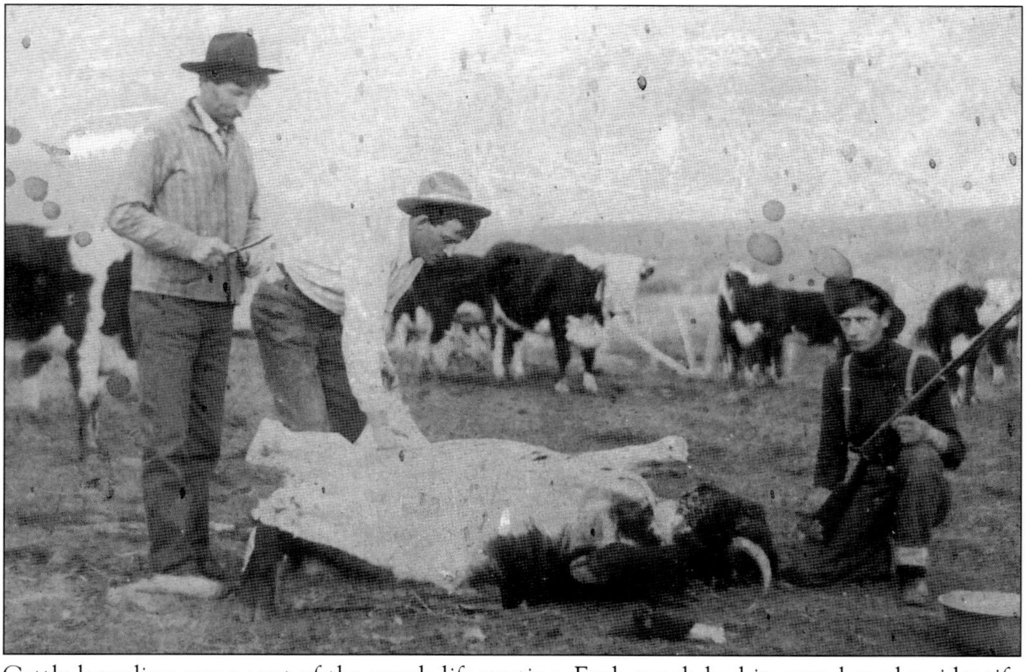

Cattle branding was a part of the ranch life routine. Each ranch had its own brand to identify cattle and ranch hands such as Charlie Strode (right) to do the dirty work. The Jordan Valley Live Stock Association offered a $500 reward "to be paid for the arrest and conviction of any party or parties mutilating the marks or brands, killing or stealing stock belonging to members of this association."

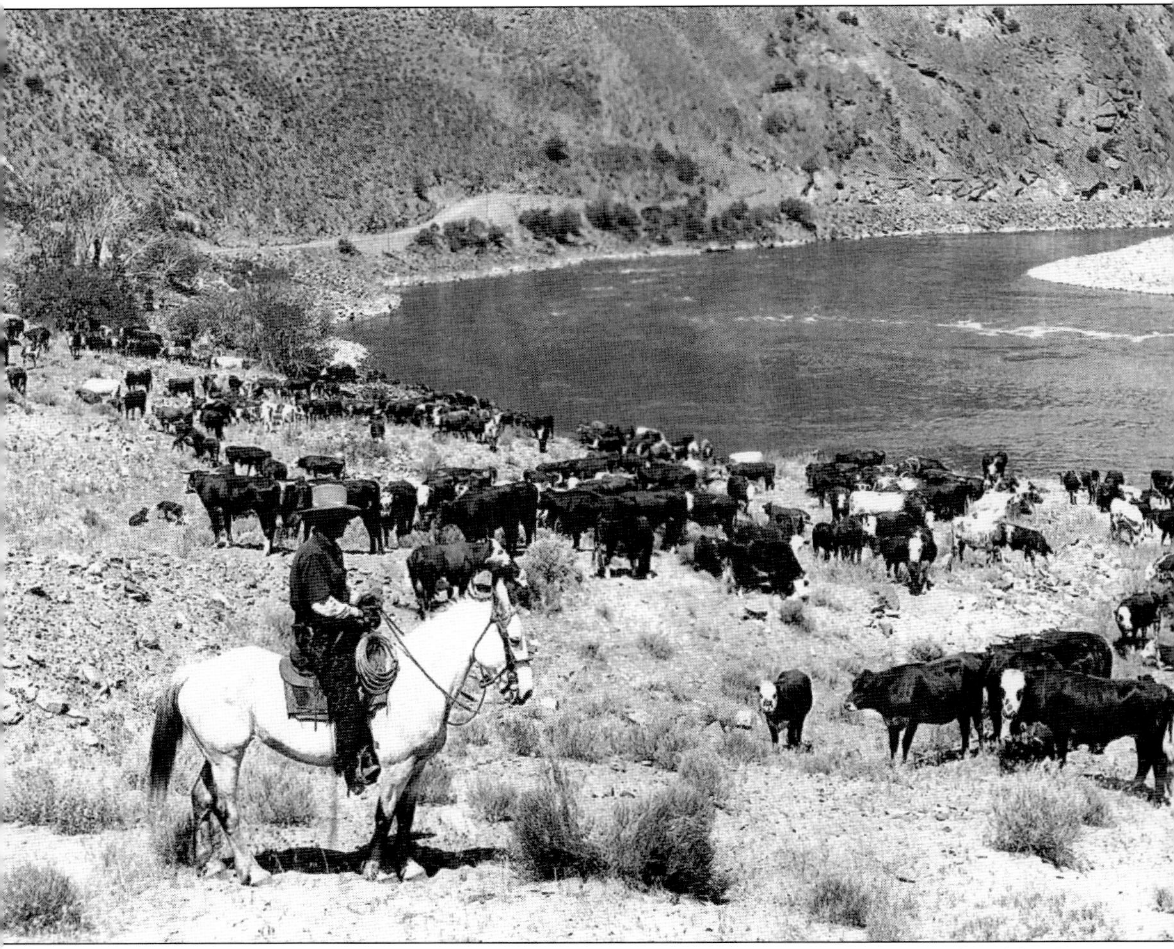

Pictured here is Con Shea's watering hole, about two miles above the Guffey railroad bridge, on the Snake River. Shea was one of the more prominent Owyhee County ranchers, and many local landmarks bear his name, including Con Shea Basin and Con Shea Road near Murphy. Shea is credited with bringing the first longhorn cattle to Owyhee County in 1868. He made two drives from Texas on his own in 1869 and 1870. (Image published with permission of the Idaho State Historical Society.)

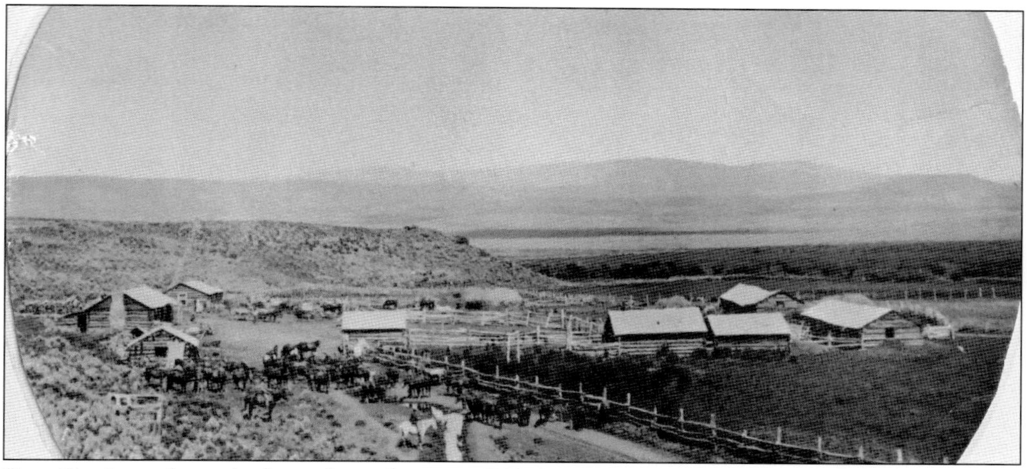

Cow Creek ranch was built on the earlier site of US Army Camp Lyons. Camp Lyon was established on June 27, 1865, to protect settlers and miners from Indian raids. The Army troops were largely ineffectual, and the camp was abandoned in 1869. The location developed as a ranching area, located on the Idaho-Oregon border. (Courtesy of G. Walmsley.)

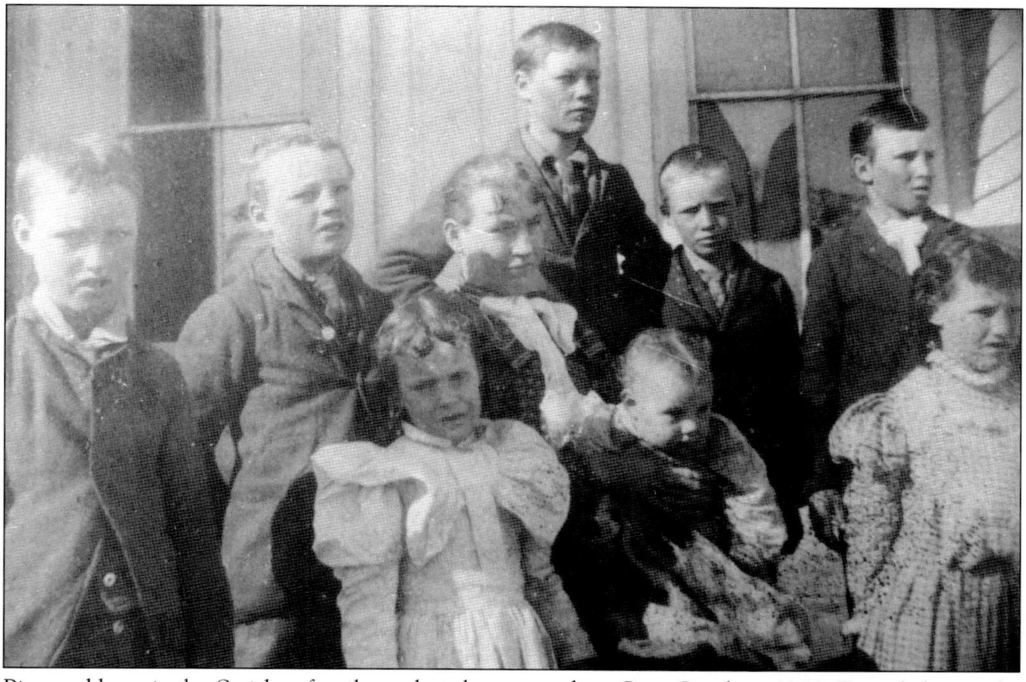

Pictured here is the Swisher family at their homestead on Cow Creek in 1890. From left to right are (first row) Clara, Mrs. Swisher and baby Irene, and Alice; (second row) Jim, Jack, Frank, Bev, and Nick Maysonholder. Long cattle drives from eastern Oregon and Washington across Oregon Trail routes, which crossed northern Owyhee County, began in 1876. The system reduced freight costs and provided grazing opportunities along roads that reduced depletion of grass resources in northwestern ranching areas. Owyhee ranchers took advantage of such opportunities, and Midwestern farmers took advantage of Owyhee cattle sources to acquire stock they could fatten for market. By 1882, with an approximation of its present boundaries, Owyhee County had 24,559 cattle, 15,150 sheep, and 2,046 horses. Livestock accounted for half of the county's entire assessed valuation. (Courtesy of Mike Hanley.)

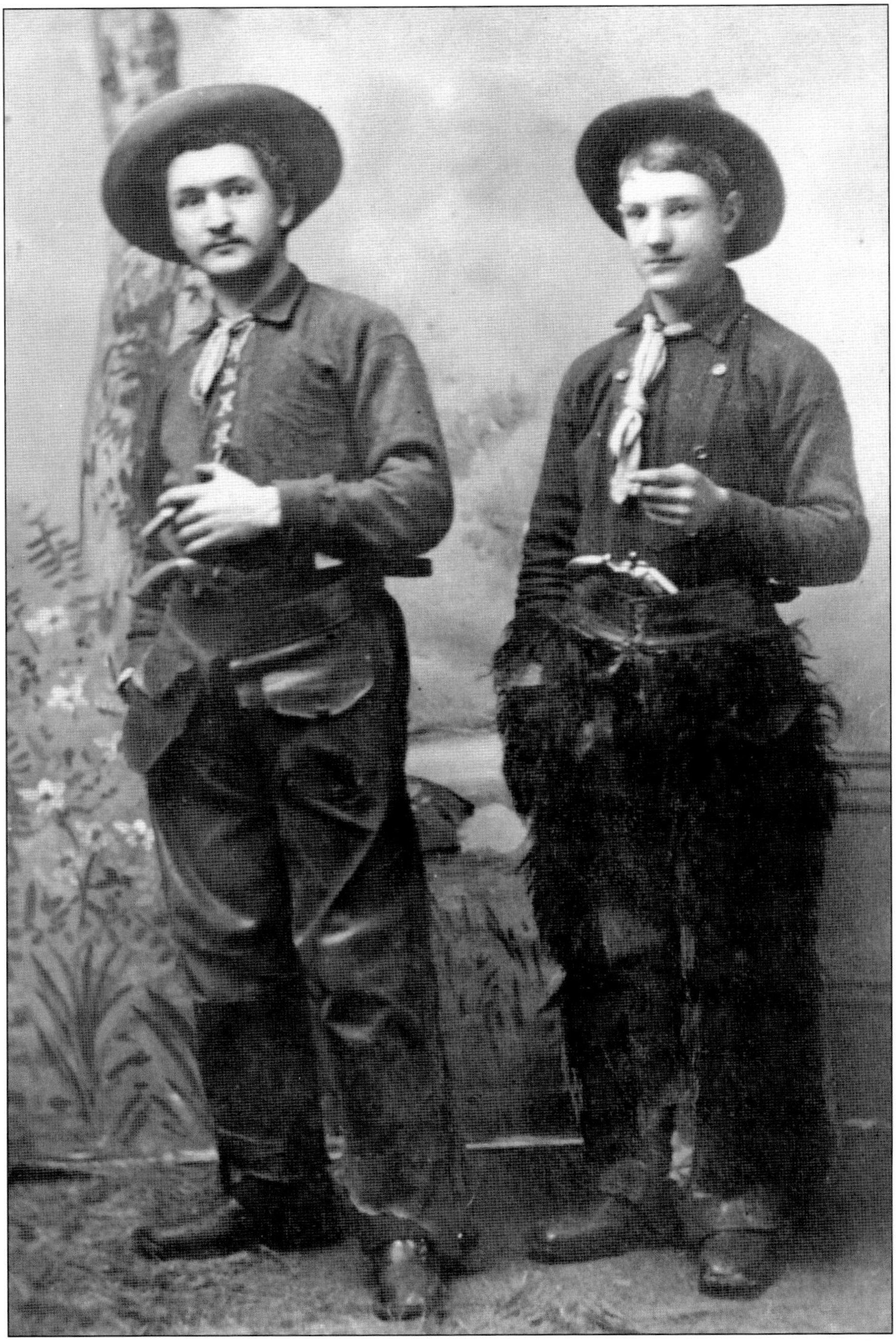

Owyhee County cowboys Walt Cook (left) and Frank McMann duded up in their best for this studio portrait in the early 1900s. A new era in Owyhee cattle ranching came by 1884, with the completion of transcontinental rail service from Portland, Oregon, to Midwestern Union Pacific lines. Ranchers could now ship directly to remote markets. (Image published with permission of the Idaho State Historical Society, donor Omar Stanford.)

Reynolds Creek was named by Michael Jordan, the man who discovered gold in the creek that bears his name. This account is from O.H. Purdy, a member of the party and well-known citizen of Silver City who was killed in the skirmish with the Bannock Indians at South Mountain in June 1878: "We crossed Snake river at the mouth of Boise river, traveling in a southwesterly direction, until we came to, at that time, quite a large stream, which we named, in honor of the laziest man in the company, Reynolds Creek."

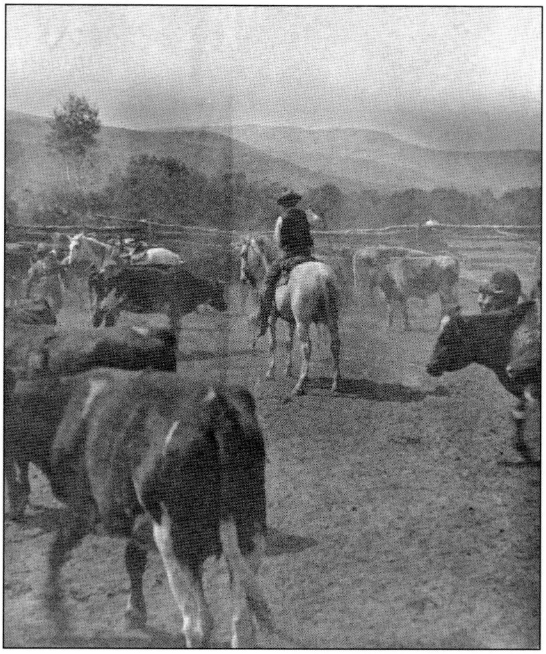

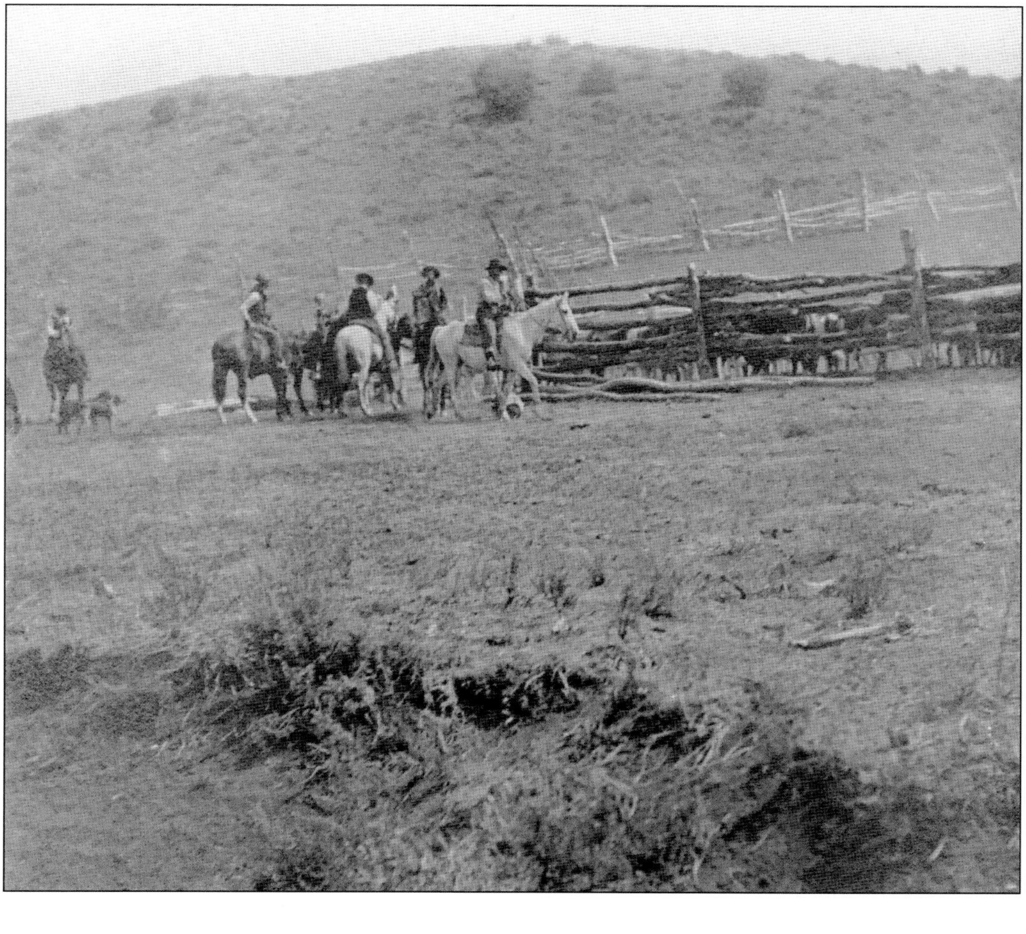

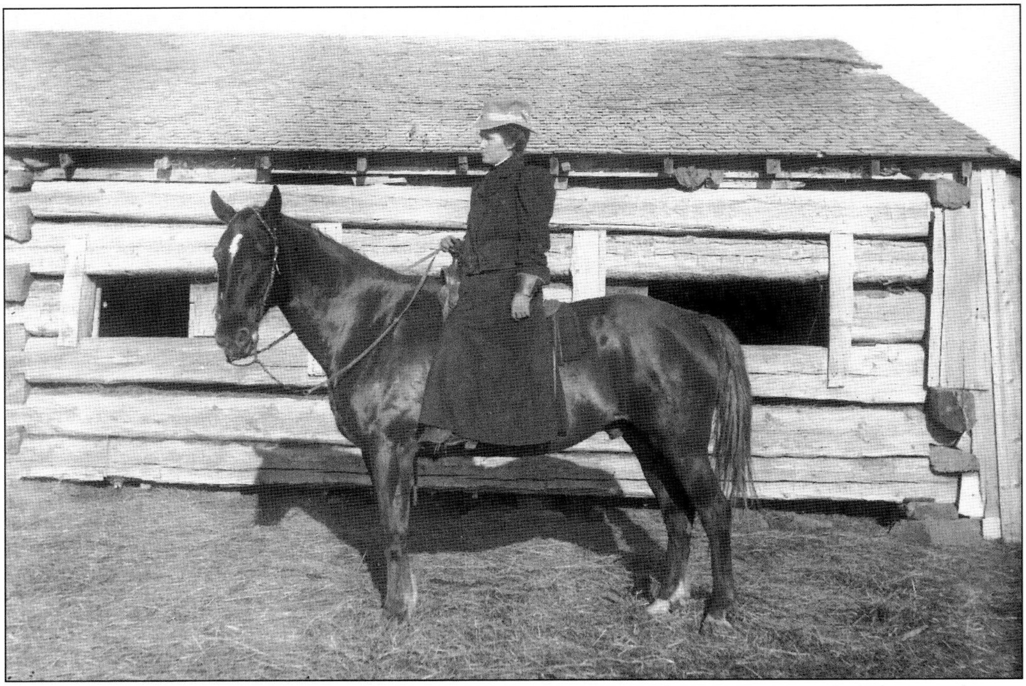

Pictured here is Nell Purcer Frost, of the Frank Purcer Ranch on Cow Creek. The ranch was also a station on the old Jordan Valley Road. During the era after 1884, local ranchers showed more interest in gaining title to their grazing lands rather than using public domain. Silver City residents began to protect themselves by taking up unpatented mining claims for a townsite, and ranchers started to hold desert land act or homestead claims. From that point, stability came with permanent ranching opportunities.

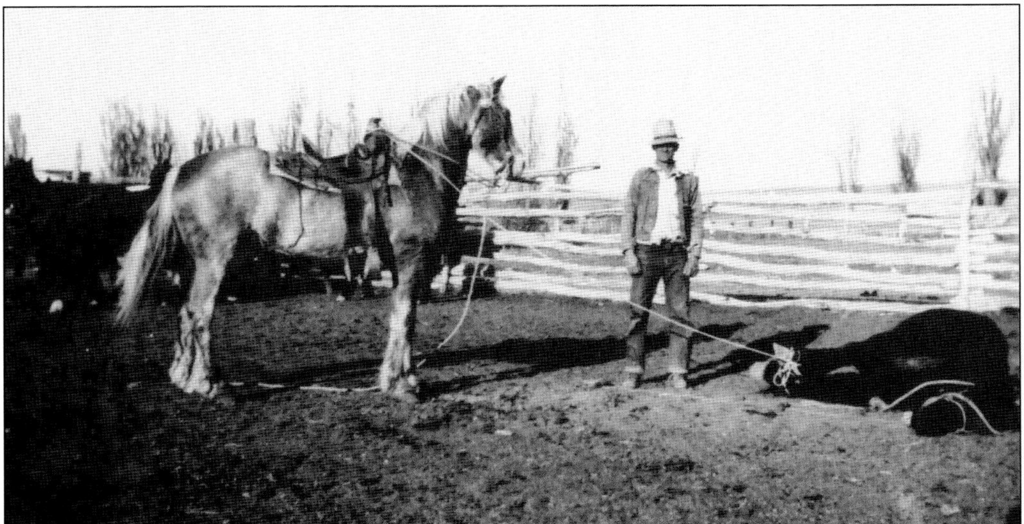

Little Valley rancher George Randall stands with his horse Askus. In the early 1900s, and especially with the advent of the automobile, cattle ranches in many parts of the West underwent a transition to farm operations. However, most major ranching operations in Owyhee County remaining cattle ranches, in part because they were remote from irrigation canal projects and thus preserved a traditional ranch culture.

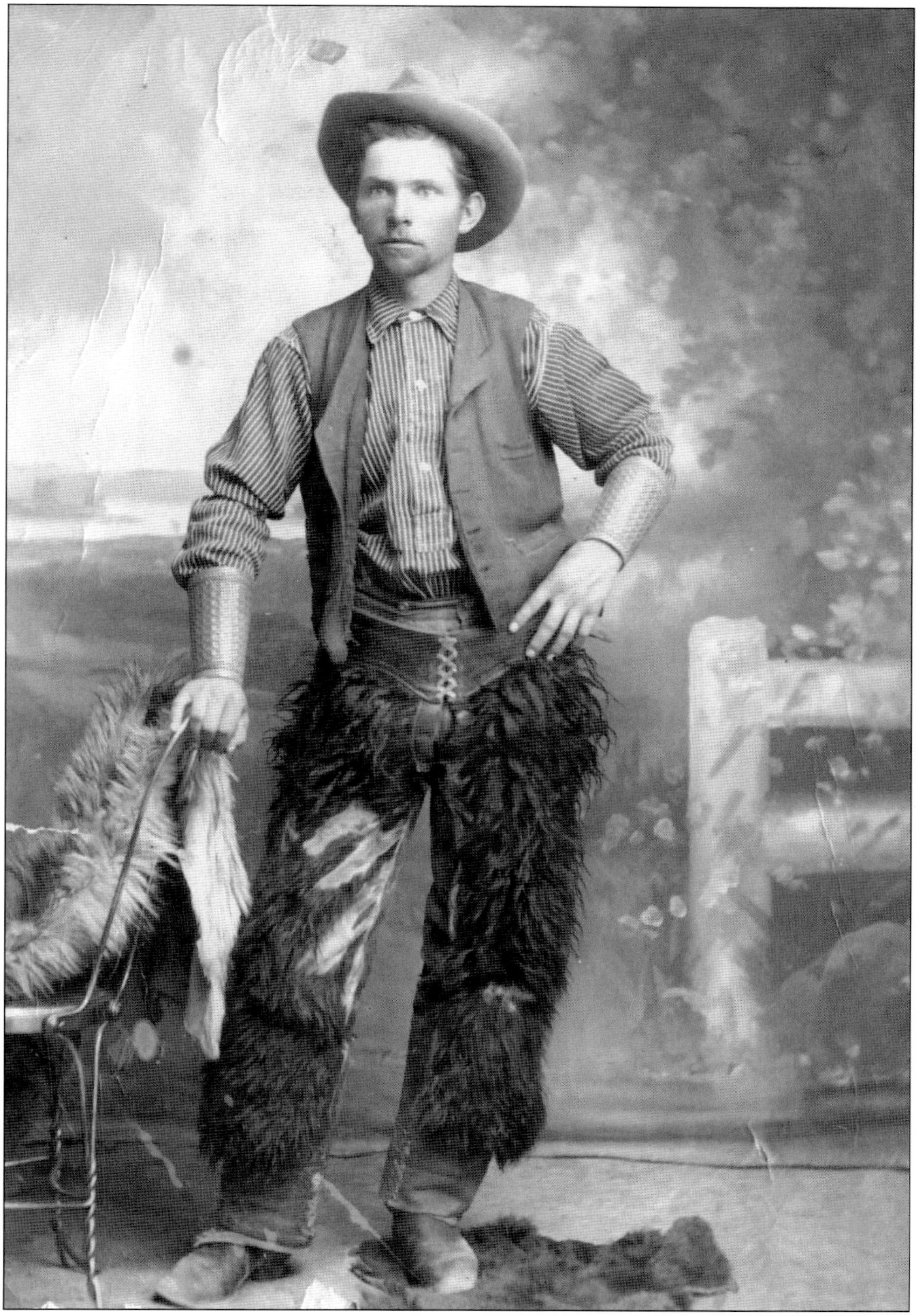

A cowboy of local renown, Ira Purjue poses for a studio portrait in 1902. Purjue, a Native American, was an example of how local Native Americans were absorbed and integrated into the growing ranching culture that replaced the hard-rock mining industry. Purjue (also sometimes spelled Purgue) was born in 1862. He and at least a dozen other family members were listed as residents of Owyhee County in the 1910 census. (Courtesy of Mildretta Adams.)

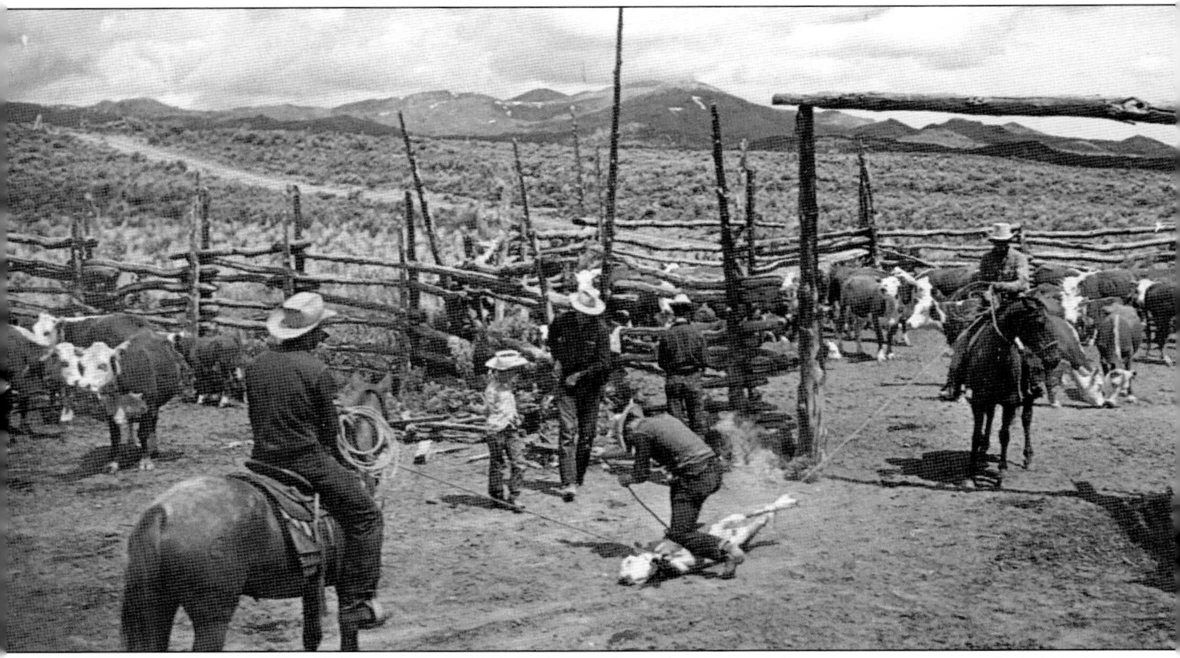

Pictured here is cattle branding at T Ranch in Triangle, Idaho. From left to right are Jack Nichols (on horse), Nick Nettleton (boy), Jim Nettleton, Matt Nettleton (branding), Tim Nettleton (back to camera), and Theron Adcock (on horse). Arid ranch land that could not be developed into extensive farms did not support any kind of dense population. Several ranches often could be grouped in a valley with an appropriate water source, while others might be located far from any neighbors. Early Owyhee ranches were broadly distributed and usually isolated. Ranch buildings would be concentrated around a home base, where owners might eventually secure title to a small tract or two, but their ranch lands extended over large, unfenced tracts of public domain that were used only by custom.

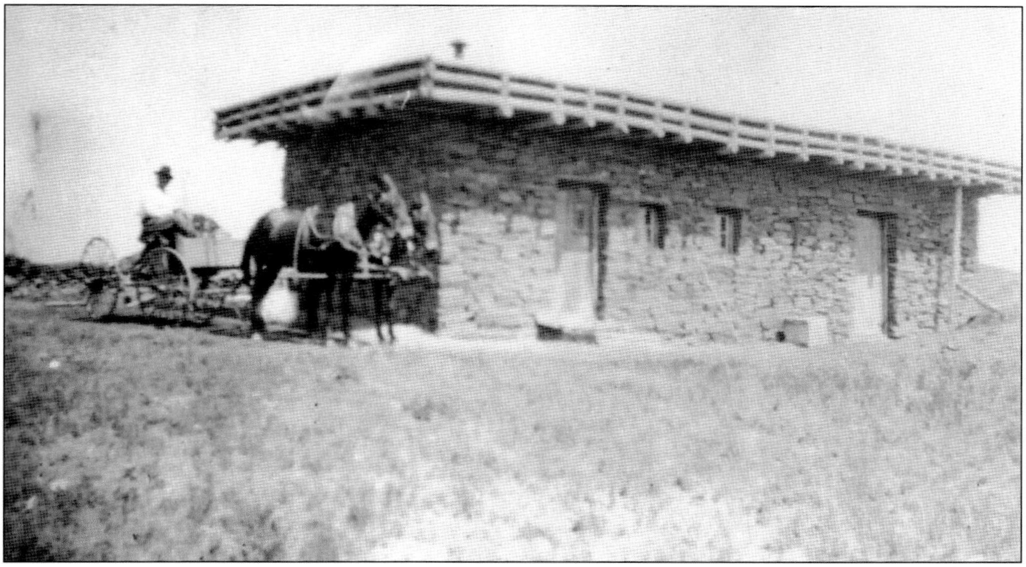

Dick Shooter built this line camp at Battle Creek around 1915. Line camps were buildings placed at the outlying boundaries of a ranch for use by cowboys. A number of Owyhee ranches grew to accommodate large herds, but they remained individual family units. Some ranchers became wealthy employers of cowboys and other staff, but they got that way as successful individual operators. (Courtesy of Neil Brace.)

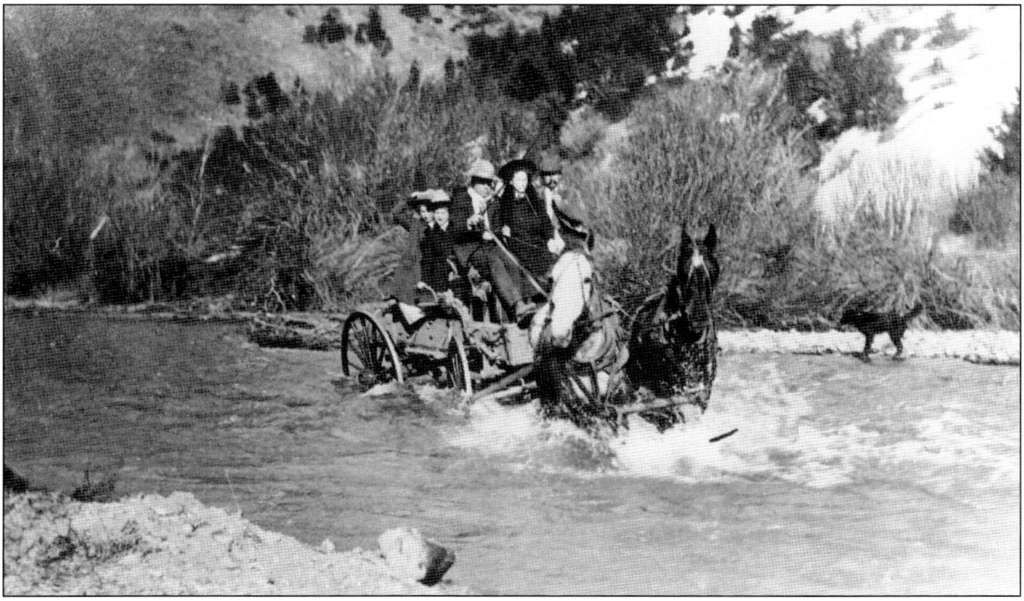

Ranch life was not for the faint of heart, as evidenced by this laden wagon bravely crossing Jordan Creek near DeLamar. Even into the 20th century, life was often isolated and rough. Highways or any kind of paved roads did not penetrate into the interior, although ranches could be reached with faster and more convenient means than earlier wagons and pack strings. Eventually, ranches needed to depend less upon local families (that needed schools and other facilities) because transient herders could be supplied from distant communities, and livestock could be transported by trucks. Herds did not have to rely on uninterrupted grazing lands along their entire route to railroad lines or Idaho markets.

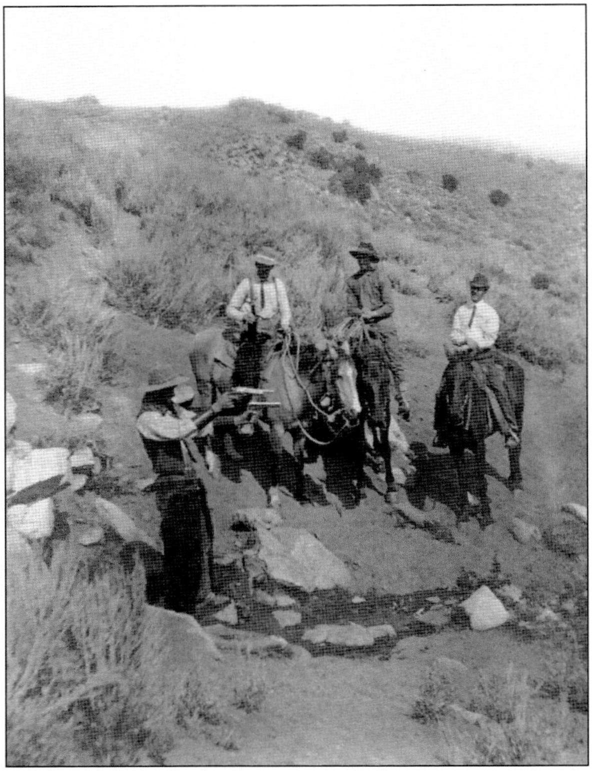

Cowboys of the Reynolds Creek Ranch put on a show for visiting dude John V. Larson of Chicago, Illinois (note the whiskey bottle and six shooters). Although not by any means a dude ranch, the Share Stage House on Reynolds Creek became a well-known resort, stage stop, and way station for the traveling public. Mr. and Mrs. Charles Share opened it in April 1877. The local newspaper provided the following description: "The house, of modern and substantial construction, is beautifully located in about 25 acres of orchard land, covered with hardy fruit of many varieties. Mr. Share also owns about 35 acres, cultivated in timothy and alfalfa, and his yield this season will amount to about 130 tons of hay. The stage house is the stopping station of the C.O. and I Stage Company and welcome to all those who have had the good fortune to partake of the hospitalities of the worthy host and hostess."

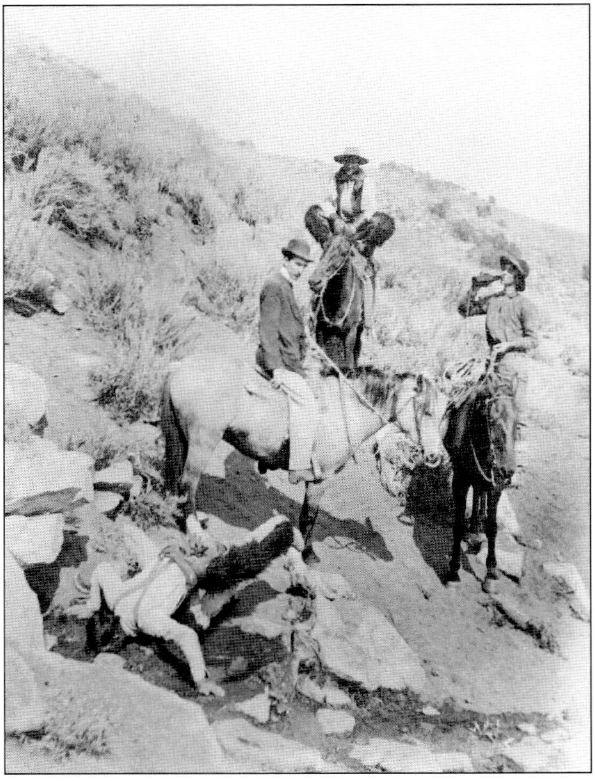

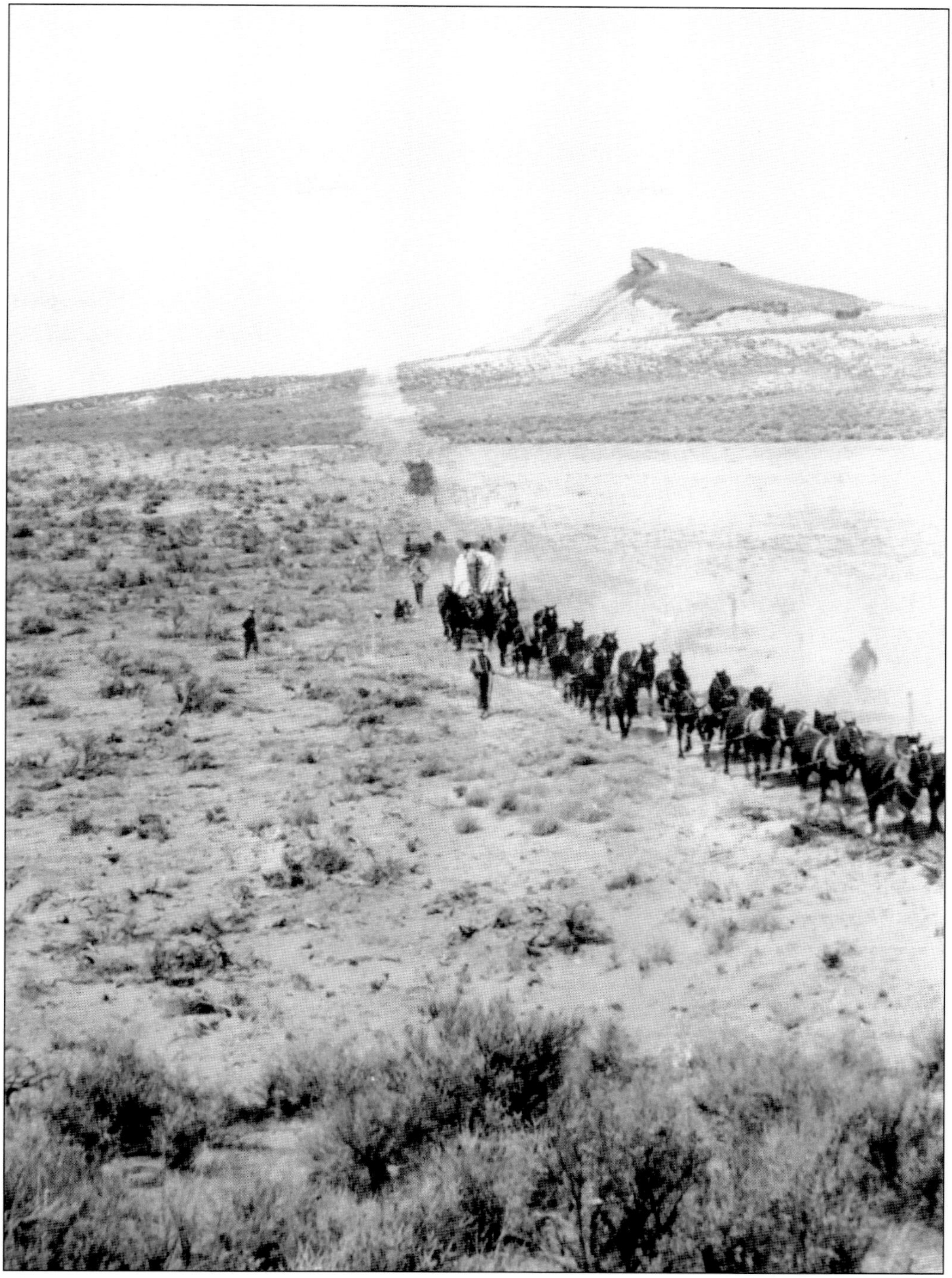

This wagon with 24-horse team is traveling along the path of the Oregon Trail, often used locally for cattle drives. Lizard Butte, the volcanic formation in the background, is one of the more prominent landmarks along the southern Idaho branch of the Oregon Trail. In this particular instance in 1912, the Morrison-Knudsen Company's wagon is hauling a large transformer for the pumping plant of the Gem Irrigation District. The town of Marsing got its start from Lizard Butte's status as a camping site on the Oregon Trail.

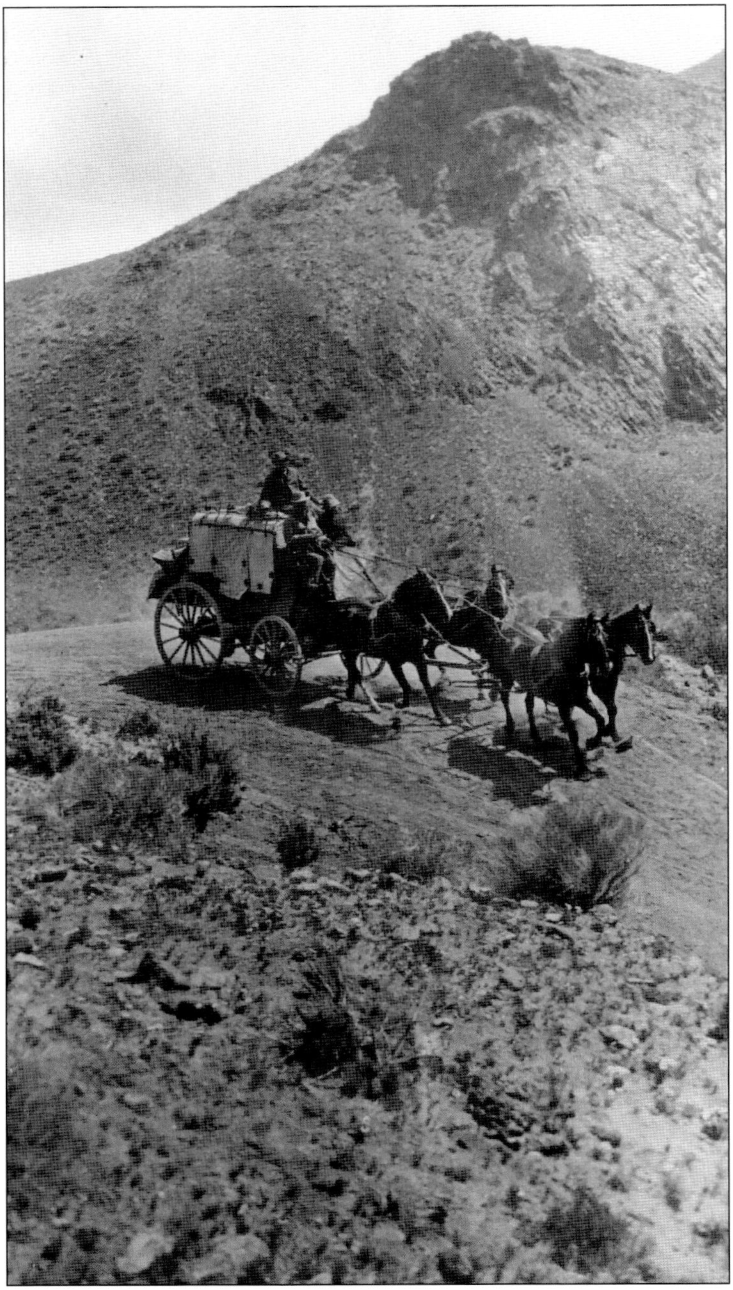

Stagecoaches remained an important means of transportation in the ranching country up until World War I. This is the Silver City stage on Whiskey Hill road in 1910. On September 2, 1865, the *Owyhee Avalanche* reported, "The Idaho and California Stage and Wagon Routes are beginning to assume an importance which we have predicted for a long time. The stage route is now protected by troops from Ruby City to Susanville, California. Captain Mullan arrived in Ruby City the day before yesterday with the first through stage from Sacramento's river—bringing a full load of through passengers. The stage stock was started from here yesterday to be distributed from Ruby City to Puebla and the first through stage will leave here for California Tuesday next—after that leaving regularly three times per week." (Photograph by Edith Farrer.)

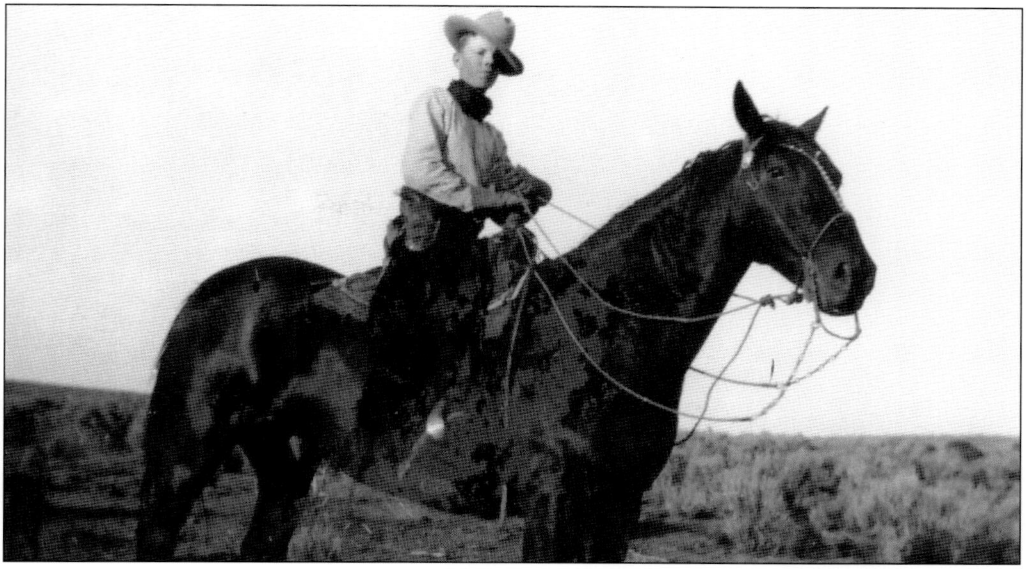

Guy Black of Bruneau poses on Duke near Jack Creek and the Potholes. The Bruneau region was a natural setting for cattle ranching, with miles of green meadows along the Bruneau River, which furnished water. Settlers moved into the area in the 1860s. The meadows provided winter feed for stock, which during the summer months was driven into the higher elevations for grazing.

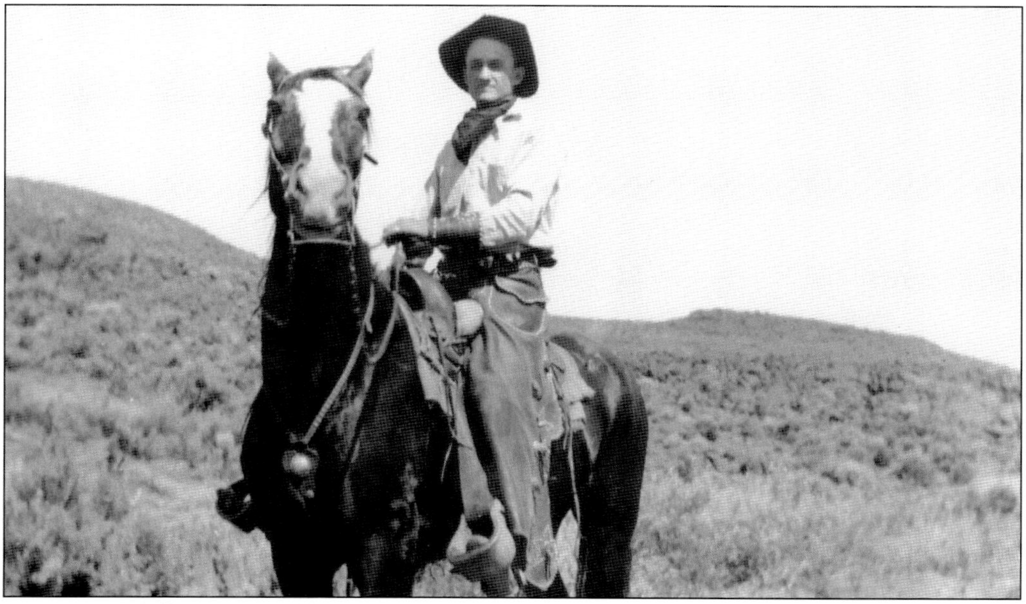

George Randall, 22 years old, poses on horseback in Little Valley near Bruneau. The Bruneau Valley is located in the northeastern part of Owyhee County, and it is approximately 14 miles in length. The Bruneau River runs through the center of the valley. Many of the old ranches were covered when the river was dammed, forming the C.J. Strike Reservoir. (Courtesy of the Ruth Randall collection.)

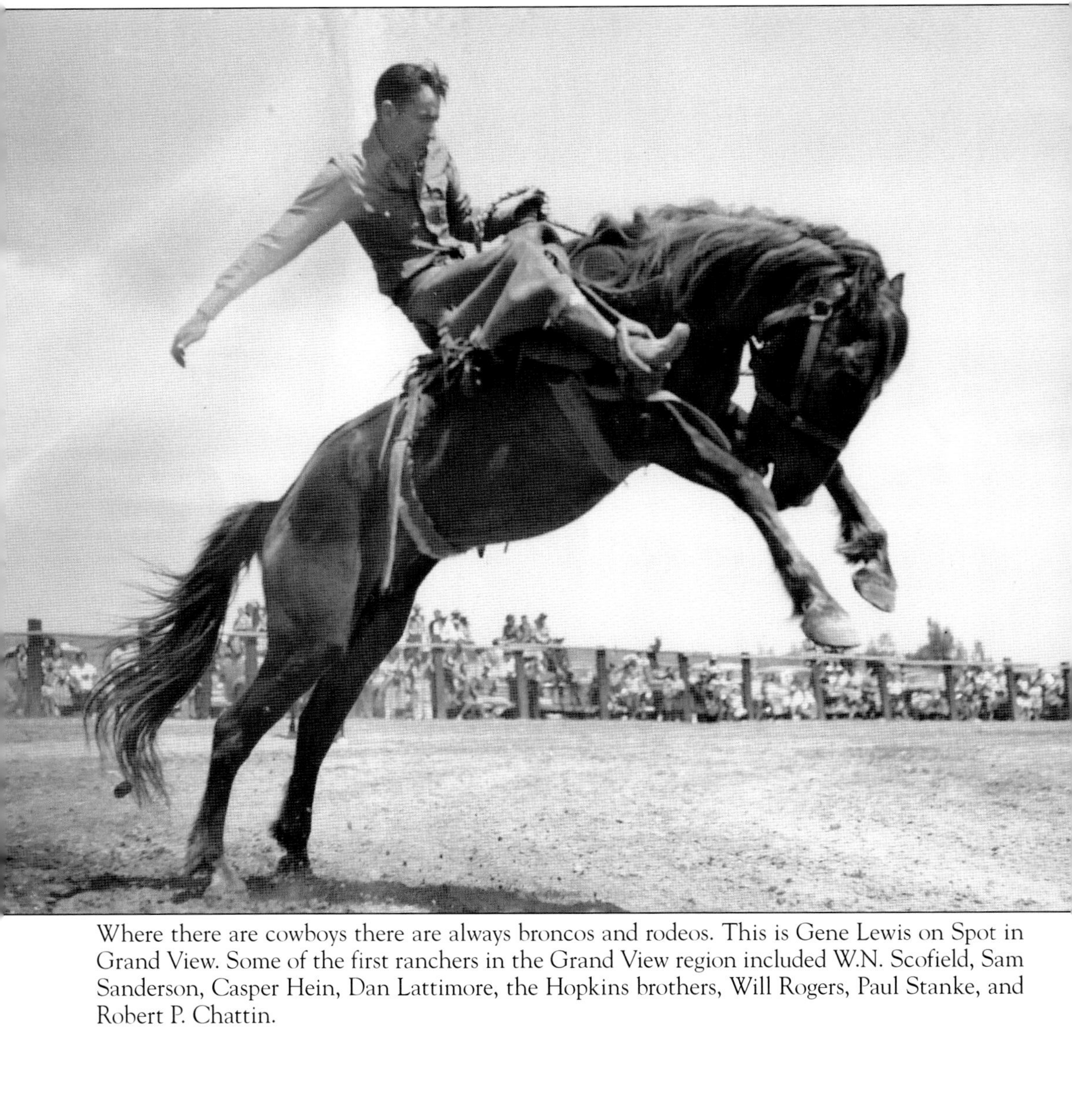

Where there are cowboys there are always broncos and rodeos. This is Gene Lewis on Spot in Grand View. Some of the first ranchers in the Grand View region included W.N. Scofield, Sam Sanderson, Casper Hein, Dan Lattimore, the Hopkins brothers, Will Rogers, Paul Stanke, and Robert P. Chattin.

Six

The Farmers

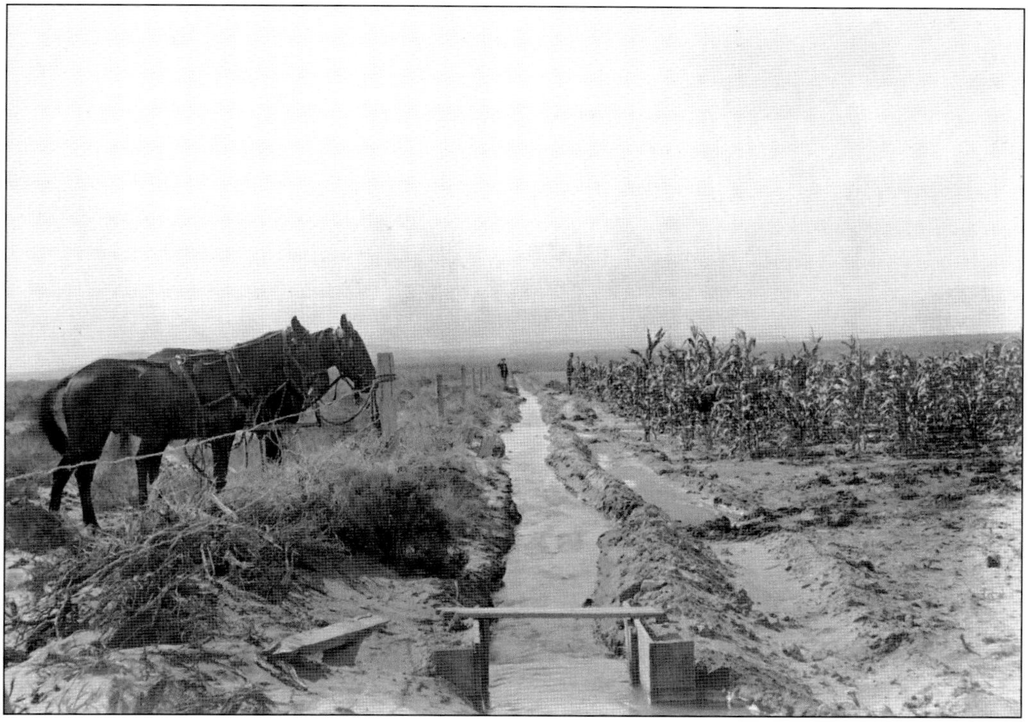

This is Ernest Bedford's first crop in Claytonia near Homedale. The town was officially established in 1913 and named Claytonia in honor of B.F. Clay, a prominent local landowner. Claytonia had a moment in the national spotlight in 1917 when the selective conscription lottery was held during World War I. A national lottery fixed the order of military liability for the 10 million young men registered. One at a time, 10,000 numbers were drawn from a great lottery jar in the US Senate Building. Secretary of War Newton D. Baker stepped up blindfolded to draw the first number—258—that of James Adelbert Dunn, of Claytonia, Idaho.

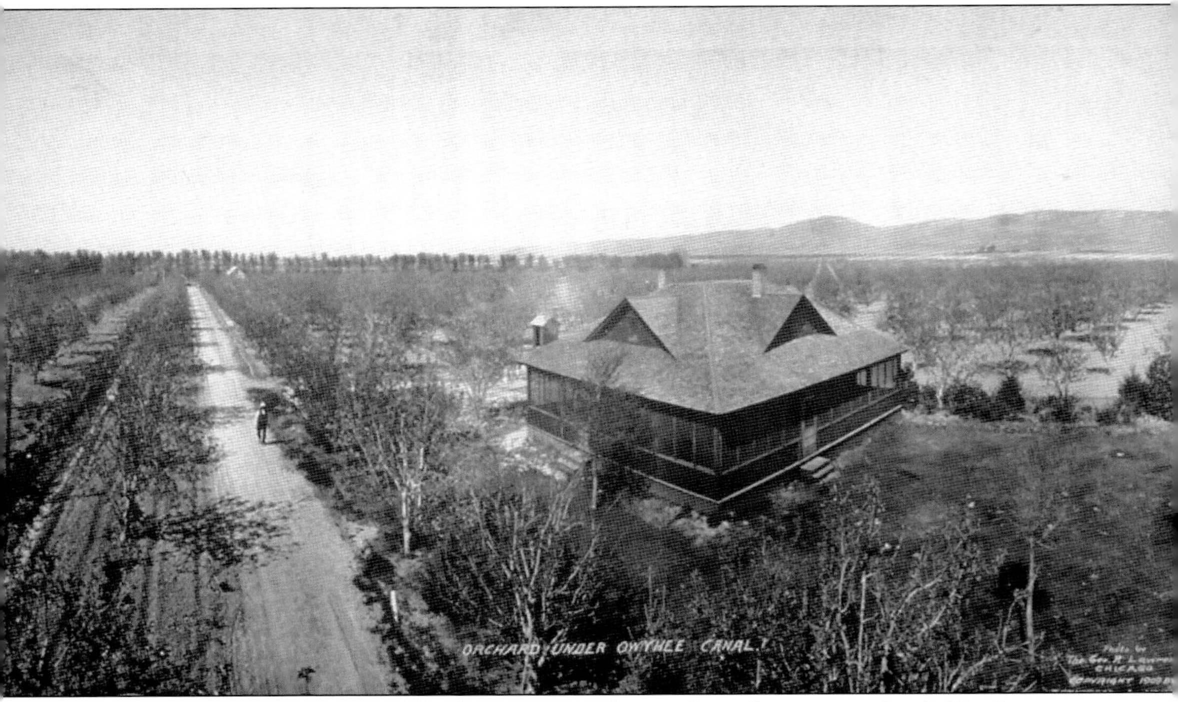

Irrigation projects converted the desert into productive farms featuring orchards like the one seen here. The Owyhee Mountains are in the background. The Gem Irrigation District, established in the early 1900s, brought water to the growing farm communities along the Snake River in Owyhee County, particularly in the Homedale and Marsing regions. It was soon practical to raise crops such as corn, sugar beets, alfalfa, and onions. (Courtesy of the Library of Congress.)

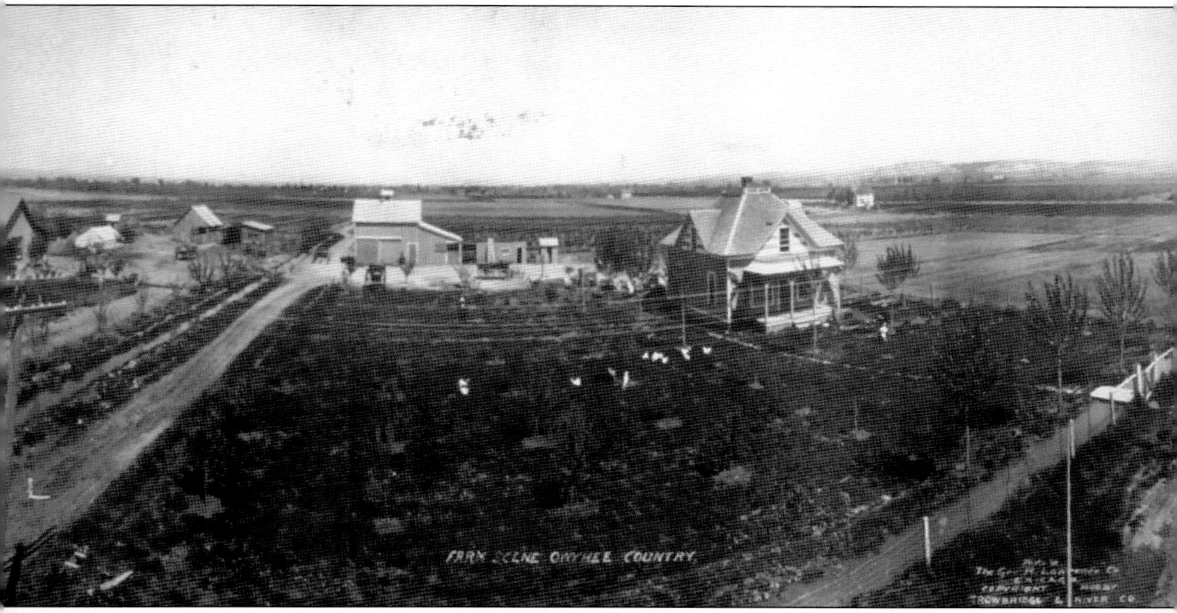

This is an early 1900 farm scene in Owyhee County along the Snake River. In 1914, forty Austrian immigrants purchased land along the Snake River near Homedale from the Idaho Title and Trust Company. They arrived by rail boxcar with all their possessions and were greeted at the train station by a local delegation. However, the newly arrived immigrants soon discovered that the promoters were fraudulent, and their title to the land was worthless. They were forced to repurchase the land from the State of Idaho in 1919. The group included the families of Frank Cegnar, John Jesenko, Frank Kushlan, Joseph Dolence, John Dempshar, James Marcheck, and Jerry Miklovich. (Courtesy of the Library of Congress.)

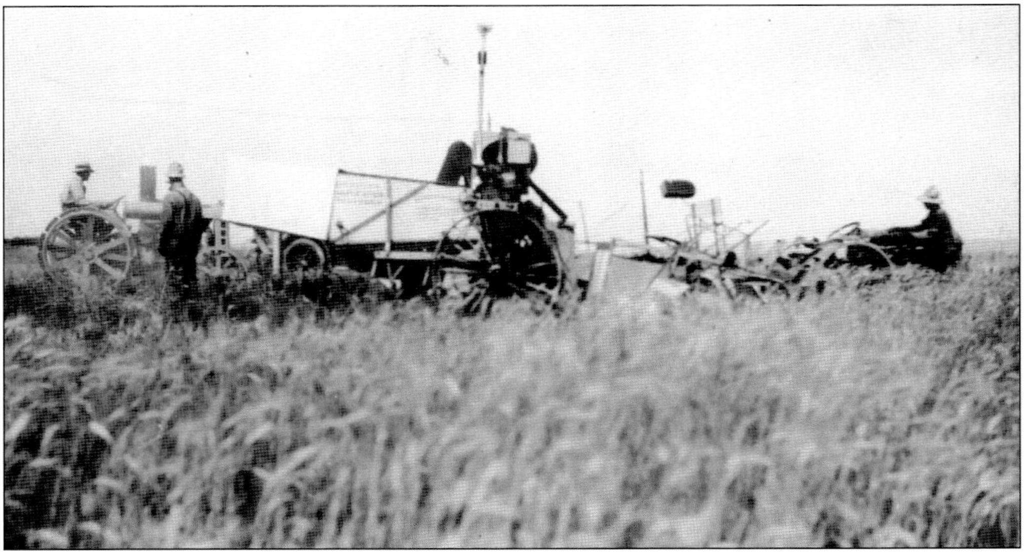

The Gem Irrigation Company started pumping water from the Snake River above Marsing in June 1913, and the miles of arid greasewood and sagebrush land surrounding Homedale turned into fertile agricultural fields. Wheat was a major crop in the early years.

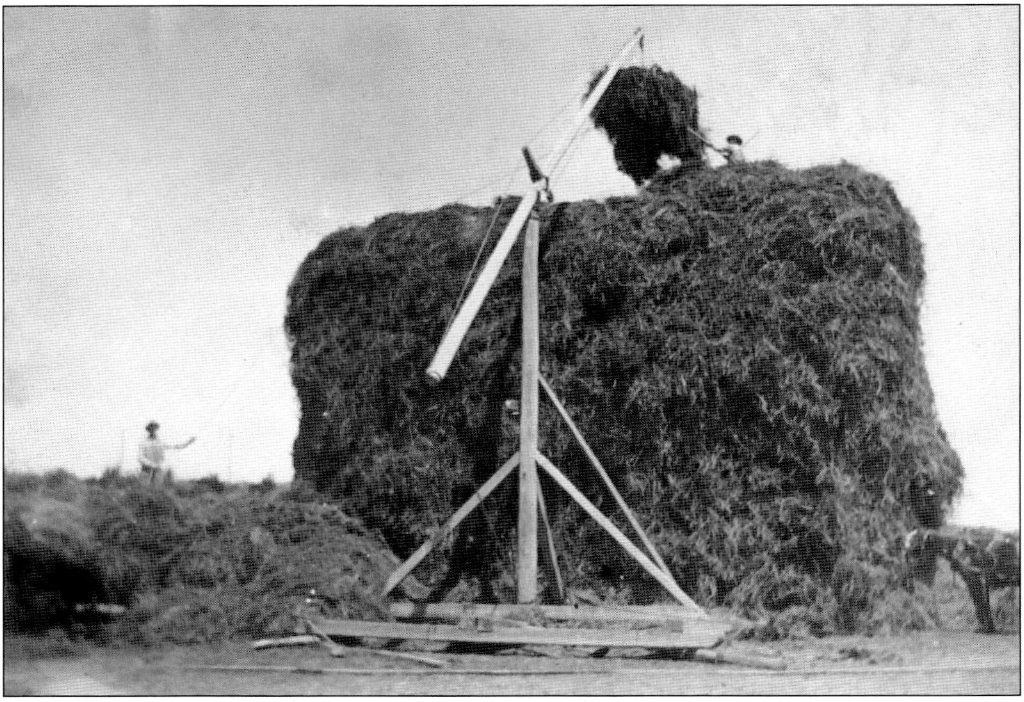

Hay, a major crop used to feed livestock, is being harvested in Homedale in this photograph. Two developments, the coming of the railroad and the advent of irrigation systems, meant an eventual conversion from crops like hay to higher-value crops such as vegetables and fruits. These needed more water, provided by irrigation, and also required a means of moving produce to markets quickly and economically, provided by trains. The Oregon Short Line reached Homedale in 1913, constructing a two-story depot, section house, icehouse, well, and a 50,000-gallon water tank. (Photograph by Edith Hyslop.)

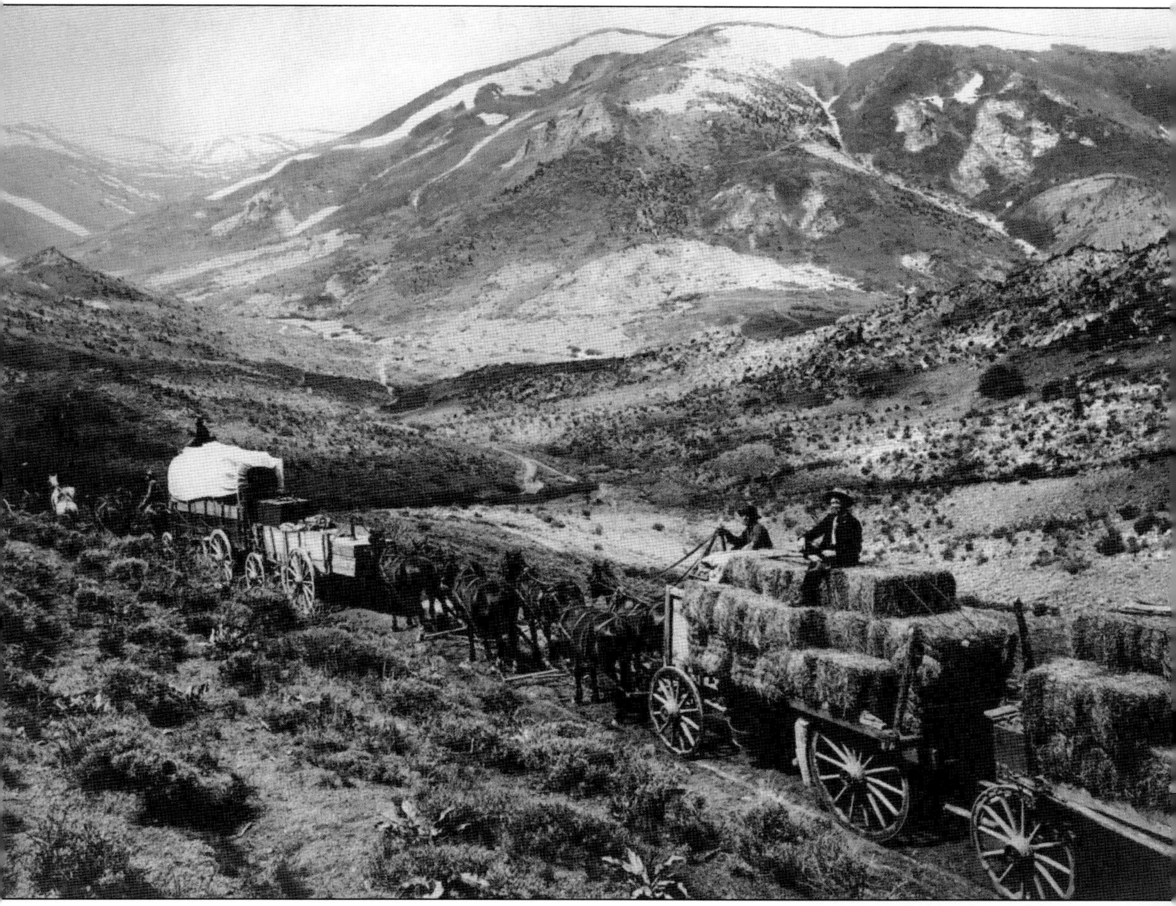

Hay wagons are moving over the New York Summit between Silver City in the mountains and the meadow hay fields along the Snake River. The productive meadows along the Snake and Owyhee Rivers, as well as smaller branches of the two, provided excellent hay production. Hay was essential to communities that depended heavily on horses and cattle. While grazing was plentiful in the vast sagebrush country, and the higher elevations provided excellent forage during the summer months, bitter cold winters accompanied by heavy snows meant that stored hay was critical to the local economy. Hay meadows are still a common sight in Owyhee County, but technology has made ranchers less dependent on local feed, and irrigation and better transportation slowly transformed most of the arable land to more lucrative crops such as fruits and vegetables.

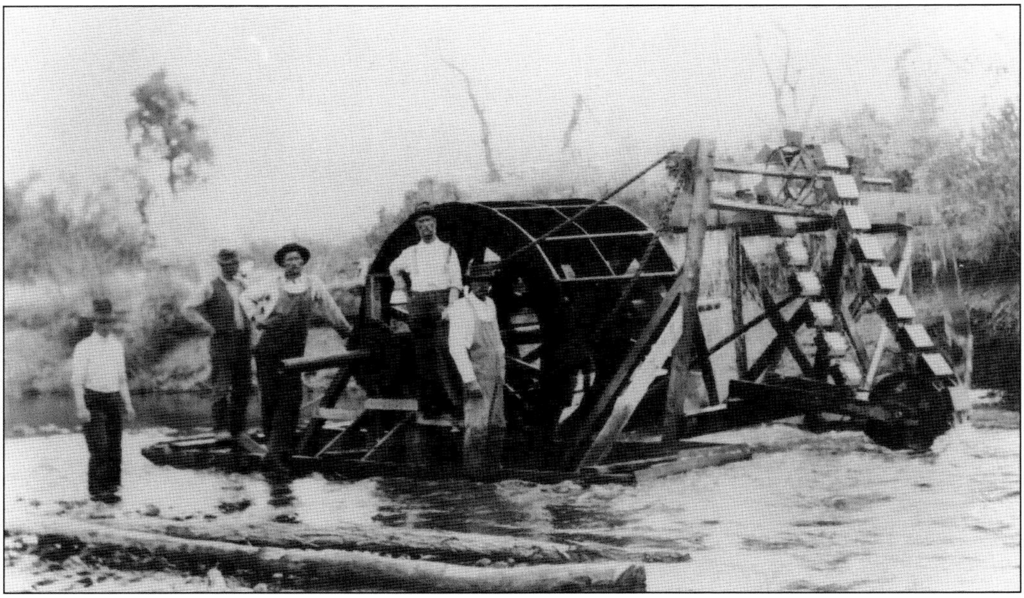

This water wheel on the Snake River near Bruneau was used to remove water from the river for irrigation purposes. In 1890, rock blasted from the high bluffs above the Bruneau River was used to build a dam for irrigation purposes for the ranches of Howard Gress and Clarence Whitted. The dam was washed out in 1892 and rebuilt from timber. (Courtesy of the Ruth Randall collection.)

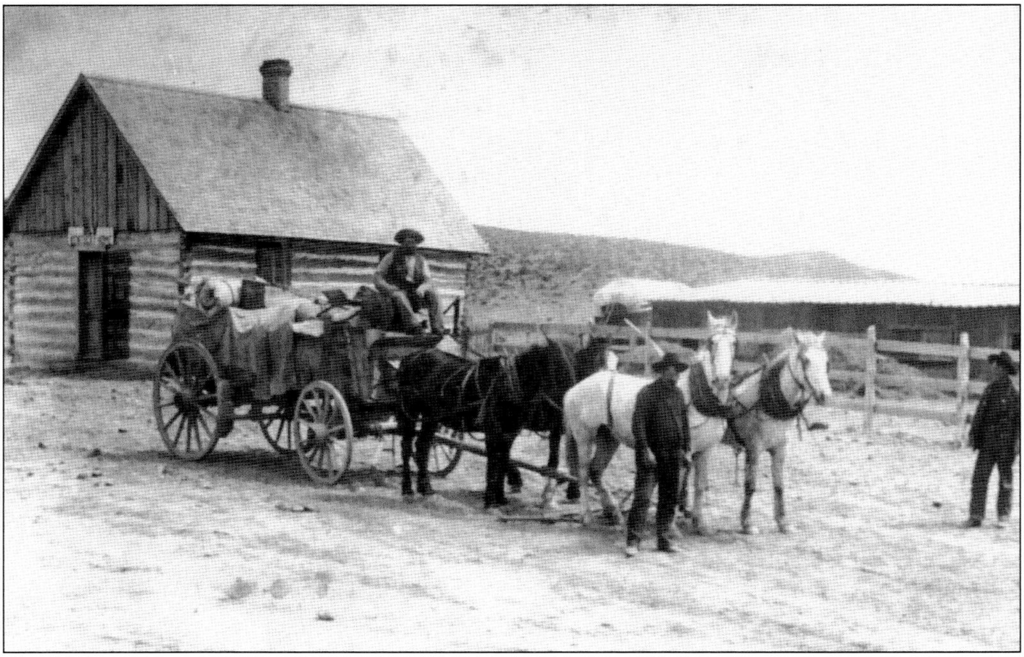

Pictured here is the Randall Farm, typical of a 19th- or early 20th-century farm operation. Life was not easy for the early farmers. One scourge was jackrabbits, which destroyed crops. Farming communities conducted regular rabbit drives, where the population would turn out to surround large areas and drive the rabbits into concentrated areas where they would be clubbed. Owyhee County did not produce a successful potato crop until disease decimated the rabbit population in 1904.

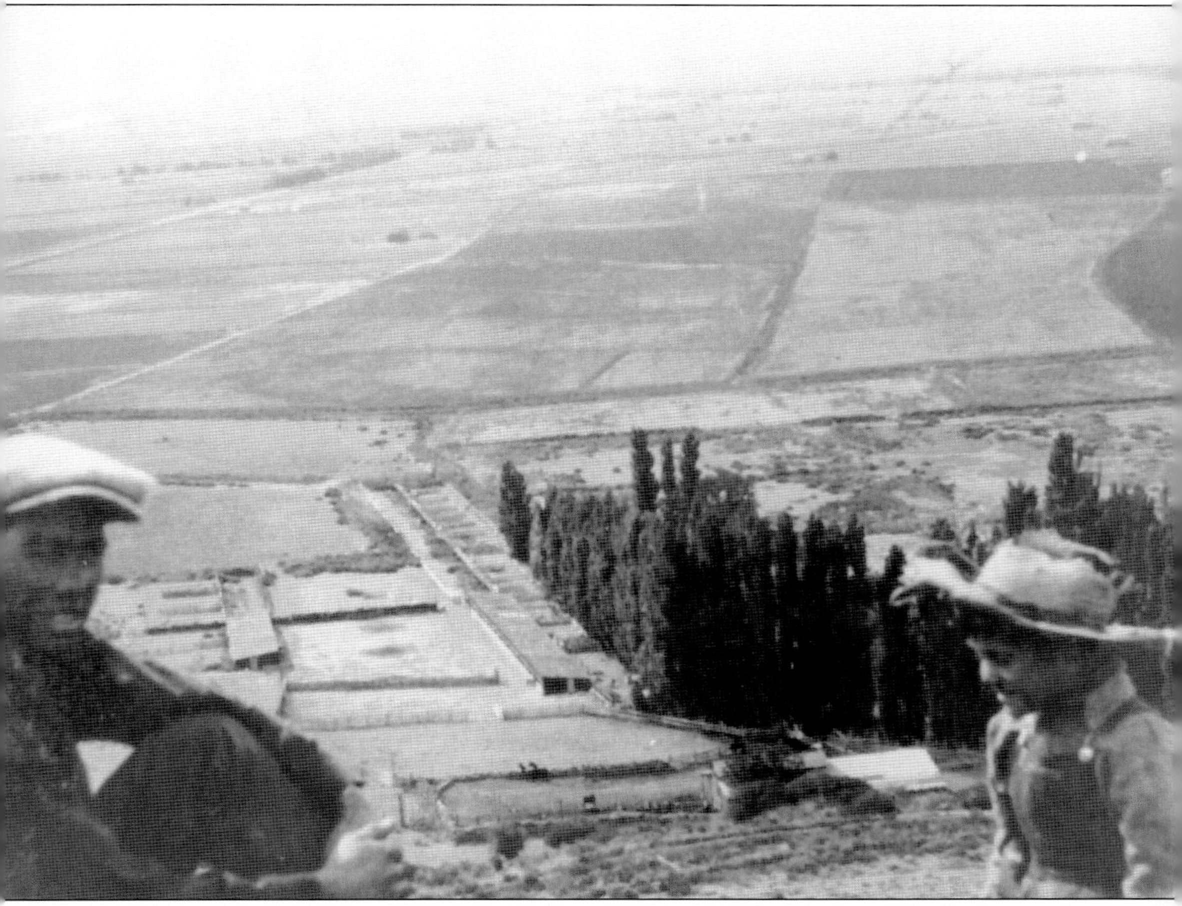

Pictured here is Grand View, with a view of the sweeping agricultural area in the background. The vast majority of the best and most level agricultural land in Owyhee County is found along the banks of the Snake River. The *Owyhee County Blue Book of 1898* states, "Grand View is located on the south side of the Snake River, distant forty-five miles from Mountain Home. It is an outlet for a large scope of agricultural country, there being several fine ranches in the back country and vicinity. It is also the headquarters of the Owyhee Land and Irrigation Company, who are the owners of a fine, substantial hotel and store, besides the ferry. The earliest settlers were Captain White, John McVann, Wenzel Turmes and Henry Dorsey."

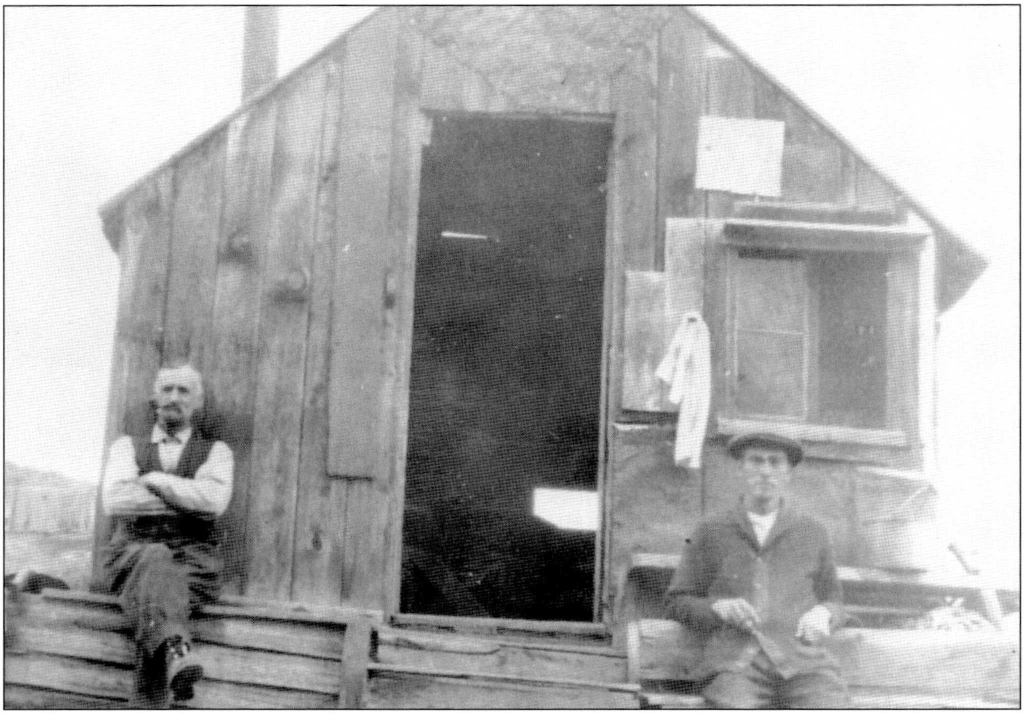

Ed Huntley (right) and Prof. Henry Cox pose at the Cox cabin on Succor Creek between Berg Mine and Rooster Comb Creek. Succor Creek often overflowed its banks, depositing silt from the rich—and uncommon—potash deposits upstream. Potash was commercially very valuable as a fertilizer.

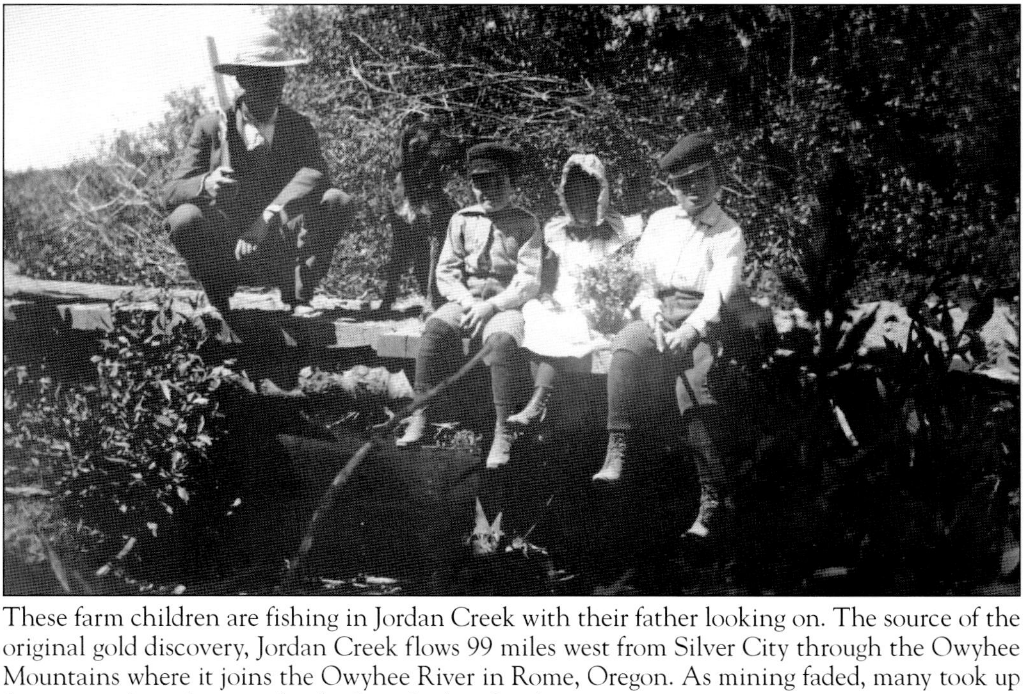

These farm children are fishing in Jordan Creek with their father looking on. The source of the original gold discovery, Jordan Creek flows 99 miles west from Silver City through the Owyhee Mountains where it joins the Owyhee River in Rome, Oregon. As mining faded, many took up farming and ranching on lands along Jordan Creek.

Seven

Homedale and Marsing

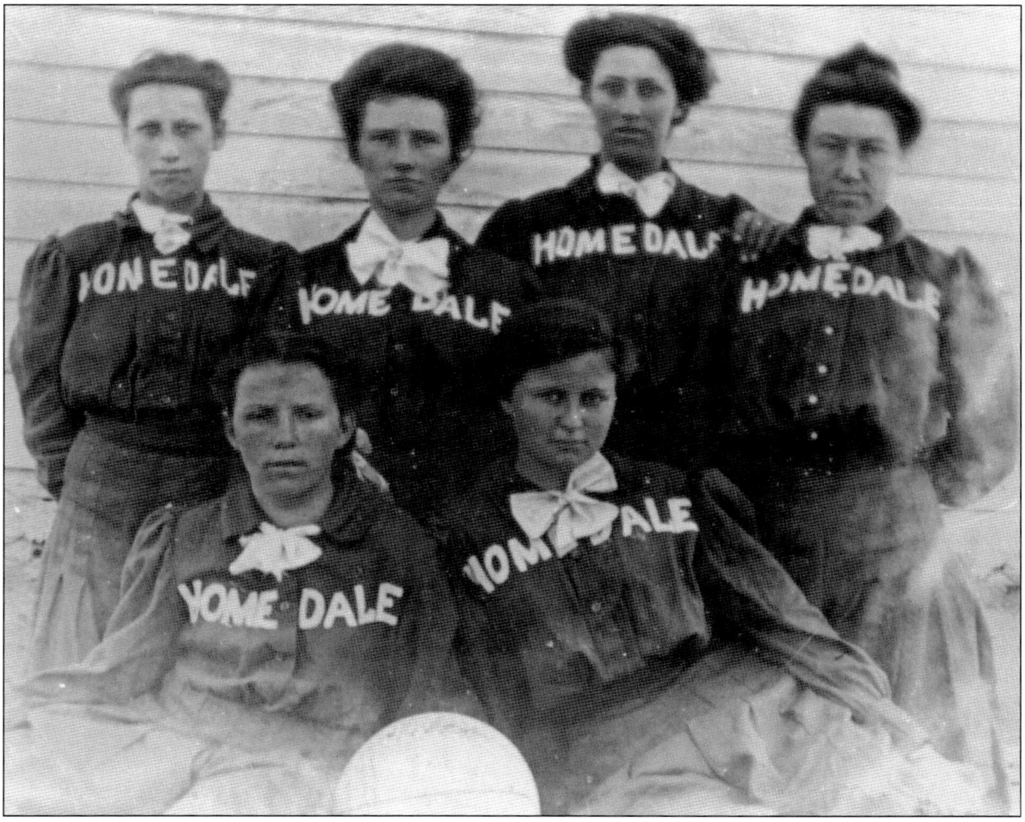

Homedale originated as a ferry crossing on the Snake River and sprang to full bloom as an agricultural community after irrigation projects converted the desert to productive land. Today, it is Owyhee County's most populous town. Members of the 1910 girls' basketball team include, from left to right, (first row) Electrica McDowell and unidentified; (second row) Hazel Sample, Meloina McDowell, Julia Sample, and Mabel Fletcher.

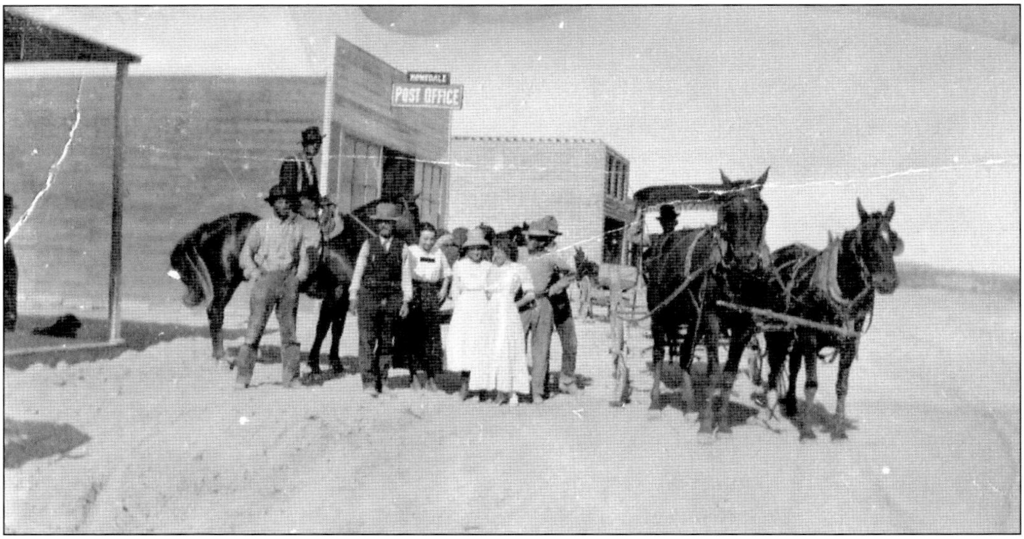

The first Homedale Post Office was established on Owyhee Avenue on May 22, 1900. Ada Mussell became the first postmistress, followed in the next 82 years by Cora McDowell, David Cox, Jacob Mussell, Sherman Mussell, Fern Bitner, Frank Troller, Theodore Nye, Russell Plummer, Frank Daws, J.D. Wright, Ida Helton, Vic Uria, and Joyce Turner. The photograph above was taken in 1914, when Fern Bitner was postmistress. Below is a slightly earlier image of the post office with Mae Mercer. (Courtesy of Edith Hyslop.)

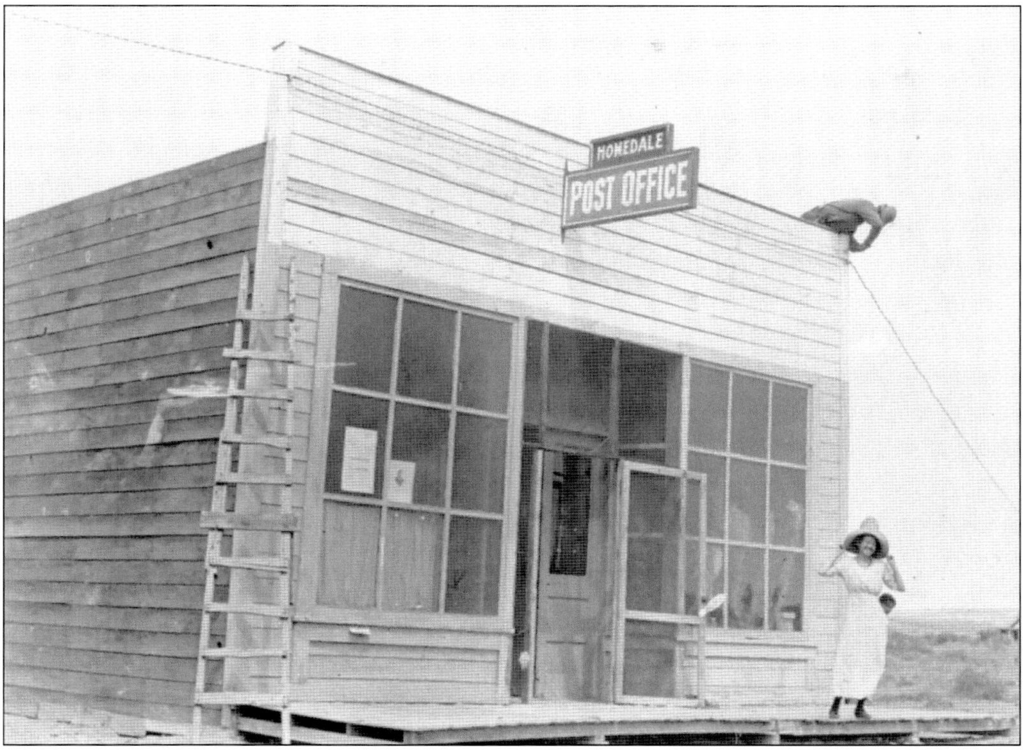

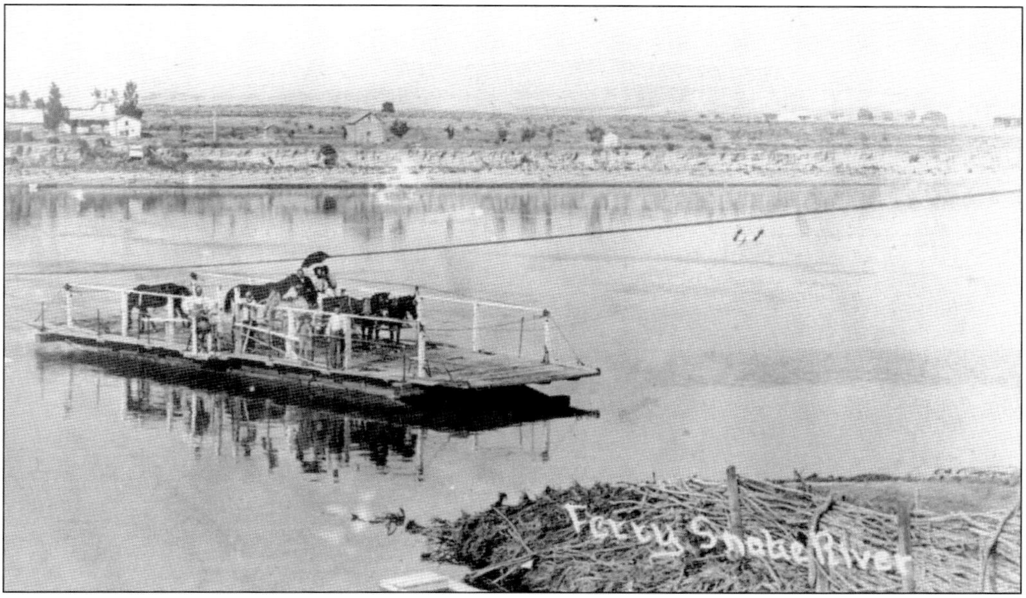

Pictured here are two views of the Homedale Ferry from around the late 19th to early 20th centuries. The Homedale Bridge was built in 1920 and put the ferries out of business. Ferries were not always practical, particularly in the winter. In January 1917, the *Homedale Empire Press* reported, "As a result of the extreme cold weather, Snake River is filled with floating ice and none of the ferries have been able to operate since Monday. No mail was received Tuesday and Wednesday. Thursday's mail was brought around by way of the Big Bend bridge [Adrian], which is about 15 miles below Homedale. Friday's mail was brought in by train. But for our train service we would be completely shut off from the outside world. With our daily train service it is cheaper and quicker and more pleasant to go to Nyssa or Ontario to do business than it is to go to Caldwell."

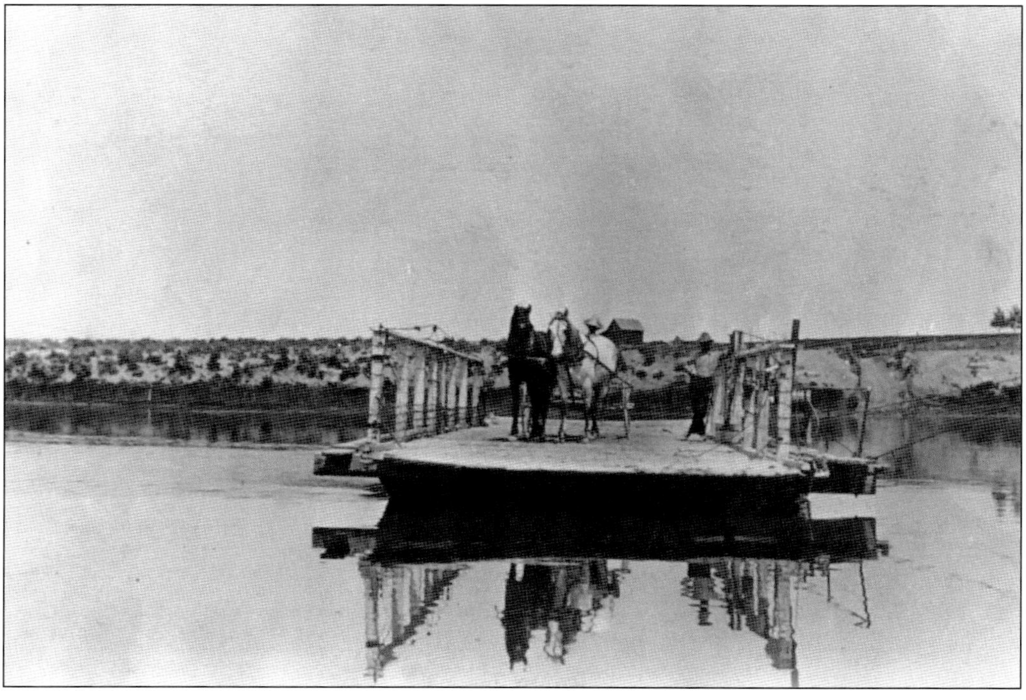

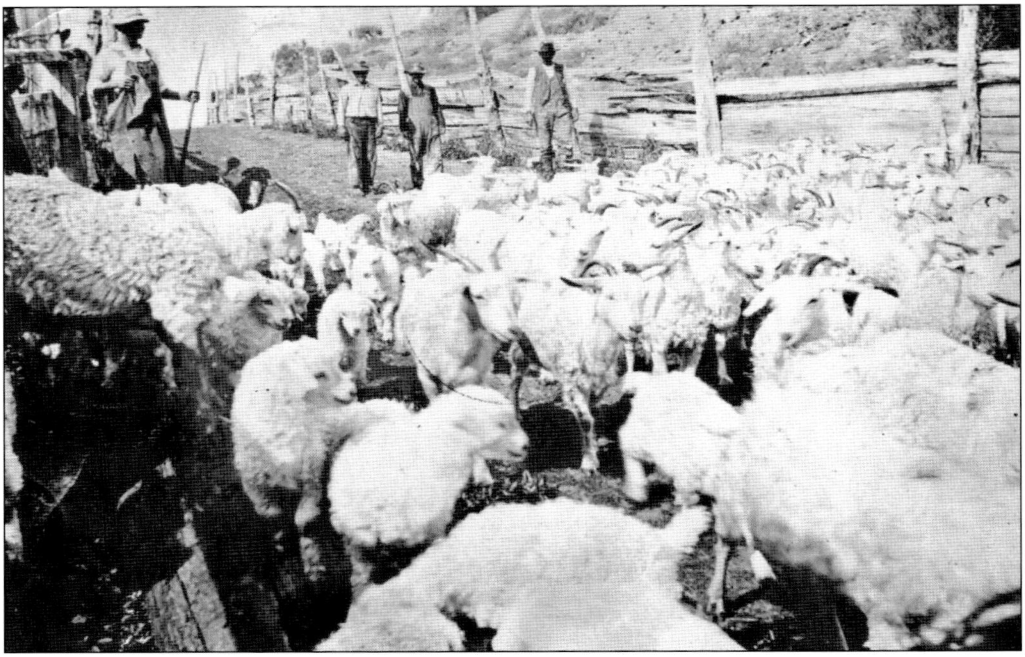

Sheep were an important early resource in Owyhee County, including the area surrounding Homedale. Basque immigrants brought shepherding skills in the early 1900s. Their culture still exerts a strong influence throughout the region.

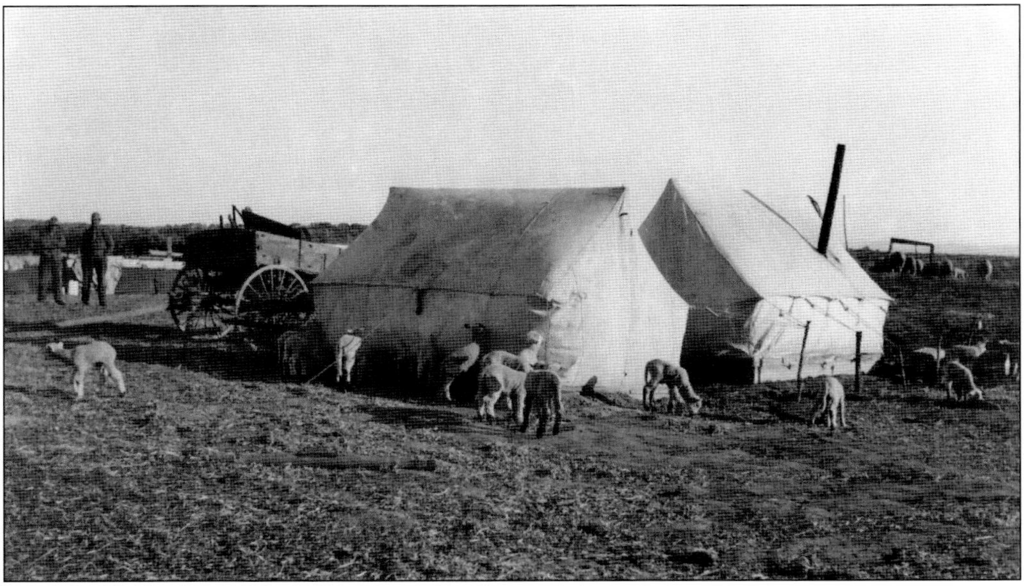

This photograph shows a typical Homedale sheep camp. Prior to the coming of the railroad and establishment of the Gem Irrigation District, the Homedale area was poorly suited for most agricultural purposes, and the land was put to use raising stock. Sheep were particularly well suited to the sparsely vegetated, primarily sagebrush country.

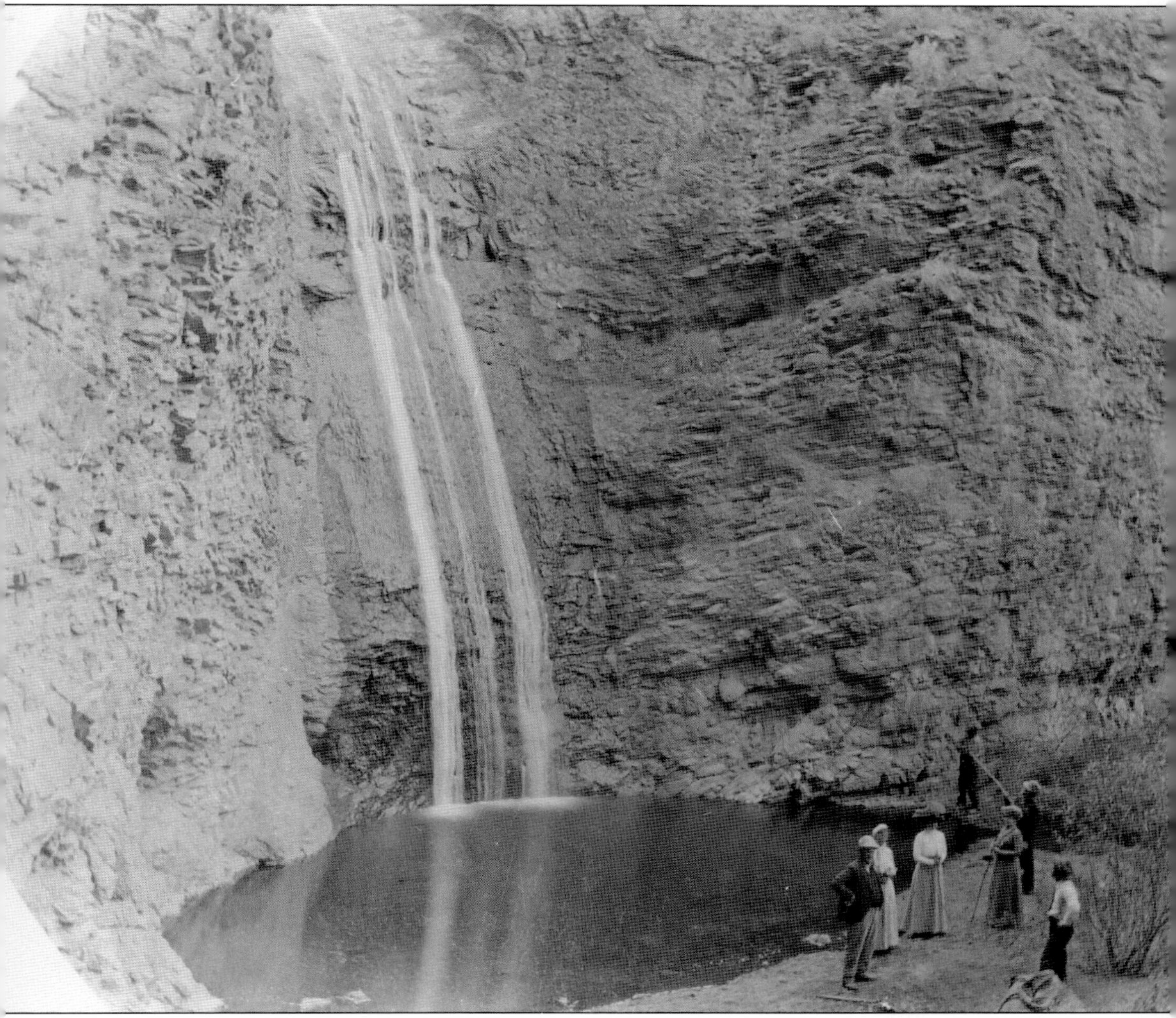

This photograph of Jump Creek Falls, southwest of Homedale, was taken in 1910. Long popular, the site receives close to 20,000 visitors per year according to Bureau of Land Management. It is used for camping, hiking, fishing, swimming, picnicking, gold panning, and rock climbing. It also serves as a staging area for off-road vehicles, horseback riding, and hunting.

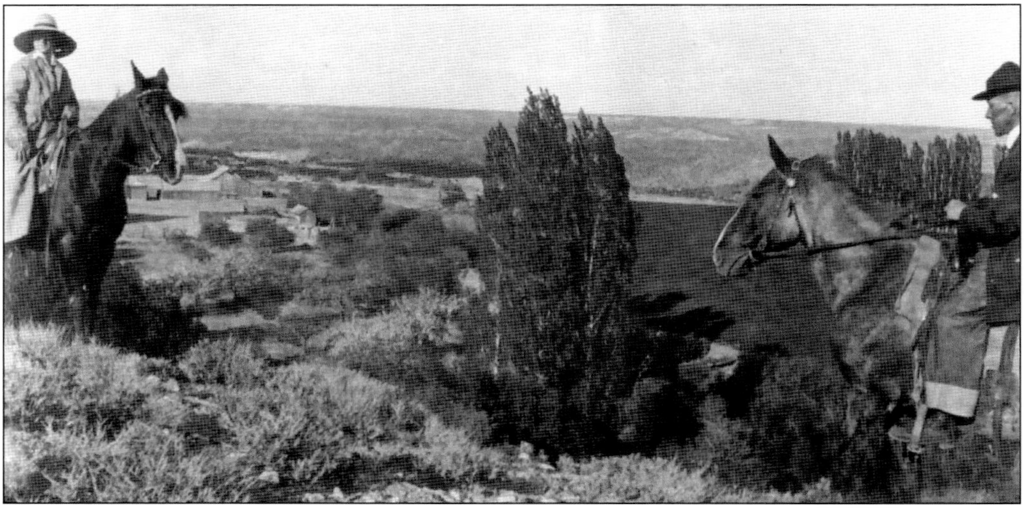

In the early 1900s, Mabel Wilson and Charles Heath enjoy a horseback ride near Jump Creek in the Homedale area. The horse remained the primary means of transportation well into the 20th century. Modern roads and cars were late in coming to Owyhee County, and they were rare in the Homedale region until bridges began to span the Snake River in the 1920s and 1930s. (Courtesy of Edith Hyslop.)

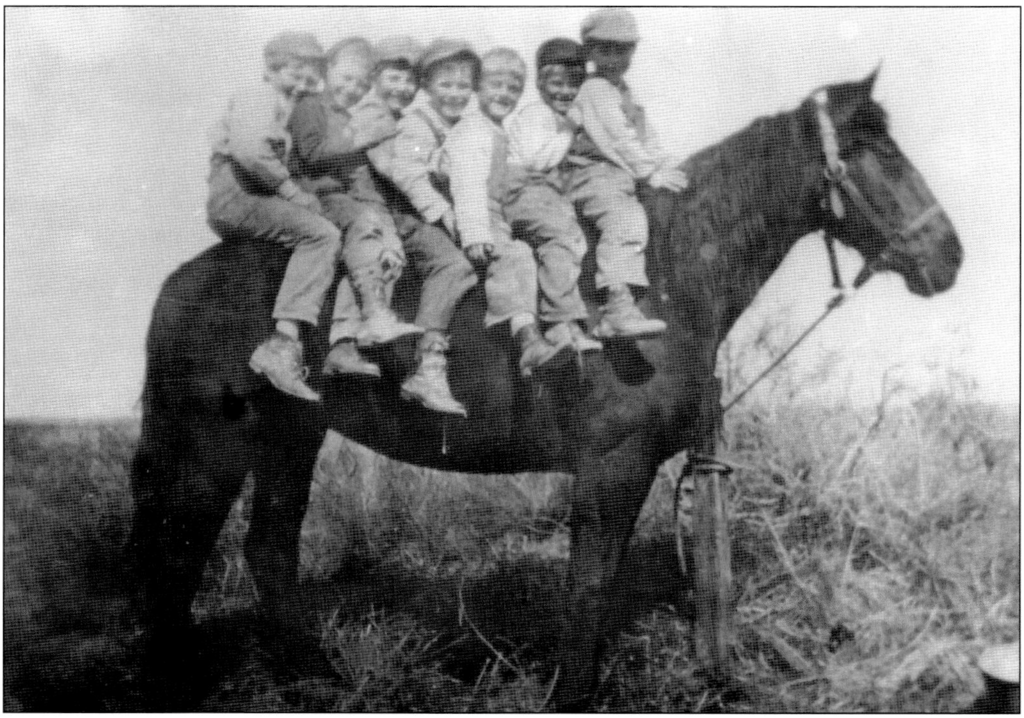

The children of Homedale grew up in the bucolic agricultural America of the early 1900s; however, farm children had many responsibilities. Once crops were planted, the men of the farm often went away to work to make extra money, leaving the women and children to maintain the farm. Range horses and cattle would eat the haystacks in the fields unless deterred, and children were often called upon to sleep overnight in the stacks to protect them. Pumpkins in the field were guarded by children against the always-ravenous jackrabbit population.

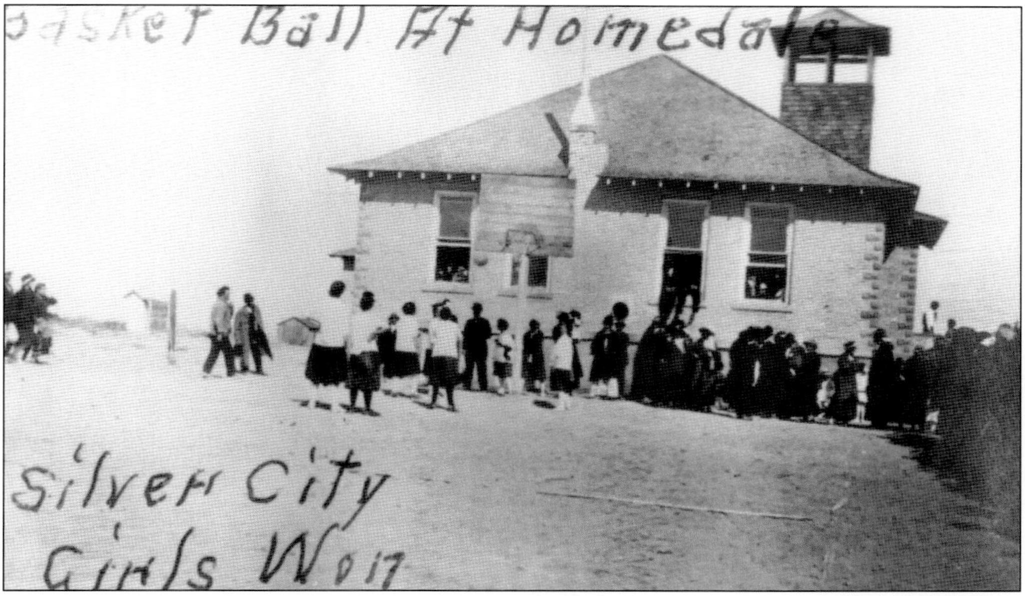

School sports were an important community event that brought people together. The Silver City girls triumphed over Homedale in this 1917 meeting. Schools were often the center of the small but tight-knit communities, and sports rivalries were a source of entertainment and significant pride.

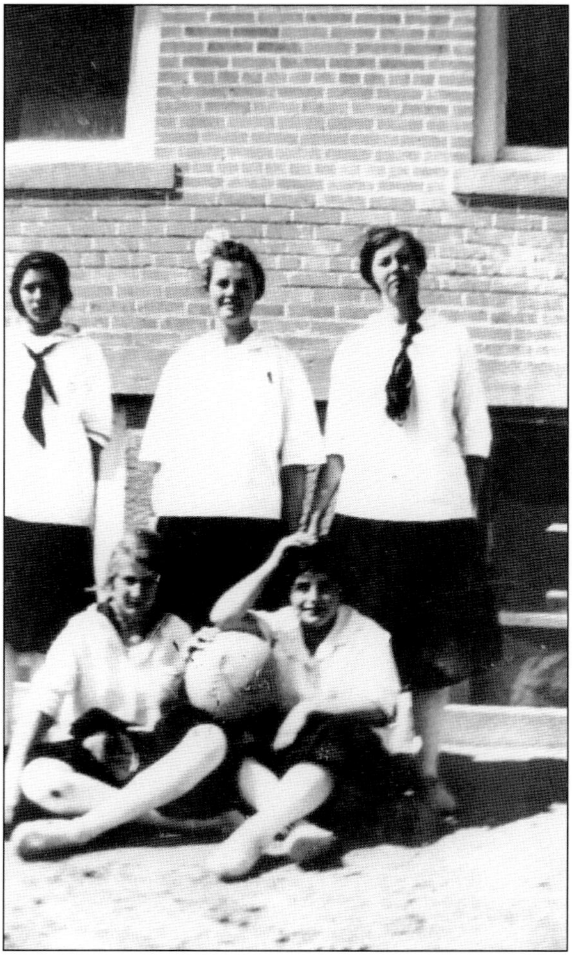

Pictured here is the Homedale girls' basketball team in 1917. The photograph was taken in Grand View during a tournament. The small towns were spread widely across sparsely populated Owyhee County. Travel could be a difficult and time-consuming experience. Rather than playing a schedule against opposing teams, as schools do today, it was more common for a central location to be chosen and a tournament held when all schools could participate. Residents would host teams.

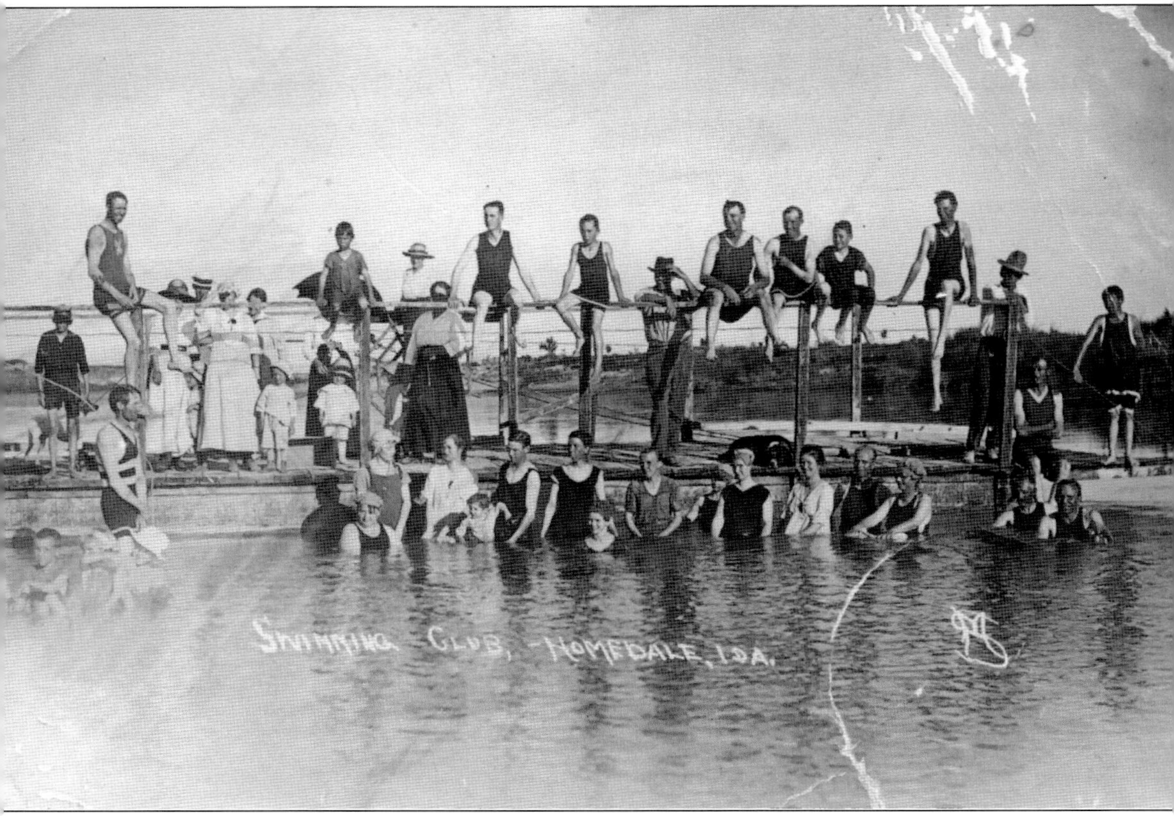

Pictured here on June 5, 1915, is the Homedale Swimming Club at Helton's Island, including the Frank Trotter family; John Upton and children Esther, Grace, and Laraine; Anna Fessner and boys Ernie and Bill; Mr. and Mrs. Tony Freeburn and their small daughter; Dick and Ida Helton; E.C. Preston and daughter Helen; George Ramsey; J.D. Welch and Oscar and Elwood; Mr. and Mrs. R.A. Vanderhoof; O.A. Megorden; and Mrs. Yaden and son Boyd. (Courtesy of Mac Parkins.)

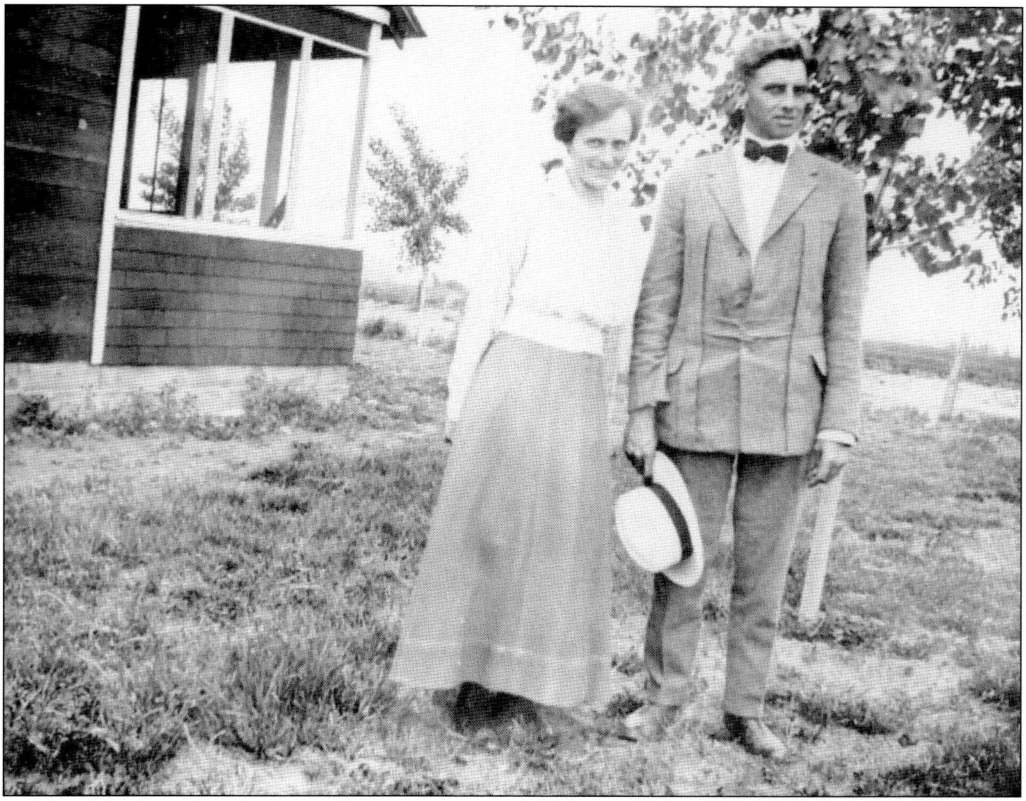

Edith Hyslop, pictured here with her husband, Logan, was a prominent and longtime resident of Homedale. She is responsible for many of the photographs of Homedale published in this book. Logan, below, was a Homedale lawyer. About the time these photographs were taken, a company was created to promote Homedale and the surrounding region. It opened offices in St. Paul and Minneapolis, Minnesota, and Chicago, Illinois, in hopes of attracting settlers to this part of Idaho.

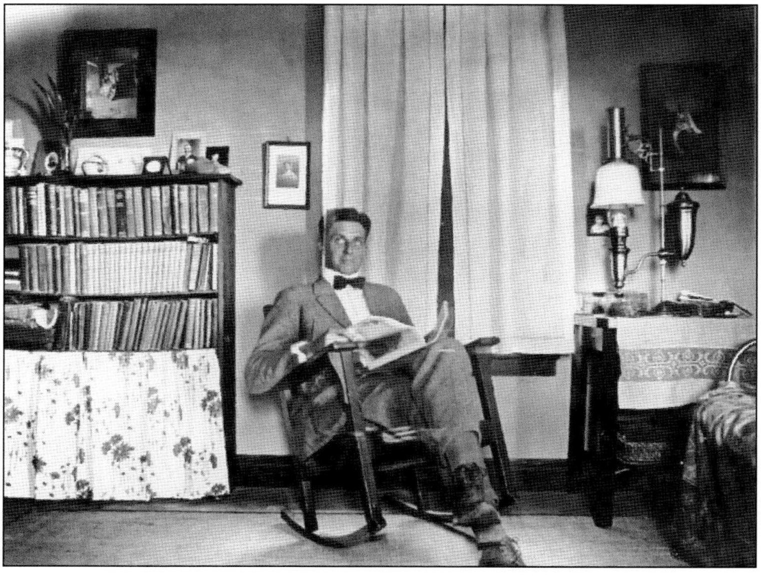

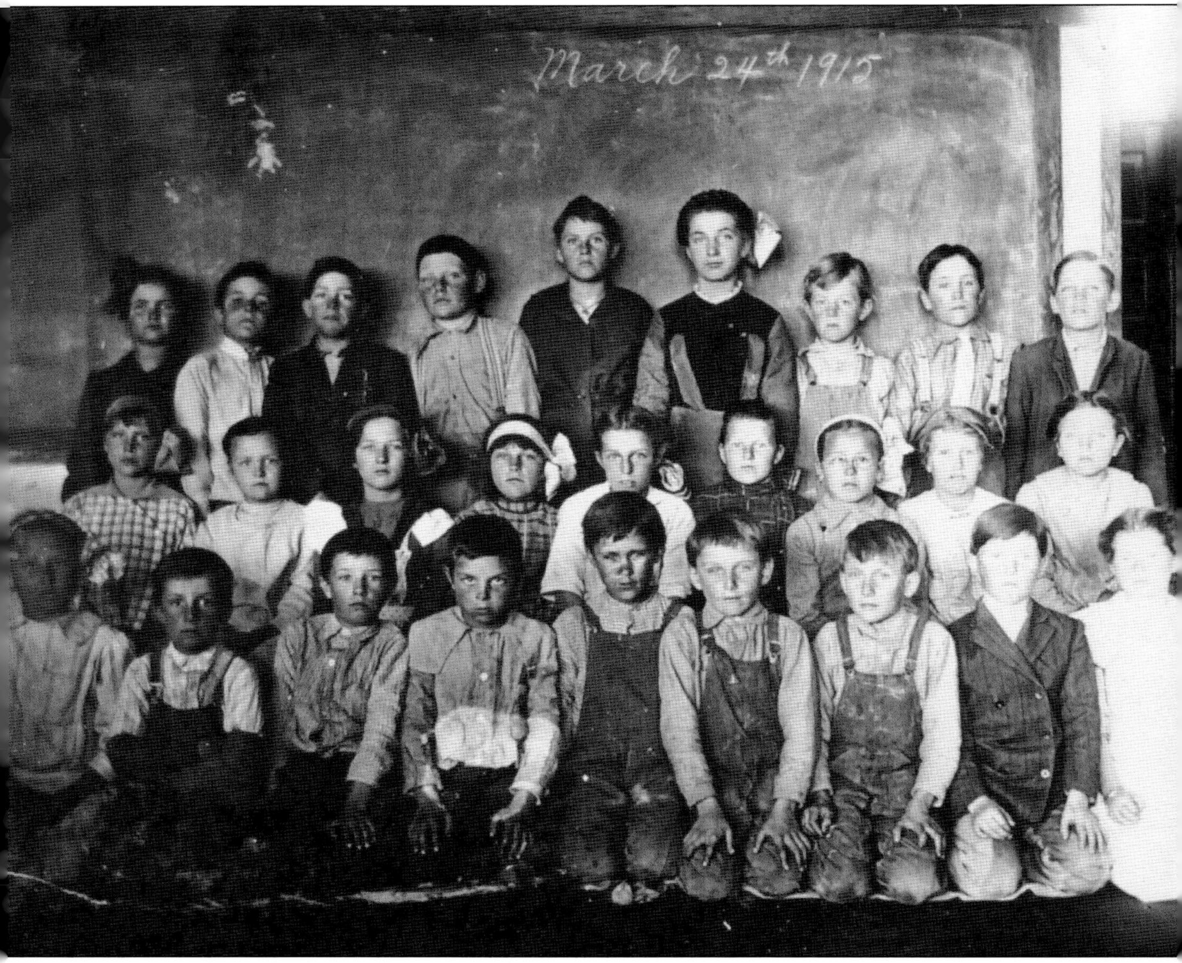

During the early days, schools were built near the center of the population. School was first held in the living room of the Mussell family. The first schoolhouse was built a mile west and a mile south of town; it was a one-room building painted white with a bell and flagpole. In 1913, a $12,000 brick schoolhouse was built on a block donated by the town company. It is pictured here on March 24, 1915.

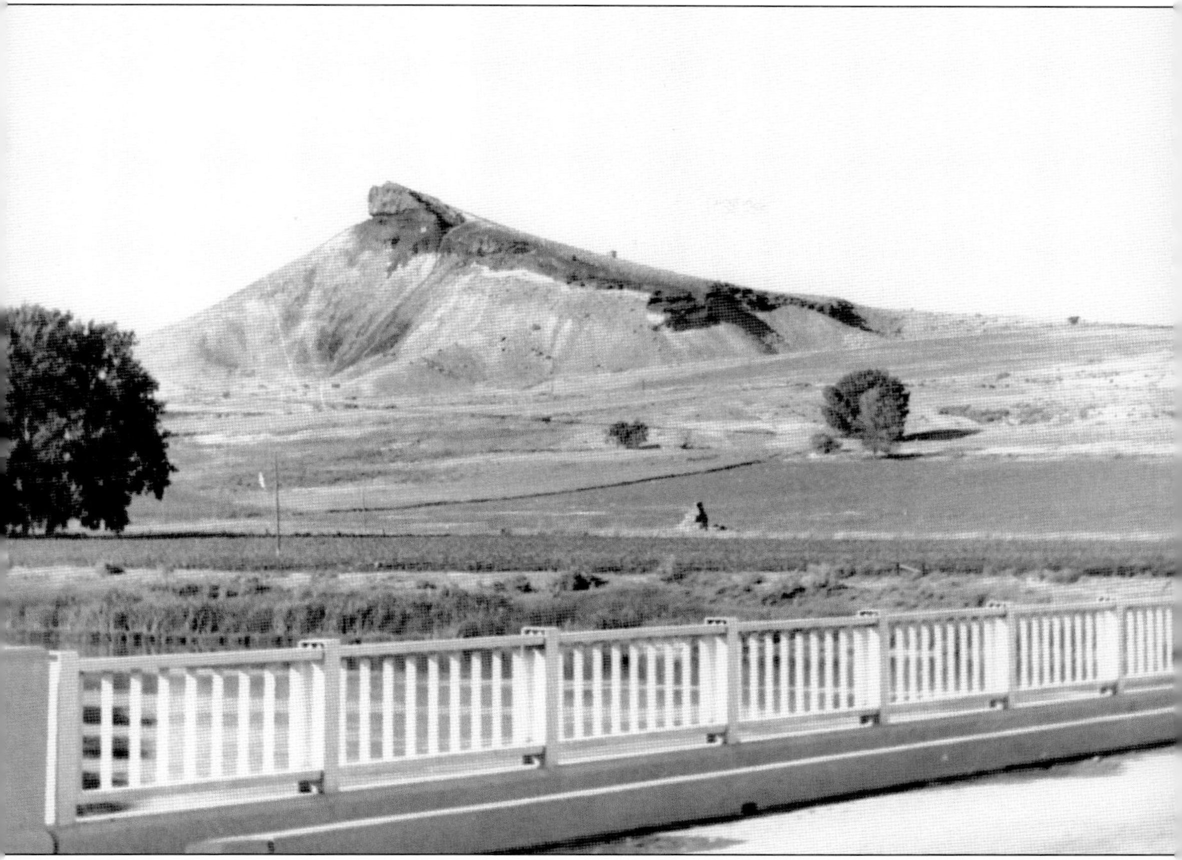

Lizard Butte has been a prominent southern Idaho landmark dating back to the days of the Oregon Trail. This view is from Marsing looking north across the Snake River. Marsing was sagebrush country until the Gem Irrigation Project converted it to productive farmland; 52 miles of main canals were built with 20 miles of laterals.

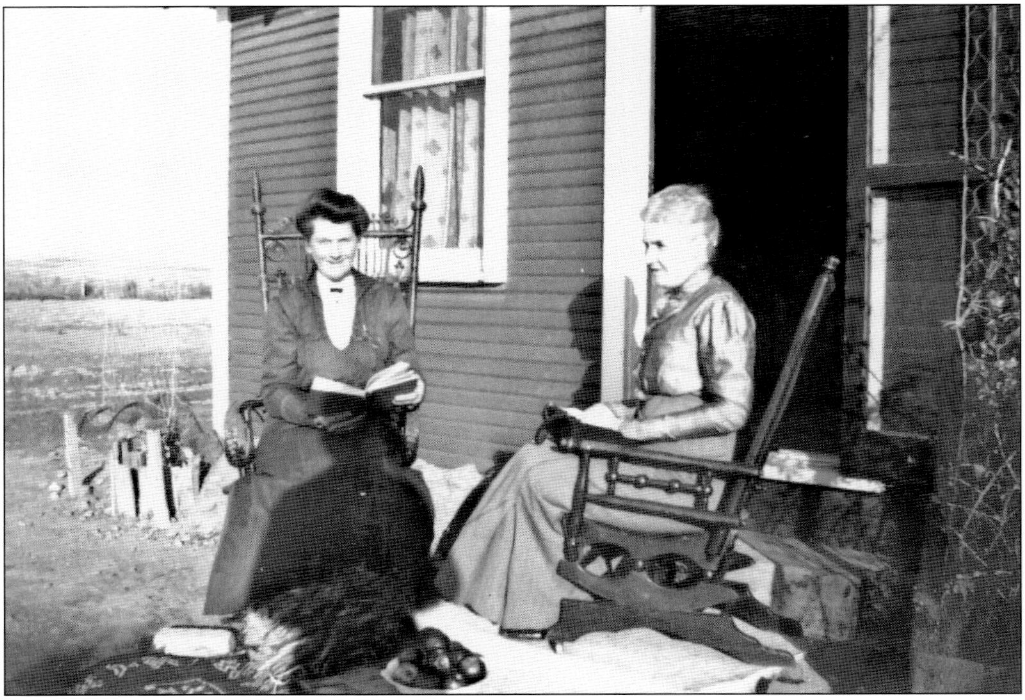

Pictured here is the Dugsdale home in Marsing not long after the Gem Irrigation District was formed. Laura Wilson (left) and Mary Dugsdale are enjoying a rock on the front porch. Marsing only truly developed as a town after completion of a bridge across the Snake River, dedicated on June 1, 1921. The bridge dedication celebration included speeches, songs by schoolchildren, and an amateur rodeo.

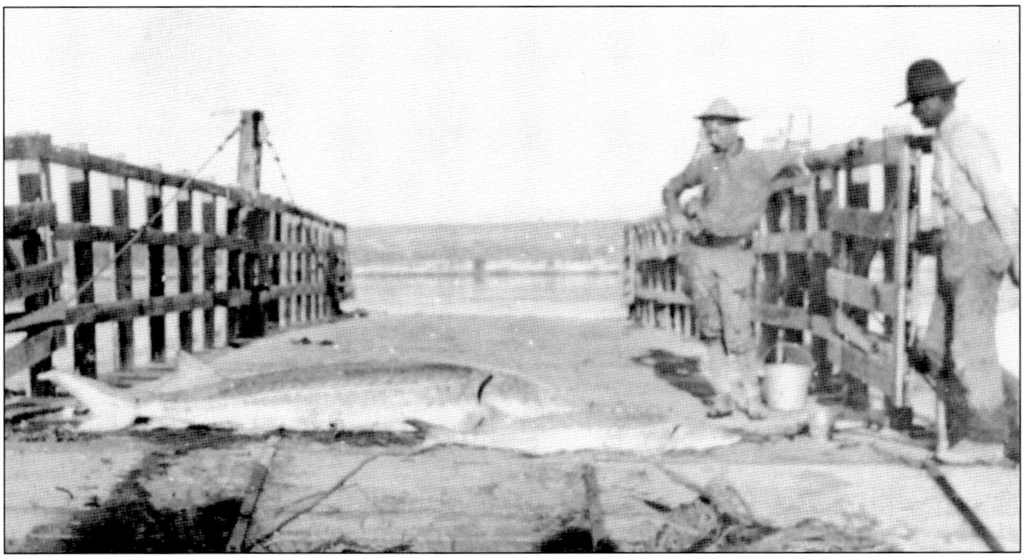

Elmer Maxwell and Billingsly "the Ferry Man" admire sturgeon caught in the Snake River close to the Froman's Ferry near Marsing. The location of Claytonia was chosen near Froman's Ferry, as the town's developers felt it would be the natural site to be on the line of a proposed railroad from Caldwell, Idaho, to Winnemucca, Nevada. When the railroad failed to materialize, Claytonia was doomed to eventually fade away.

Eight

Bruneau and Grand View

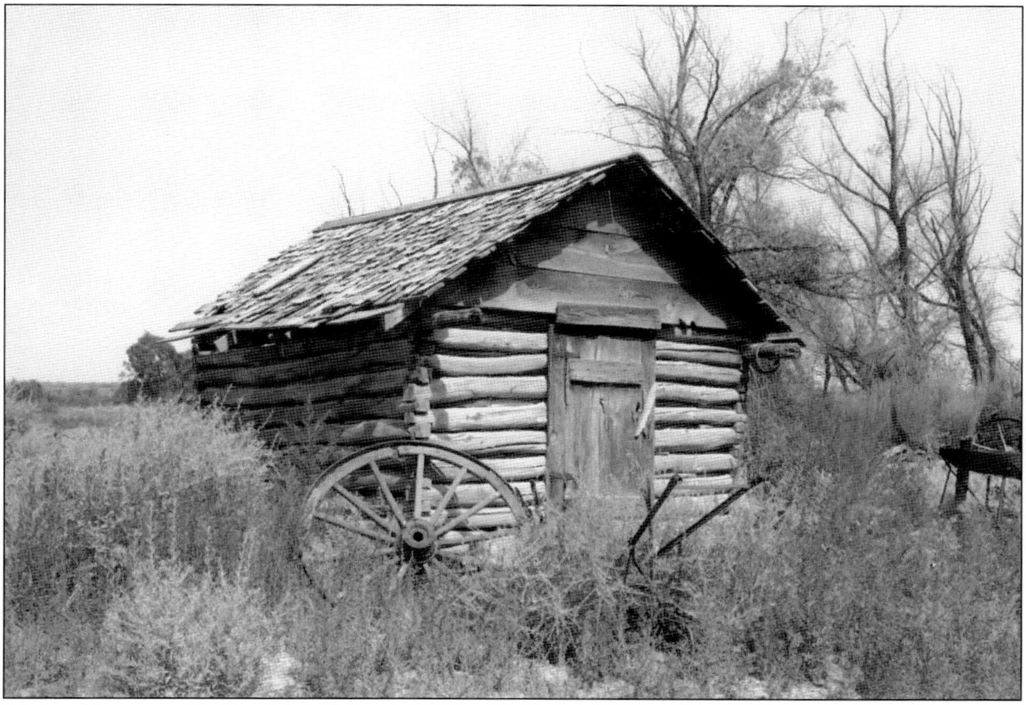

Pictured here is an early settler's log cabin near Bruneau. The Bruneau Valley lies in the northeastern part of Owyhee County, and the Bruneau River runs through the center of the region. Settlers moved into the region in the 1860s due to its suitability for ranching and agriculture. Meadowlands along the river were ideal for growing winter feed for cattle, which were taken to higher elevations for summer grazing.

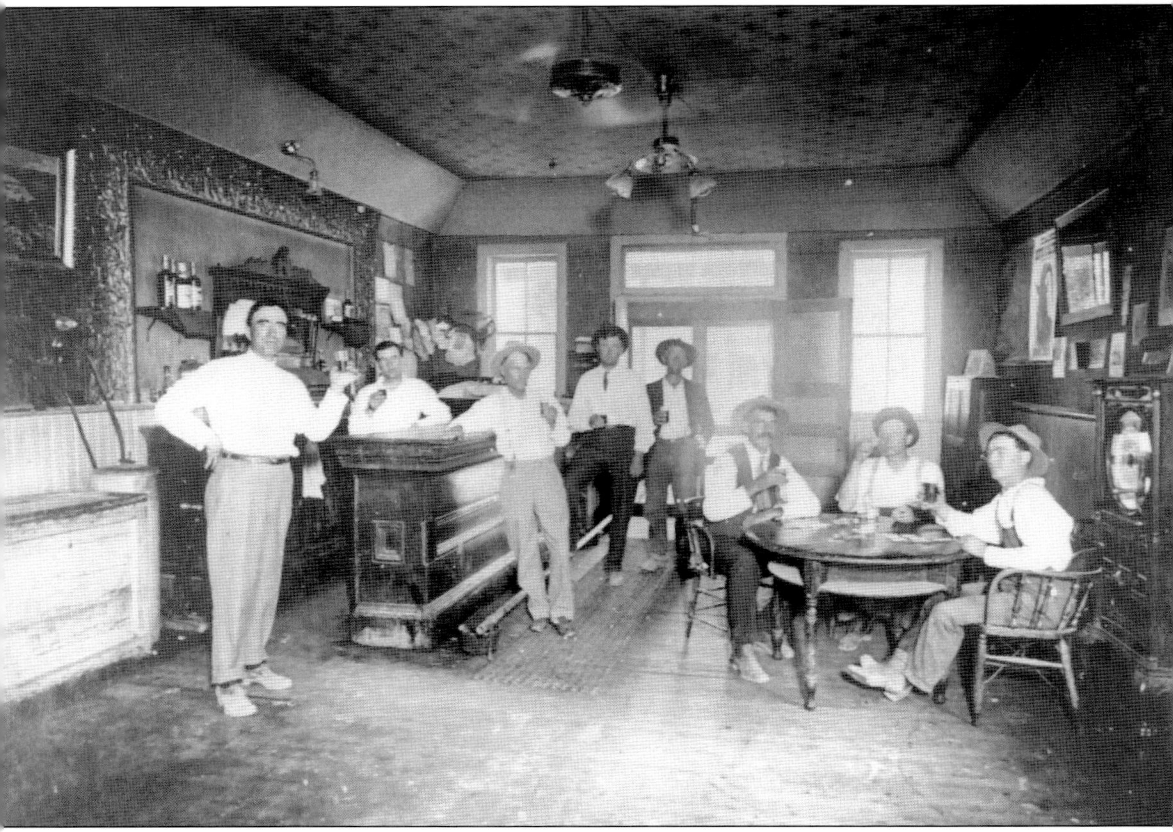

Enjoying a drink in the saloon are, from left to right, Charley Thomas (barber), Tommy Clark, F. Black, R. Randall's father Len Stawn, Tom Jabe, Oscar Tate, and Albert Lawson. The watering hole is the Buckeroo Resort, also known at one time as the Oscar Tate Resort. (Courtesy of Ruth Randall.)

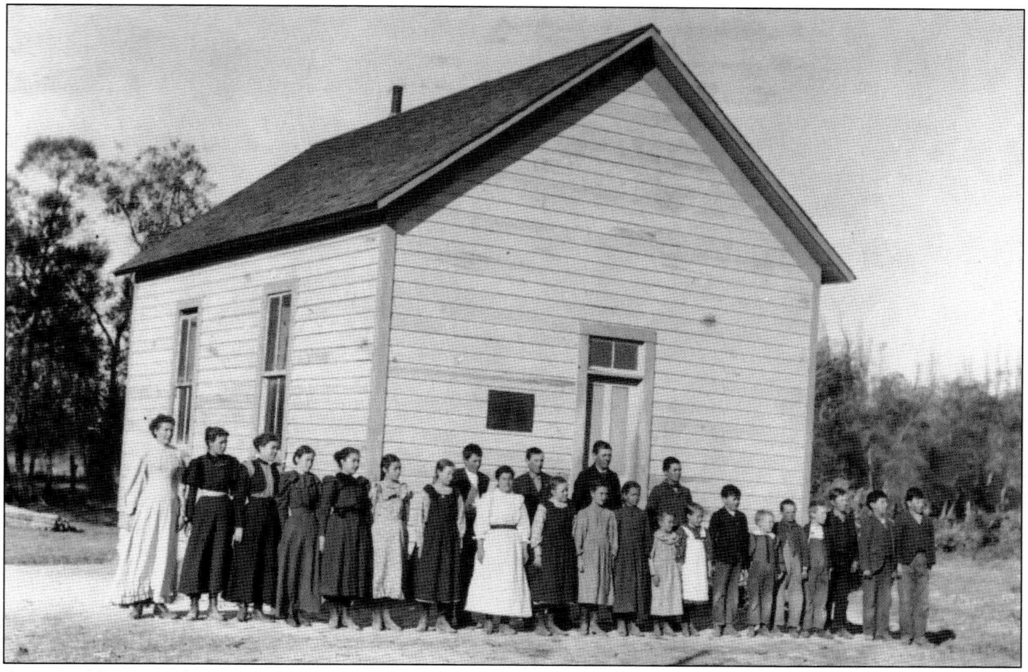

Pictured here is the Hot Spring School in 1893. Located at the upper end of the Bruneau Valley, eight miles from town, the district known as Hot Spring was named after the many hot springs to be found in the area. In 1869, Arthur Pence, Abe Roberson, and his son Stephen located ranches in the area. Hot Spring was located on the old road from Bruneau Valley to Duck Valley and was used by ranchers and stockmen.

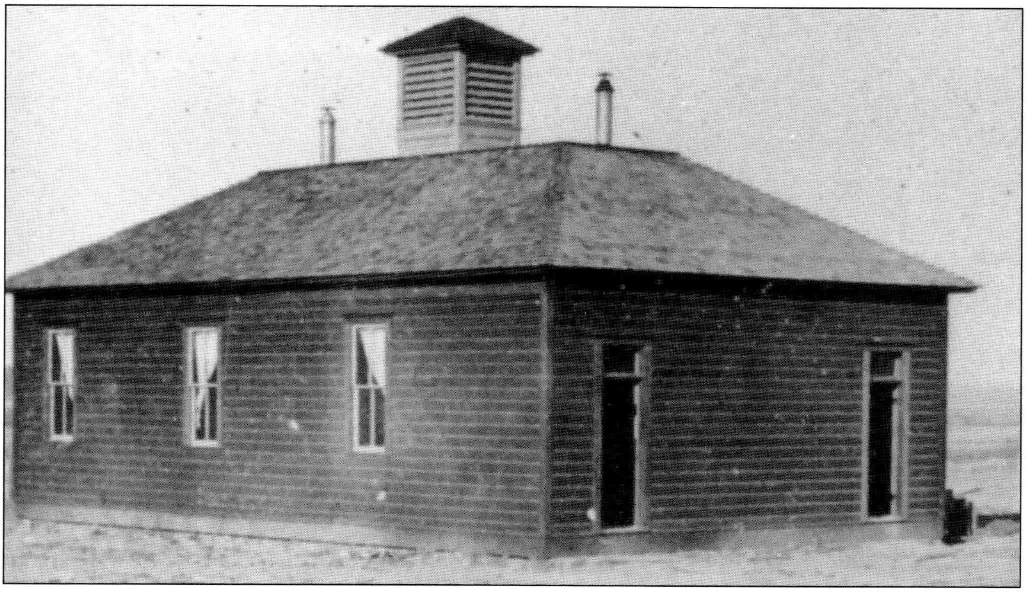

This Bruneau school is pictured in 1900. The *Owyhee County Blue Book of 1898* listed prominent valley ranchers such as John Turner, John Portlock, the Harvey brothers, and Barney Horn. The famous T Ranch was established in the 1860s, when George T. Miller and Con Shea brought a longhorn herd to the valley from Texas. Rancher John Turner's daughter Adelaide Turner (Hawes) wrote a book about life in the Bruneau Valley, *The Valley of Tall Grass.* (Courtesy of Dick Benham.)

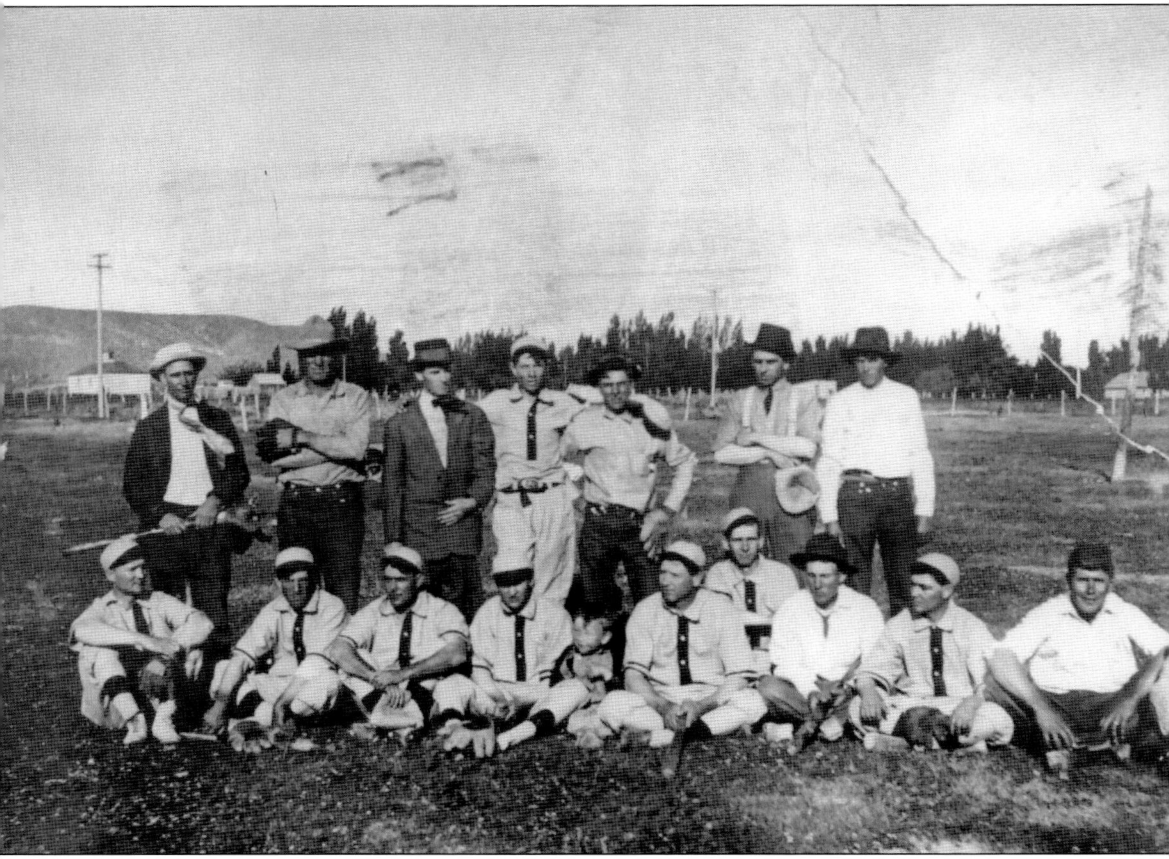

The Bruneau baseball team of 1918 poses for a photograph. Pictured here are, from left to right, (first row) M. Polsom, unidentified, John Fisher, Tommy Clark, Walter Tate, Oscar Tate, Donald Barney, Alvard Harley, Albert Lawson, Happy Howard, ? Vail, and unidentified; (second row) ? Mahoffer, Dave Baker, ? Mahoffer, Roy Koller, Joe Harley, G.R. Jones, and George Hutchinson. (Courtesy of Ruth Randall.)

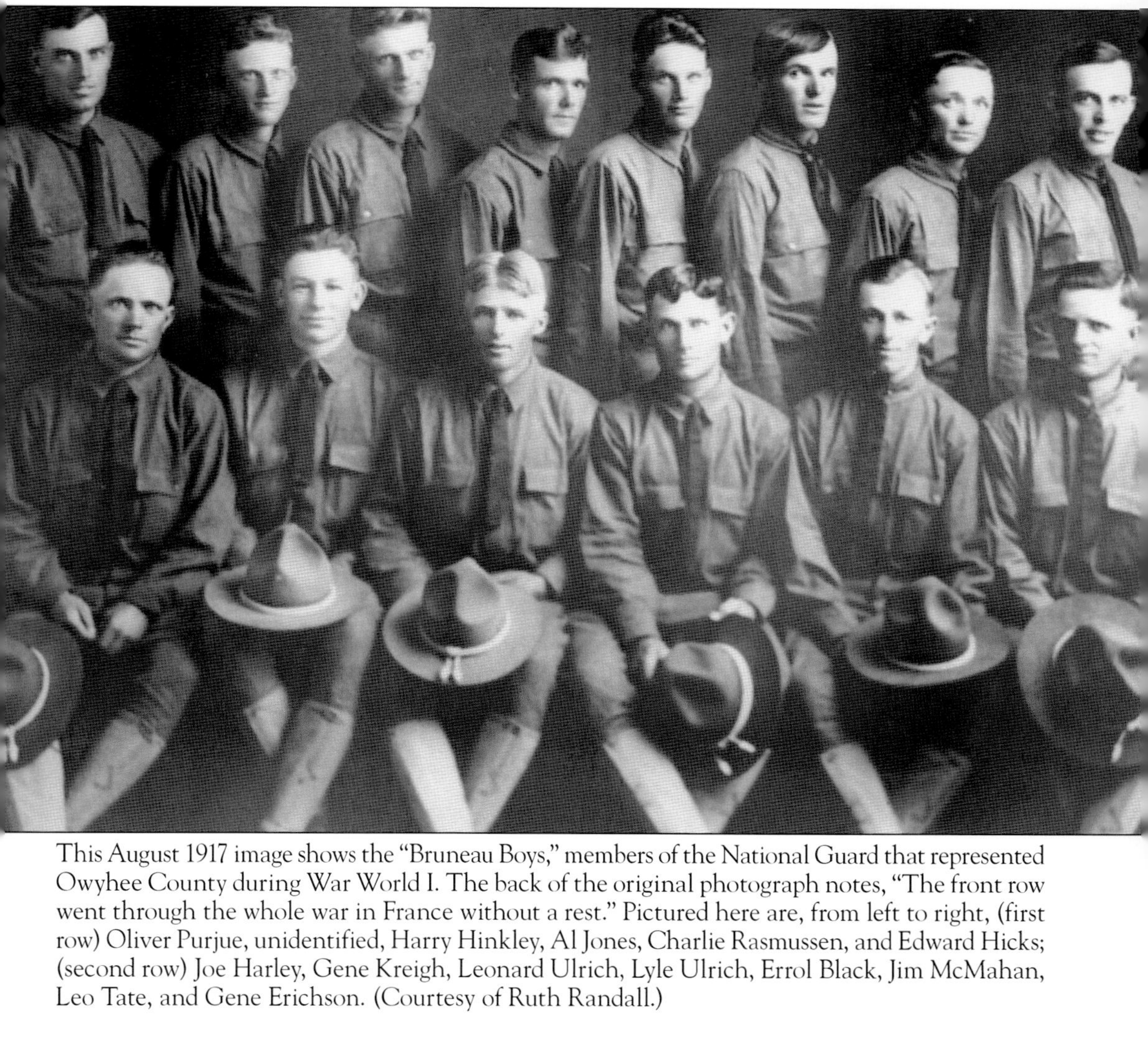

This August 1917 image shows the "Bruneau Boys," members of the National Guard that represented Owyhee County during War World I. The back of the original photograph notes, "The front row went through the whole war in France without a rest." Pictured here are, from left to right, (first row) Oliver Purjue, unidentified, Harry Hinkley, Al Jones, Charlie Rasmussen, and Edward Hicks; (second row) Joe Harley, Gene Kreigh, Leonard Ulrich, Lyle Ulrich, Errol Black, Jim McMahan, Leo Tate, and Gene Erichson. (Courtesy of Ruth Randall.)

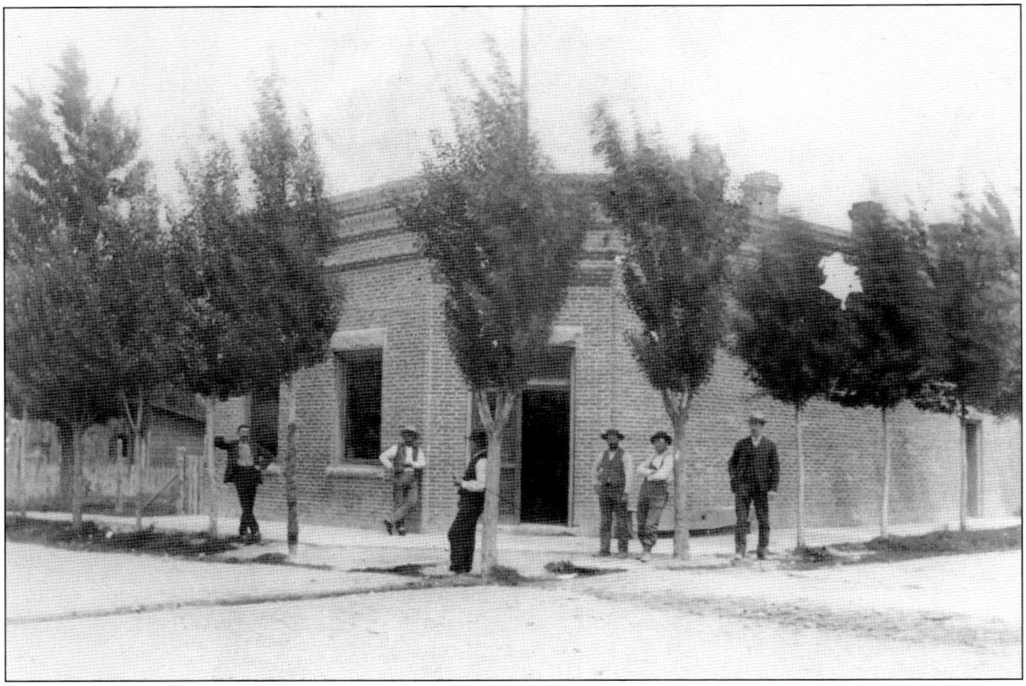

From bar to bank: this Bruneau building featured prominently first as the Hyde & Benham Saloon and then later as Bruneau State Bank. By 1912, Bruneau had a chartered state bank, a drugstore, the Basque Hotel and livery stable, Hyde's Hotel, and two barbershops (both connected to saloons). The population was 800. (Courtesy of Ruth Randall.)

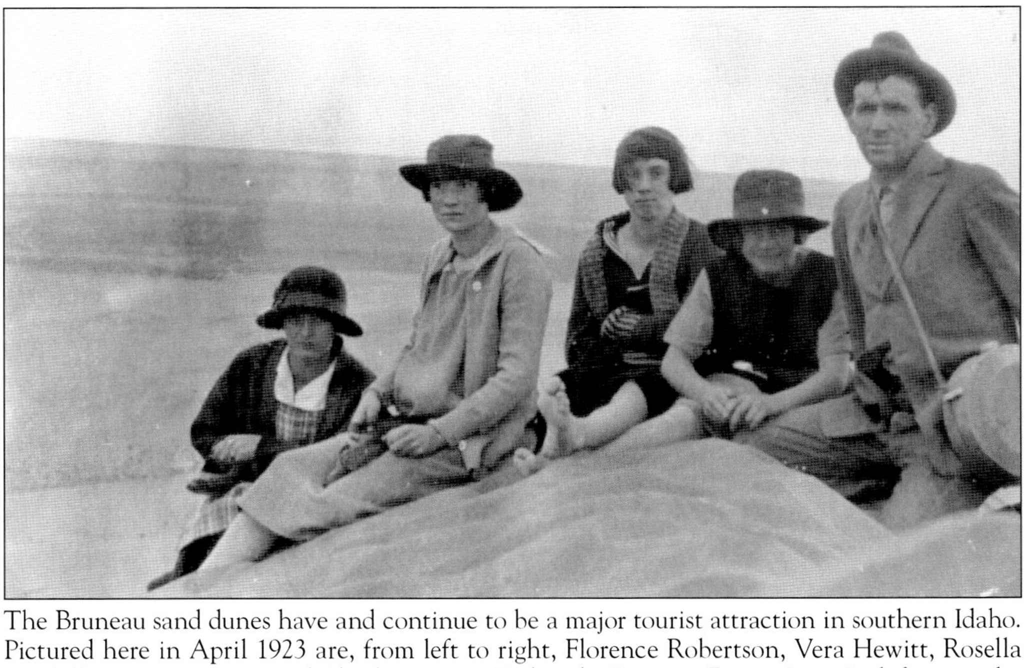

The Bruneau sand dunes have and continue to be a major tourist attraction in southern Idaho. Pictured here in April 1923 are, from left to right, Florence Robertson, Vera Hewitt, Rosella Tendall, Bernice Hewitt, and Charles Hewitt. Today, the Bruneau Dunes State Park features the tallest single-structure sand dune in North America, rising to 470 feet above several small lakes in the high desert. (Courtesy of Vena Bower.)

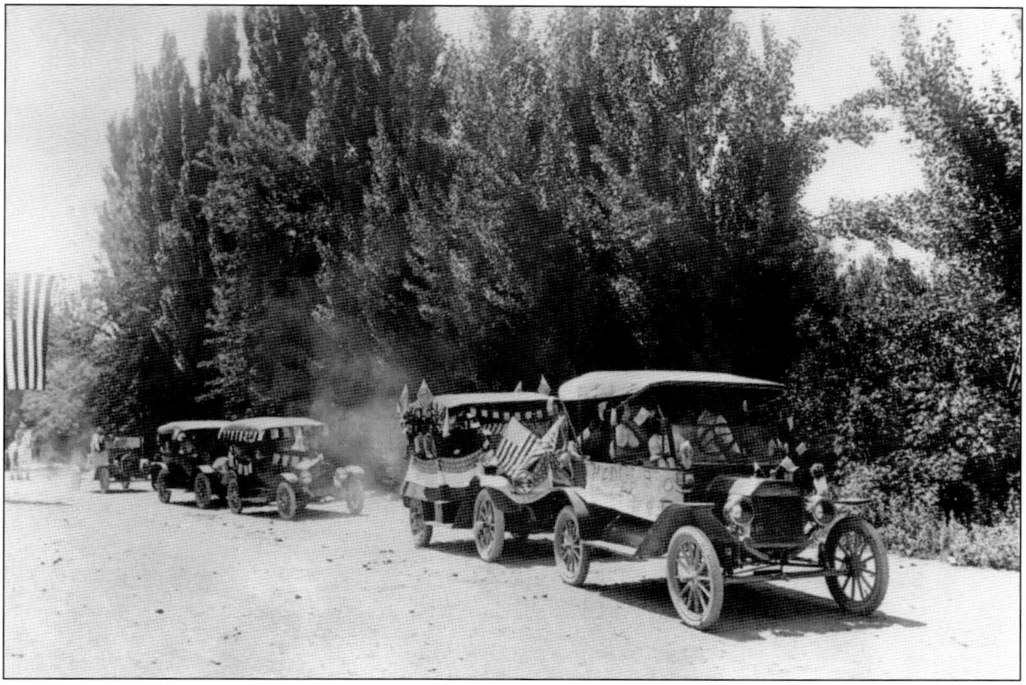

Cars form a Fourth of July parade in Bruneau. In 1910, Bruneau had the largest voting precinct in Owyhee County, with the city boasting a population of 800. When the *Avalanche* newspaper moved from Silver City in 1912, it incited a debate over moving the county seat to Bruneau, largely on the basis that Silver City was inaccessible much of the year due to snow; however, a countywide vote kept Silver City in charge.

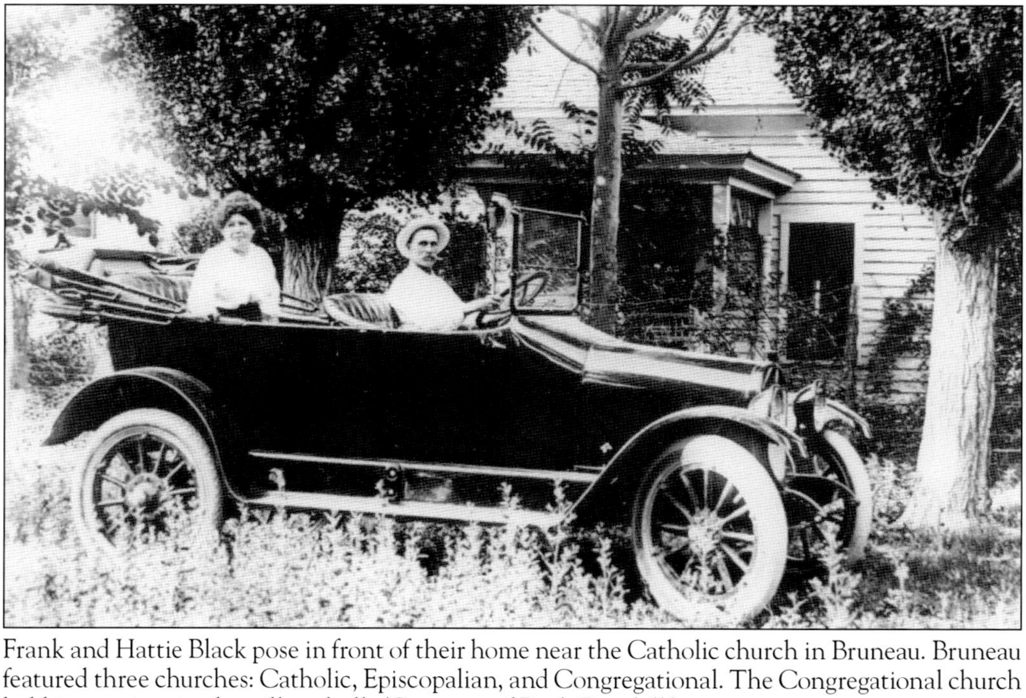

Frank and Hattie Black pose in front of their home near the Catholic church in Bruneau. Bruneau featured three churches: Catholic, Episcopalian, and Congregational. The Congregational church held its services in the village hall. (Courtesy of Ruth Randall.)

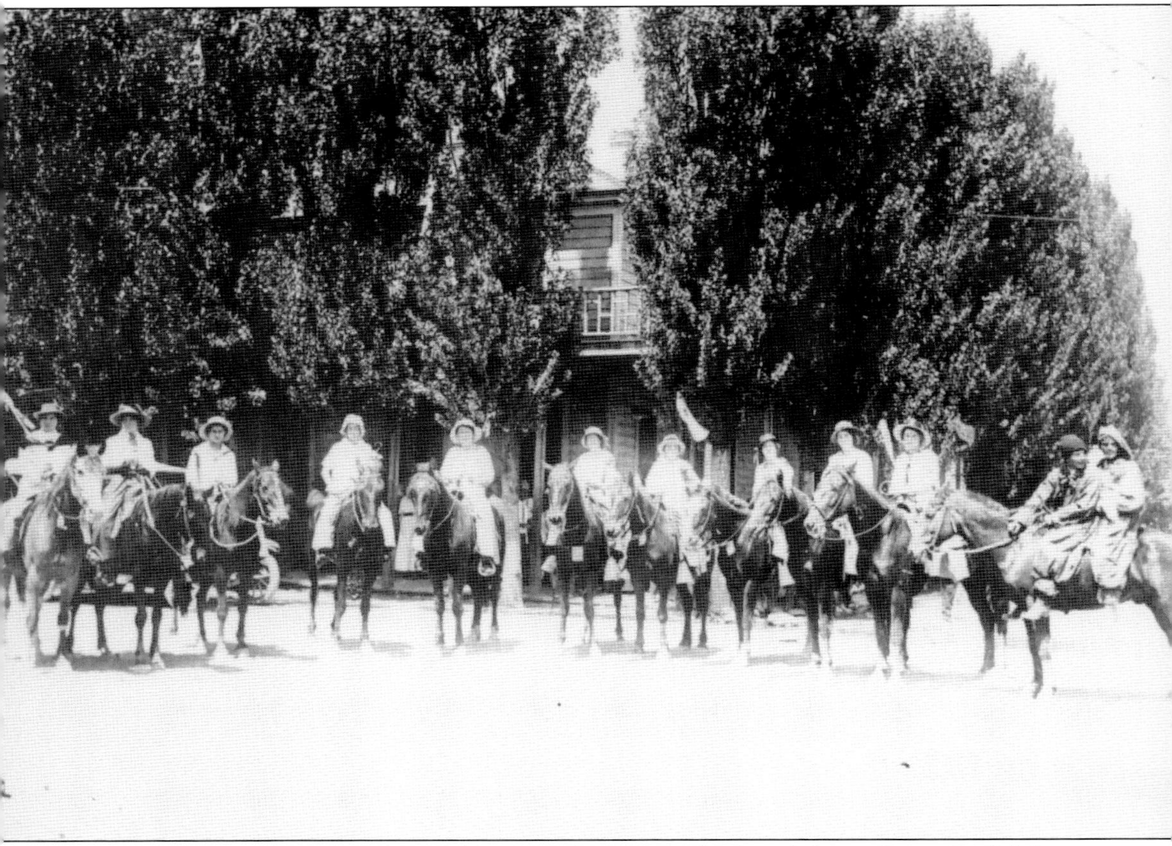

An early-1900s Bruneau riding club poses with their steeds. From left to right are Bealah Lawson, Mary Baxter, Nina Turner, Lois Gahan, Edith Calahan, Rosalind Harley, Fay Black, Ruth Black, Pearl Baxter, Emma Turner, and Frank Jones and Murrell Portlock (clowns). (Courtesy of Ruth Randall.)

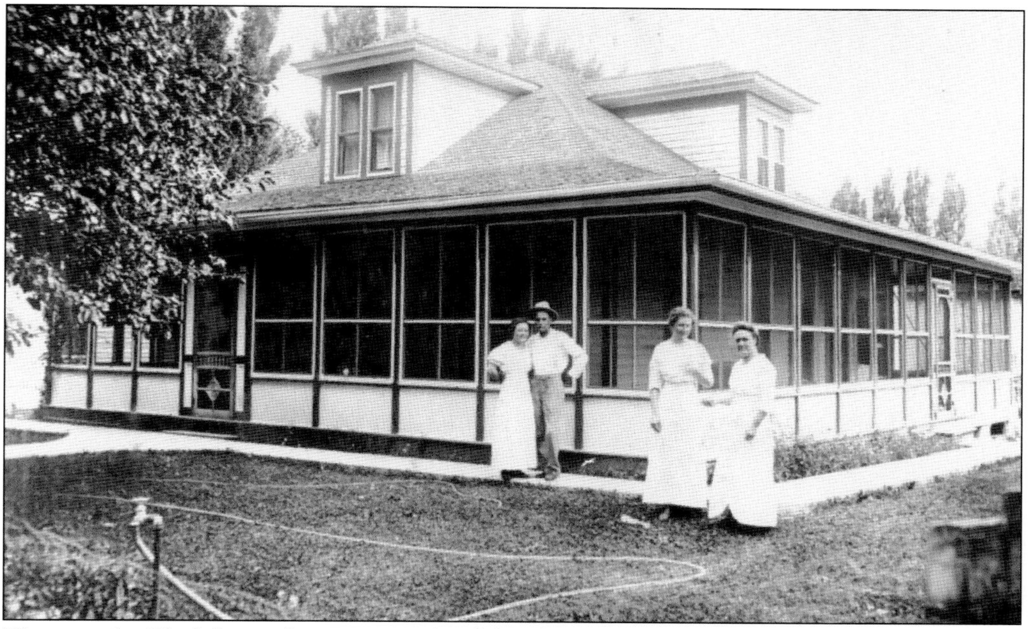

This was the Black home (a prominent local family for many years) across from Legion Hall in Bruneau. The Bruneau Valley was originally home to the Bruneau Shoshone. The most noted member of the tribe was Bruneau John, who saved the white settlers during the Bannock War of 1878 by, among other things, warning of an impending attack. Pres. James A. Garfield presented Bruneau John with a silver medal in recognition of his deeds in 1881.

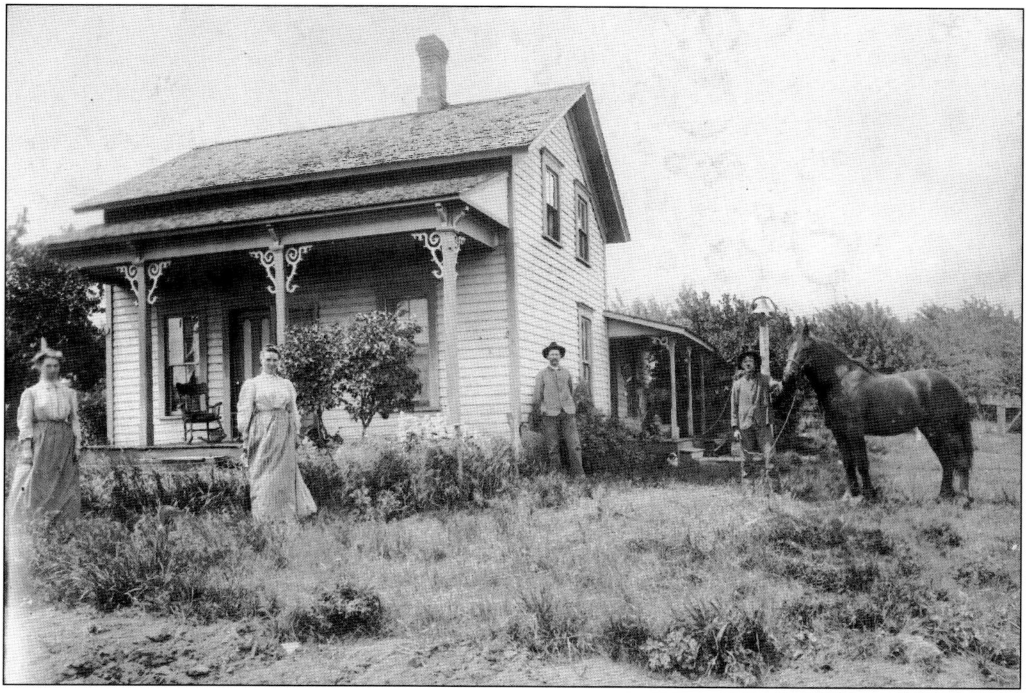

This is an example of a Bruneau home in the 1890s. Rancher David Hyde originally laid out the town of Bruneau. In the early 1890s, he built a two-story hotel, soon followed by a town hall. By 1898, the town had a store, post office, saloon, hotel, and blacksmith shop.

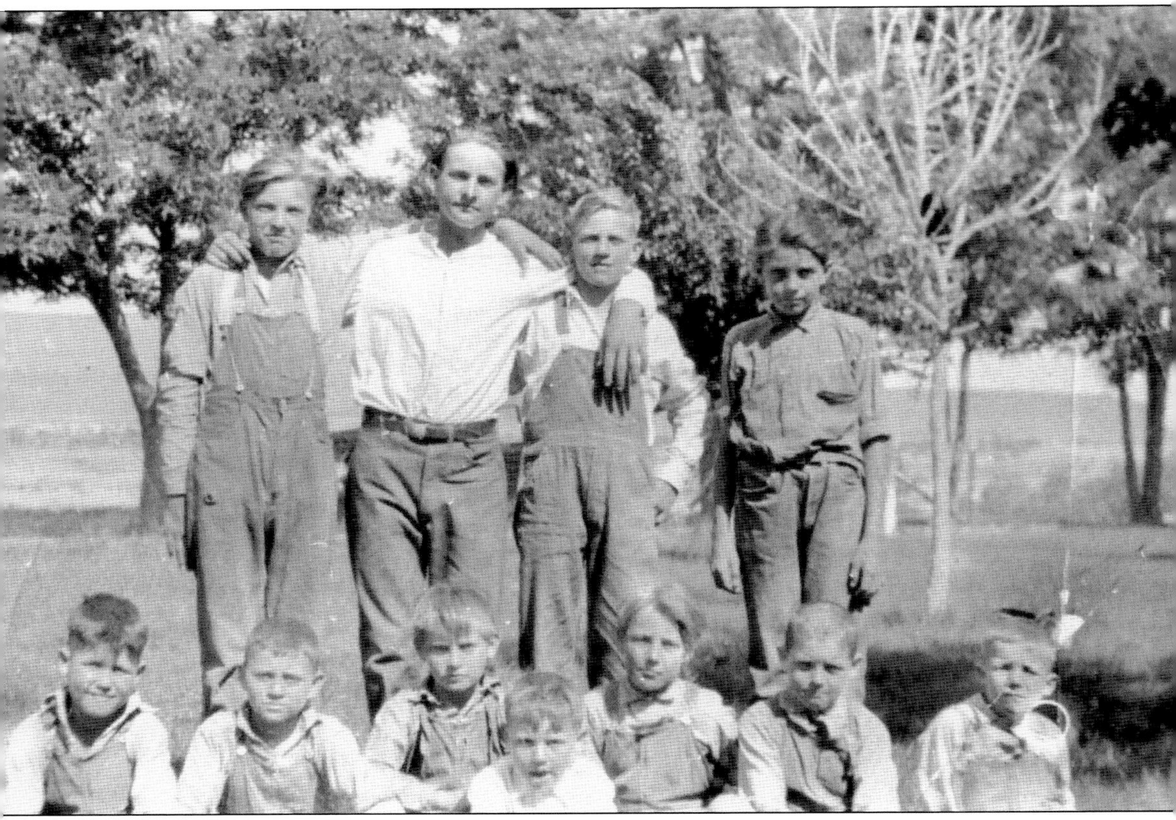

Students from an early Grand View School pose outdoors. When Grand View built a four-room, concrete-block school building in 1911, it was the largest of its kind in Owyhee County. The *Owyhee County Blue Book of 1898 states*, "Grand View is located on the south side of the Snake River, distant forty-five miles from Silver City and twenty-two miles from Mountain Home. It is an outlet for a large scope of agricultural county, there being several fine ranches in the back country and vicinity."

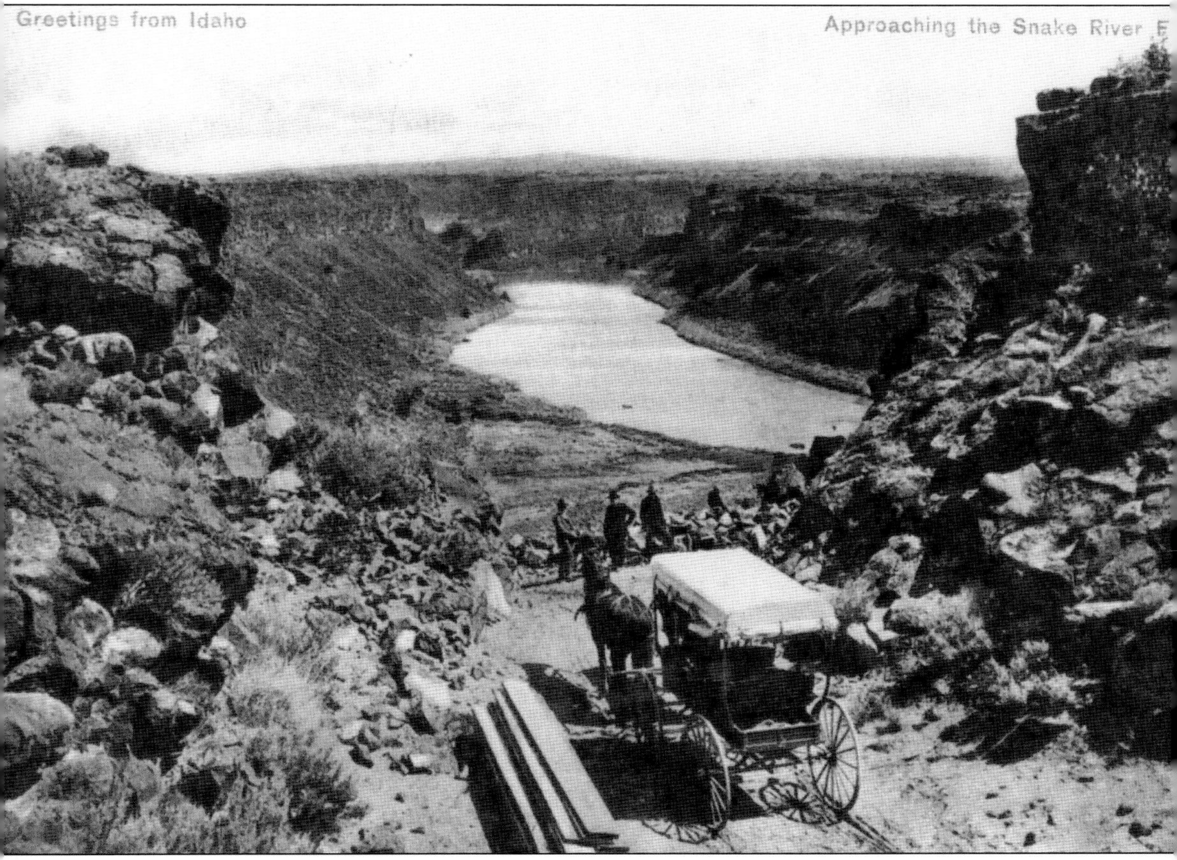

This postcard depicts the Snake River Canyon, not far from Grand View. It is near what is now the Snake River Birds of Prey National Conservation Area. It is generally believed that the Snake River Canyon was created by a cataclysmic flood caused by water released from Lake Bonneville approximately 14,000 years ago. However, some geologists believe that while the canyon was shaped by the flood, its basic structure predated it. Land along the Snake River was the most practical for agricultural use during the early history of the state, but its importance diminished as new irrigation technologies made farming practical in areas remote from the river's water. Most of Owyhee County's northern border is defined by the Snake River.

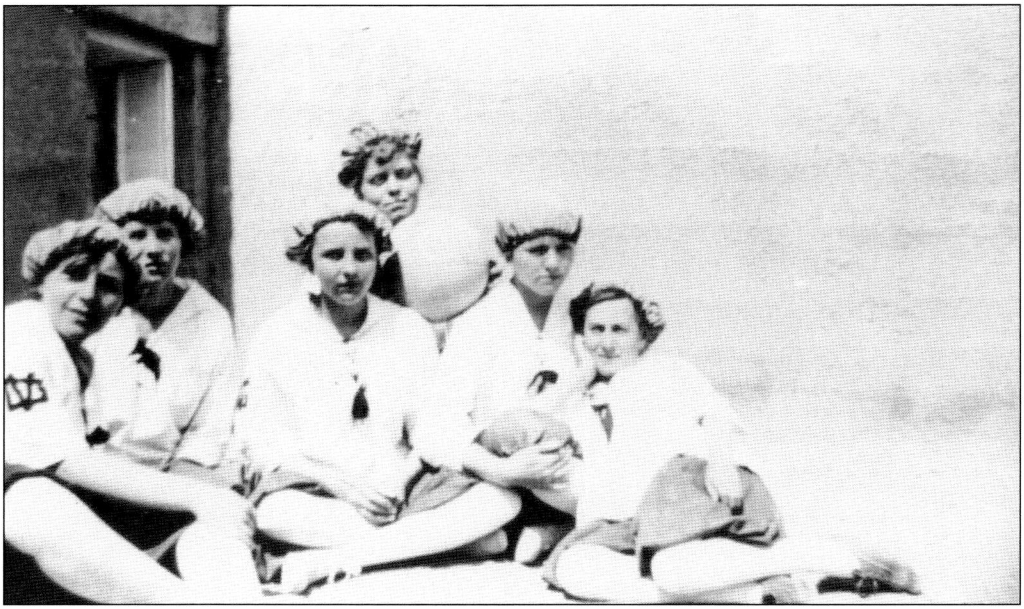

Members of the Grand View girls' basketball team in 1917 are, from left to right, Helen Ormsby, Blanche Wallace, Mildred Proctor, Jacqueline Bennett, Clara Whitted, and Gladys Rowe. Because Grand View was centrally located in Owyhee County, it was often the host for school meets with teams from Silver City, Homedale, Claytonia, Brunzell, Oreana, and Bruneau. (Courtesy of Bernice Palmer.)

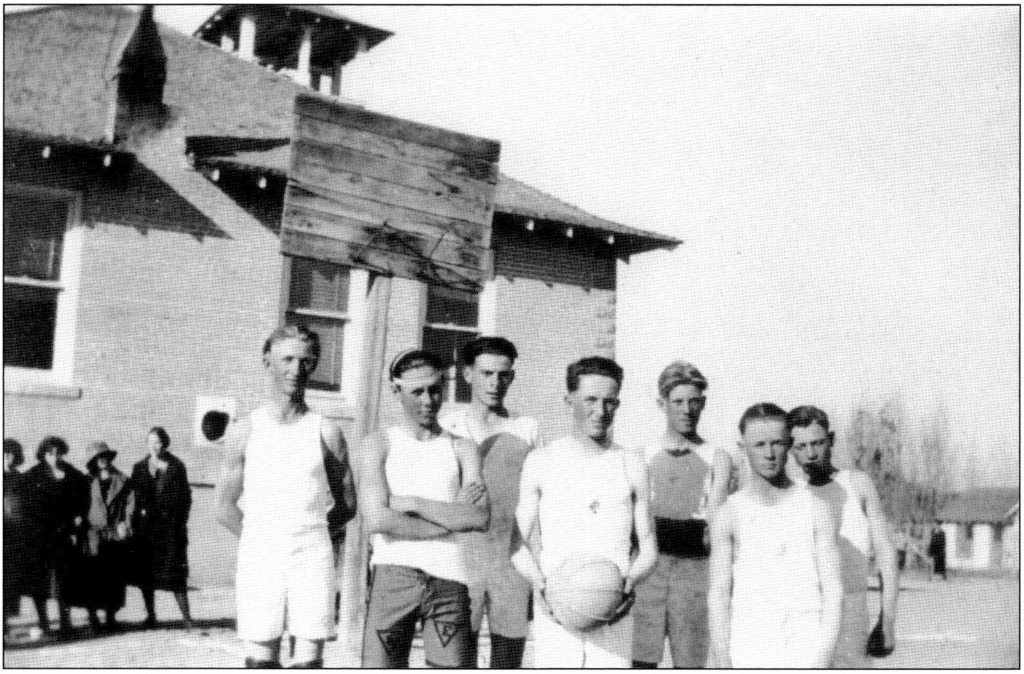

Pictured here is the Grand View boys' basketball team in 1923. Basketball was a prominent feature on the school grounds during the annual spring school meet. In addition to outdoor sports, the schools would compete in activities such as cartooning, spelling, adding, reading, and singing. Baseball and races were also favored competitions. (Courtesy of Eloa Guisanda.)

Nine

WALTERS FERRY, GIVENS, AND BERNARD'S FERRY

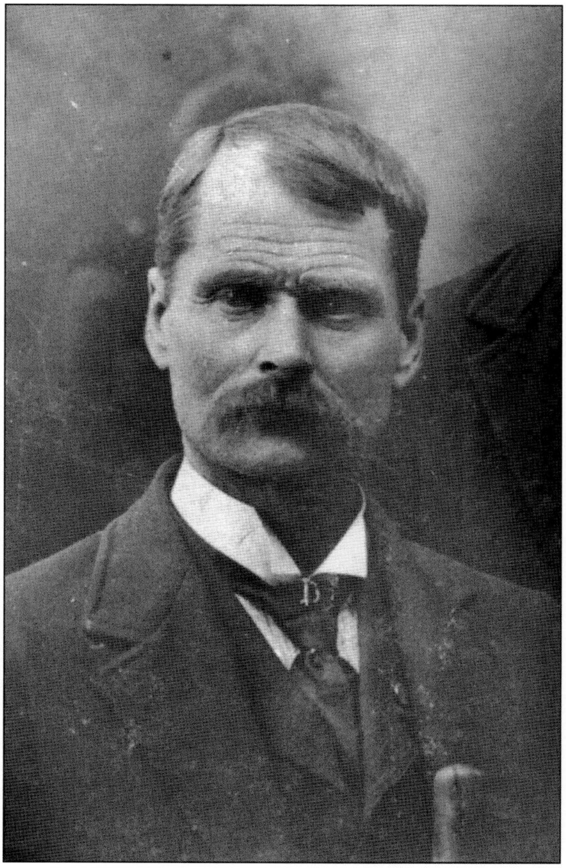

Mr. and Mrs. Milford Givens settled at the natural hot springs along the Snake River in 1881. The main source of income for the Givens was catching sturgeon, some of which weighed up to 500 pounds. In 1897, they enclosed the warm waters of the springs into a natatorium, and the Givens Hot Spring soon because a popular resort destination.

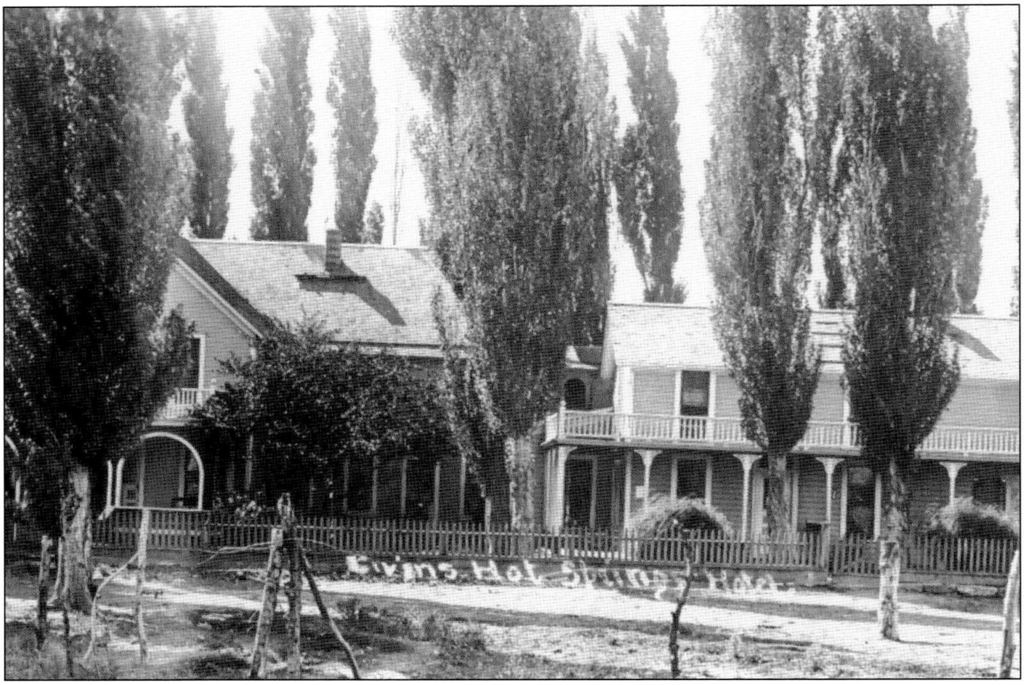

The Givens Hotel was enlarged in the early 1900s. Mrs. Givens, who later married Gus Yanke, served meals to all boarders and many who dropped by for a Sunday dinner. The hotel was completely destroyed by fire in the 1930s.

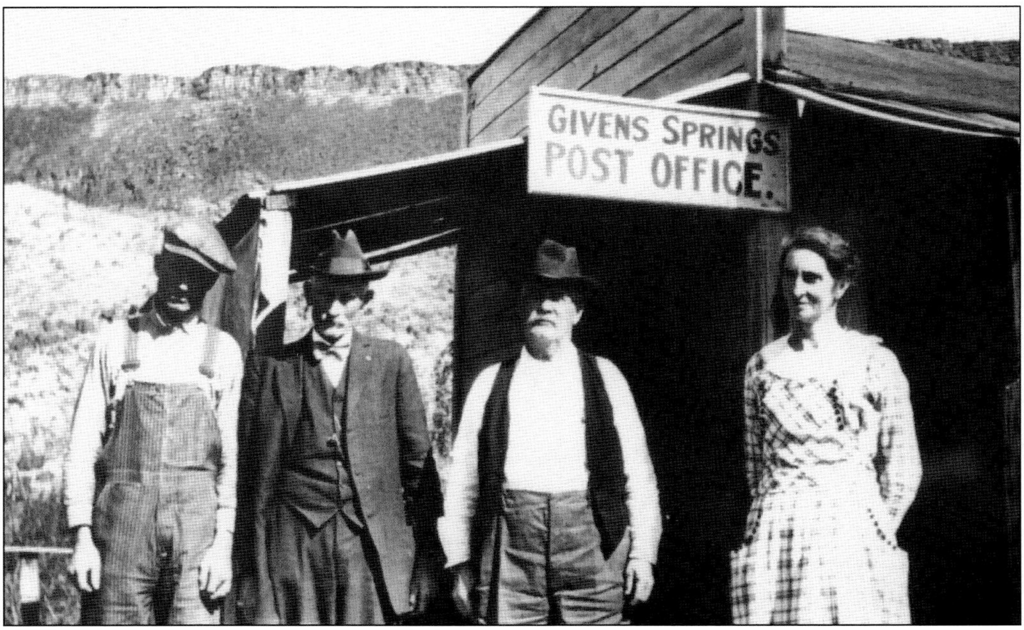

Posing here in front of the Givens Post Office are, from left to right, Andy Walker, Sam Paisley, J.A. Walker, and Mrs. Walker. Enterprise's post office was moved to Givens Springs in 1917. The operator of the Walker ferry, Joseph Walker, also served as the first postmaster, using a small building as both post office and store. Katherine Curtis became the Givens Springs postmistress in 1930. The post office was terminated in 1934. (Courtesy of Gladys Walker Teeter.)

Pictured here is the wedding of Mr. and Mrs. Berry Givens, attended by Mr. and Mrs. William Kelly, on February 2, 1910. Berry was one of five children in the Givens family. The first, a daughter, died at the age of four. The others were sons: Berry, Granville, Guy, and Jess.

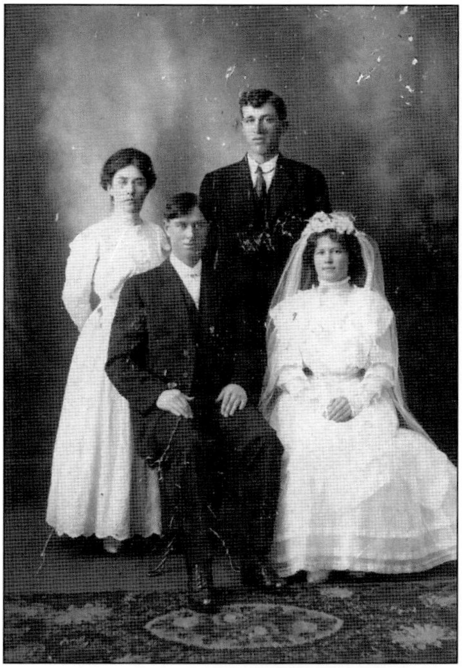

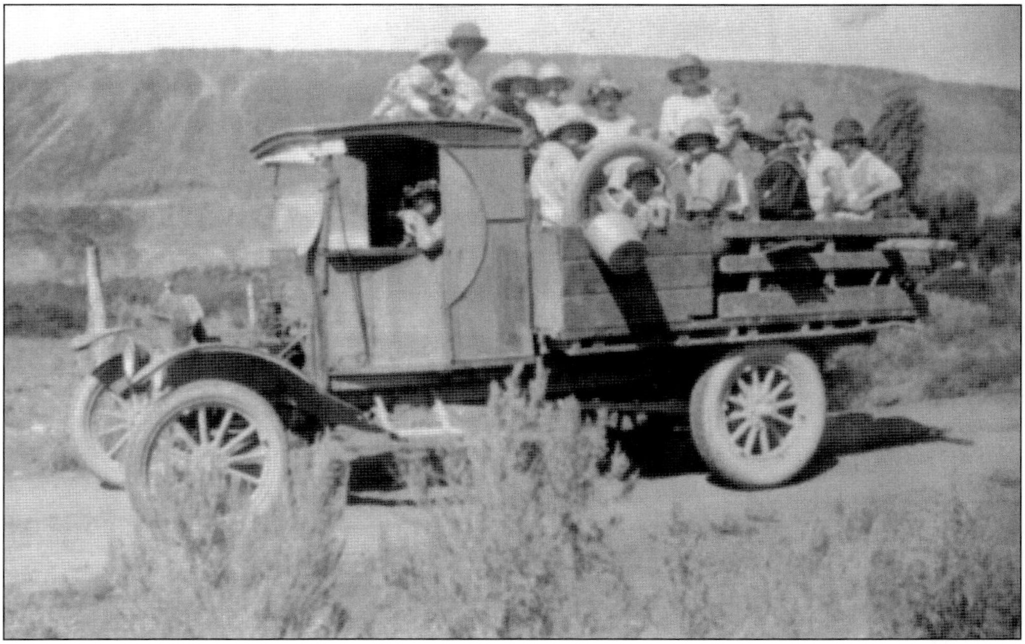

This early-1900s truck hauled visitors to the Givens Hot Spring Resort. A railroad connection announced in 1914 laid the groundwork for the springs to become a hot spot with visitors from Boise and the more populated Treasure Valley area. The *Nampa Record* reported, "Givens Hot Springs, the famous sanitarium and health resort on the Snake River 15 miles south of Nampa, at Enterprise in Owyhee County, will soon have automobile connection with the Sebree Interurban Line. Mr. Sebree offered to put on an automobile and make four trips per day from the end of the track to Hot Springs, if the Givens people would give free ferriage and put the wagon road in good condition."

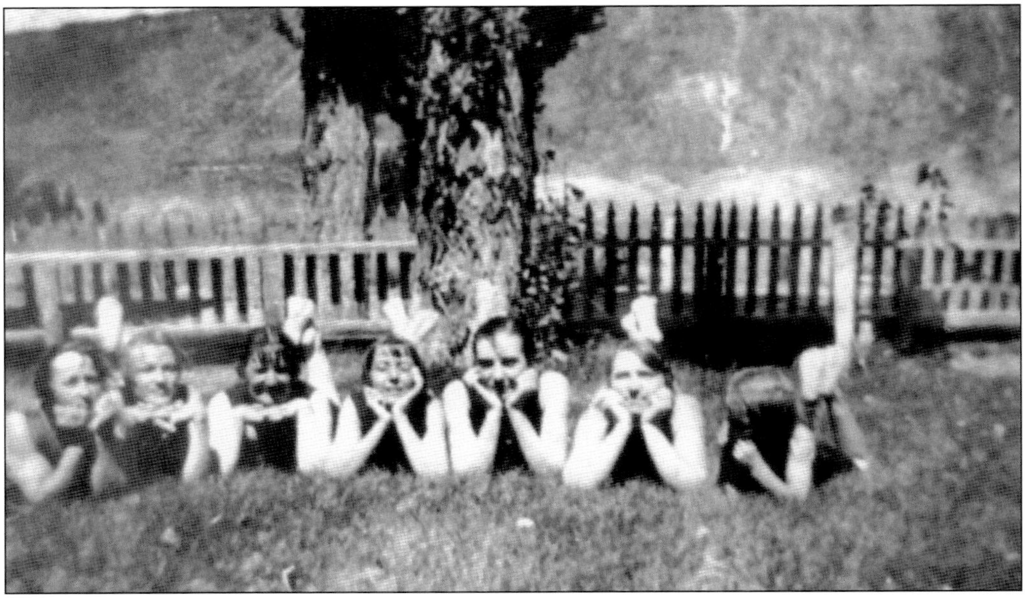

The hot springs were a poplar bathing spot for young women, as seen in these images. Below, the Wo-Ide-Lo girls are enjoying the Givens Hot Springs in 1924. Pictured are, from left to right, (first row) Lottie Benson and Vera Hamilton; (second row) Edman Marsing, Grace Marsing, Elsie Marsing, Viola Motake, and Lena Volkman. The *Owyhee County Blue Book of 1898* provided the description, "The Snake River Hot Springs is beautifully located on a bend of the river closely adjoining the Warm Springs ferry, located 35 miles from Silver City and 25 miles from Caldwell. The property embraces 154 acres, beautifully shaded by poplars and fruit trees of various kinds. The springs consist of a large thermal swimming pool 16 X 40 feet, strongly impregnated with iron, magnesia, sulphur and other health-giving properties." (Courtesy of Freita Moore Holstead.)

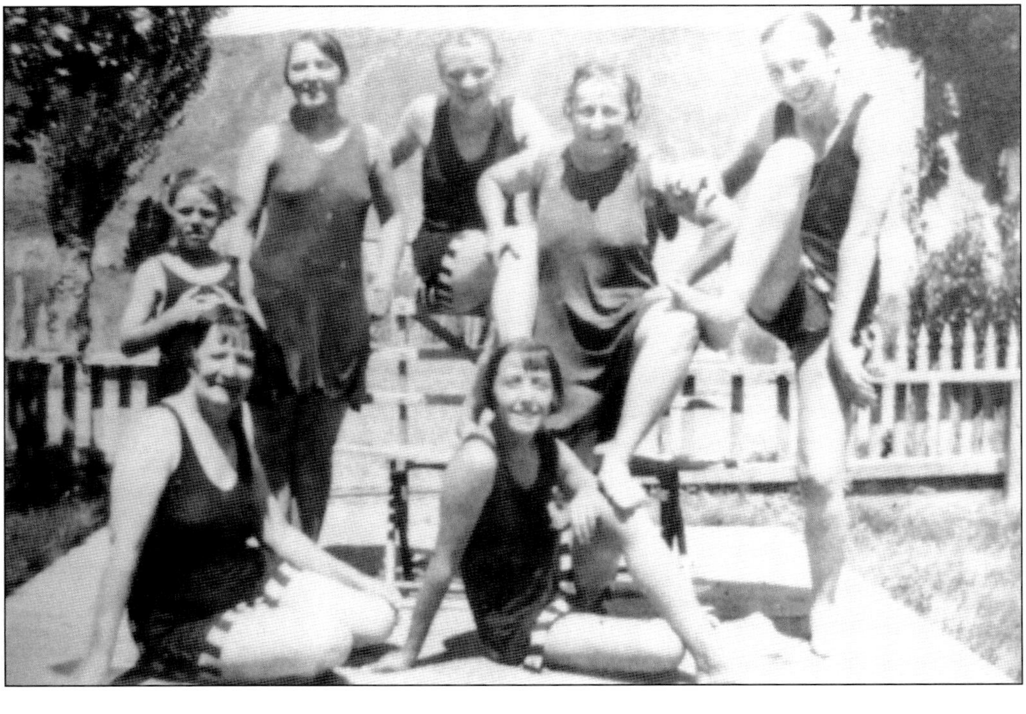

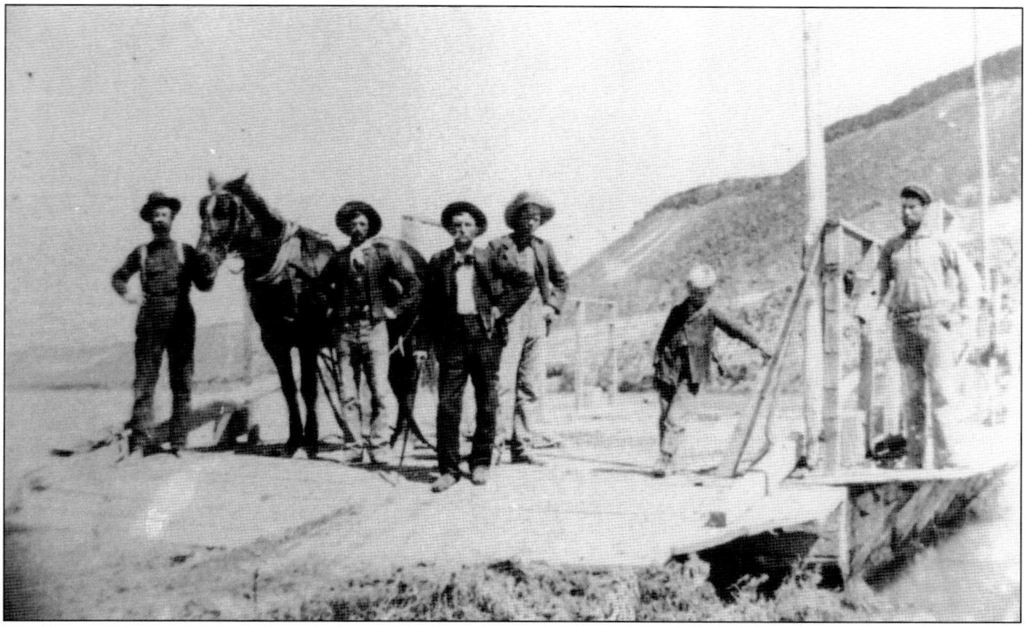

Bernard's Ferry, also called Bernard's Landing, was near Givens Hot Springs on the Snake River. This photograph is of the first Bernard's Ferry. In 1884, Bernard had the following announcement printed in the *Owyhee Avalanche*, "The public is hereby notified that the undersigned has constructed a new ferryboat, which has been placed on Snake River on the road leading from Silver City and Jordan Valley to Caldwell. TEN MILES NEARER to Caldwell, and no further to Kuna, by this route than any other, for citizens of Owyhee County and Jordan Valley. Roads in good condition; ferriage reasonable. Give me a call. J.C. Bernard." (Courtesy of Velma Bernard McKee.)

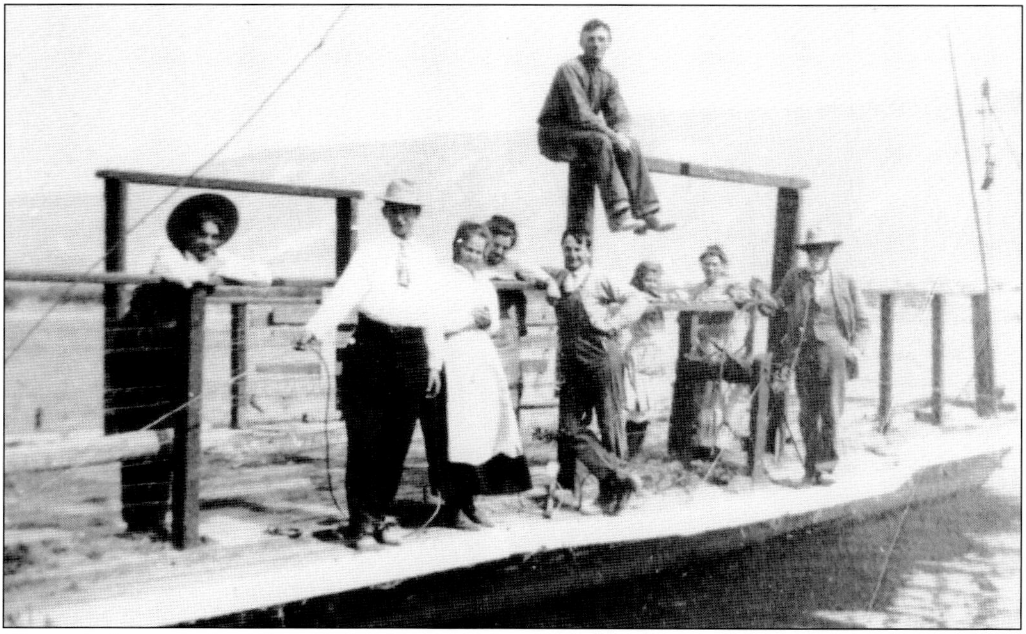

This is a photograph of the third Bernard Ferry, taken in the early 1900s. Bernard placed a sign at his ferry that read, "In God We Trust, All Others Must Pay Cash." The ferry was centrally located about four miles upriver from Givens Springs and 32 miles from Silver City.

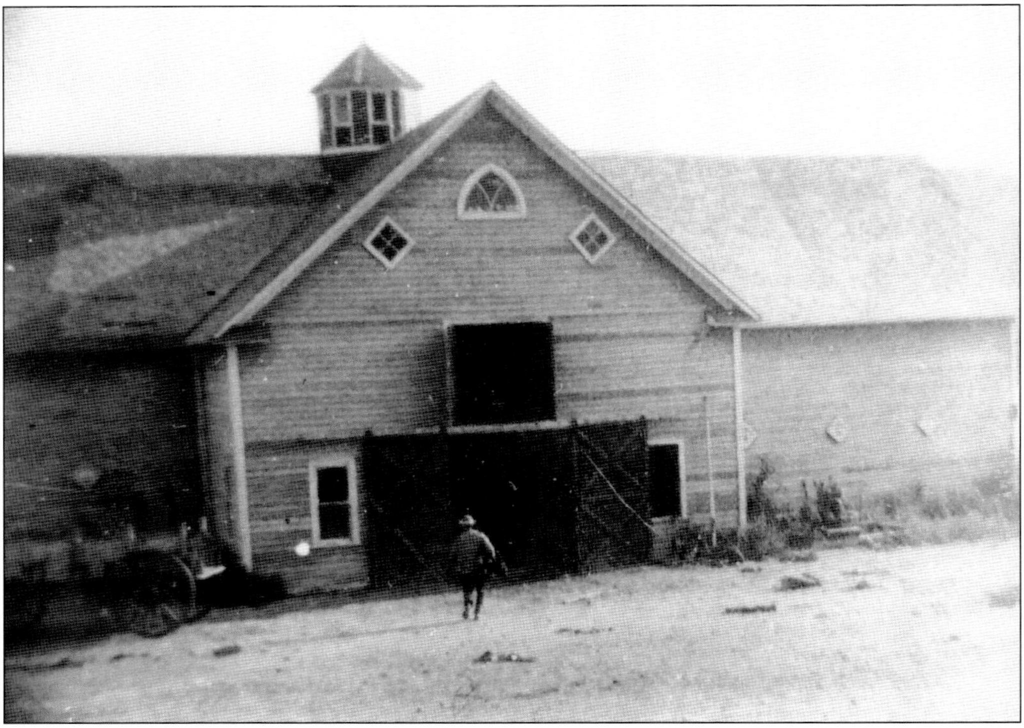

Pictured here is the ferry barn at Bernard's Landing. The following is from the *DeLamar Nugget*, July 14, 1891: "Mr. James Bernard, the Snake River ferryman, was in town Saturday. He has just finished a new ferryboat, the largest and finest one between Umatilla Landing and the head of the Snake River. He has expended some $700 for the roads on both sides of the river, and is trying to interest parties to connect his road with the new Caldwell cut-off via Wilson Creek. Bernard has the nicest ranch and house on the river and is on the shortest route from Nampa to either DeLamar or Silver City."

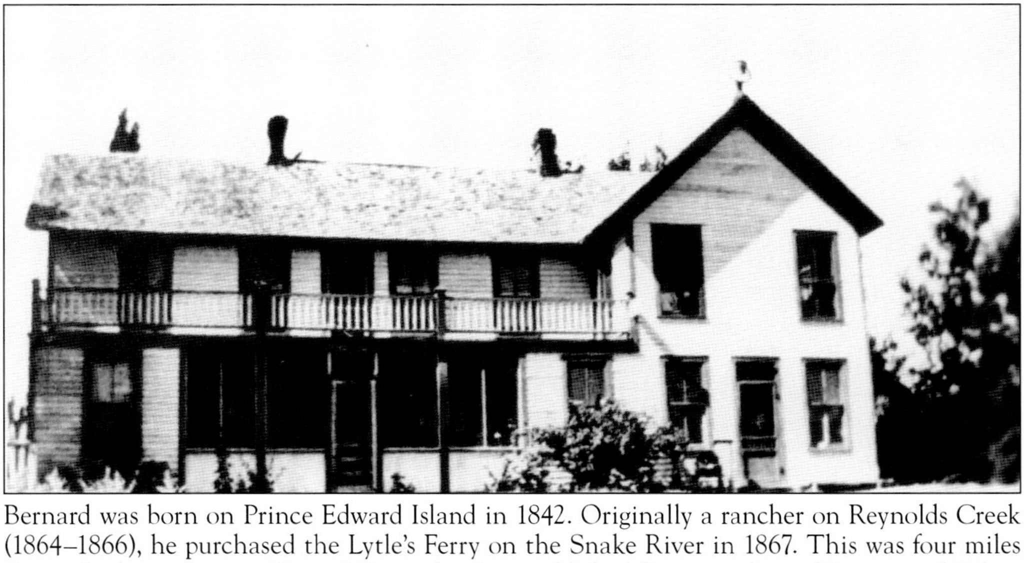

Bernard was born on Prince Edward Island in 1842. Originally a rancher on Reynolds Creek (1864–1866), he purchased the Lytle's Ferry on the Snake River in 1867. This was four miles above the better-known Central Ferry that he established five years later. (Courtesy of Velma Bernard McKee.)

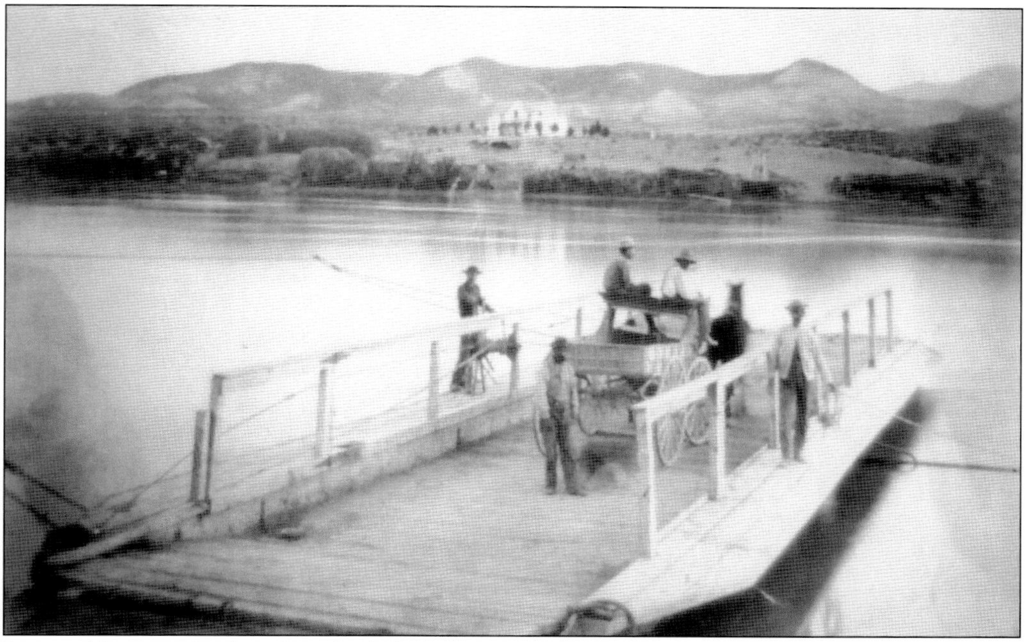

Pictured here is the first ferry built by J.C. Bernard. His first home, which burned in 1888, is in the background on the far bank. In 1866, Bernard married Ada Cox in Boise; she had come west with her family in 1864. Although the Bernards had nine children, four of them died of diphtheria, all within a single month, in 1892. After their first home was destroyed by fire in 1887, they constructed a new, larger, 14-room house, where they were known for hosting dances and parties. (Courtesy of Velma Bernard McKee.)

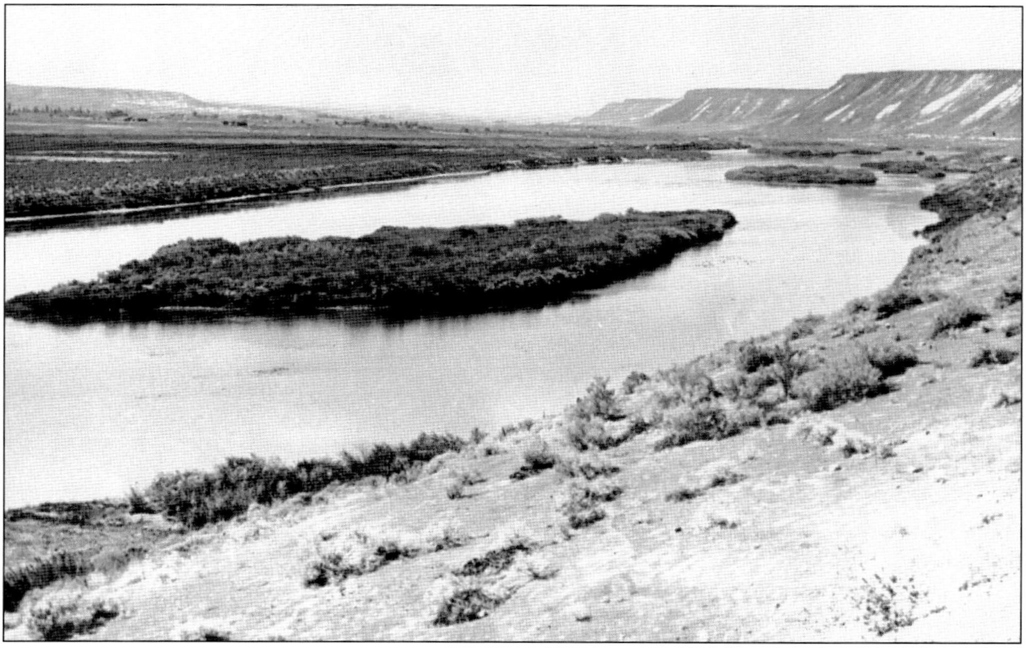

This photograph, taken just below Walters Ferry not far from Givens Hot Springs, provides a good representation of the Snake River as it winds its way from east to west. The river is the northern border of Owyhee County. (Courtesy of Mary Grammer.)

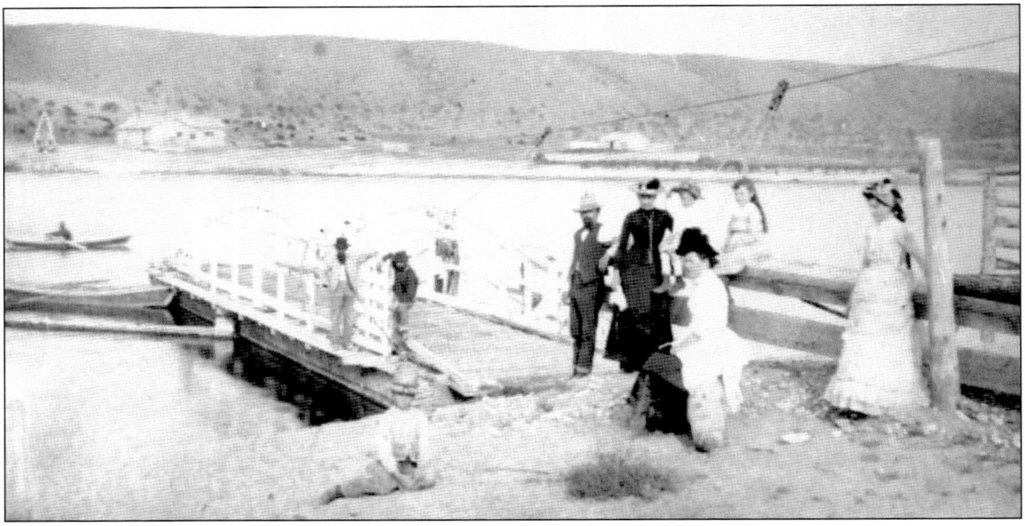

The ferry on the Snake River near Rabbit Creek was the principal connection between the Owyhee mining communities and Boise from 1863 to 1921. John Fruit launched the first ferry service on June 15, 1863. Originally little more than a raft of hand-cut logs tied together with rope, the ferry was on the Boise City–Owyhee stage and freight road. It was also called the Owyhee Ferry. L.A. Walter purchased the ferry on the Snake River near Rabbit Creek, renaming it Walters Ferry. A post office was established in 1888, with Lewellyn Walters serving as postmistress.

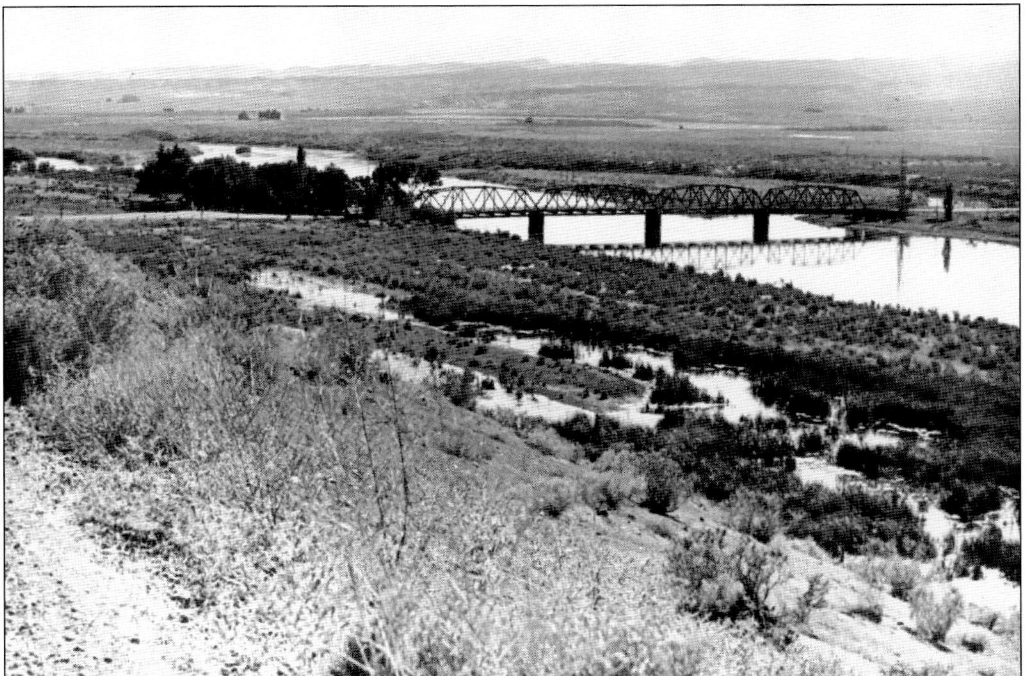

The Walters Ferry Bridge was completed in September 1921, ending ferry operations at both Walters Ferry and Bernard's Ferry. Edwin Meek was the last ferryman to operate at Walters Ferry. Today, Highway 45 crosses the Walters Ferry Bridge, where a few businesses remain and a popular boat-launching ramp operates on the Owyhee County side of the Snake River. (Courtesy of Mary Grammer.)

Ten

Guffey, Reynolds Creek, and Oreana

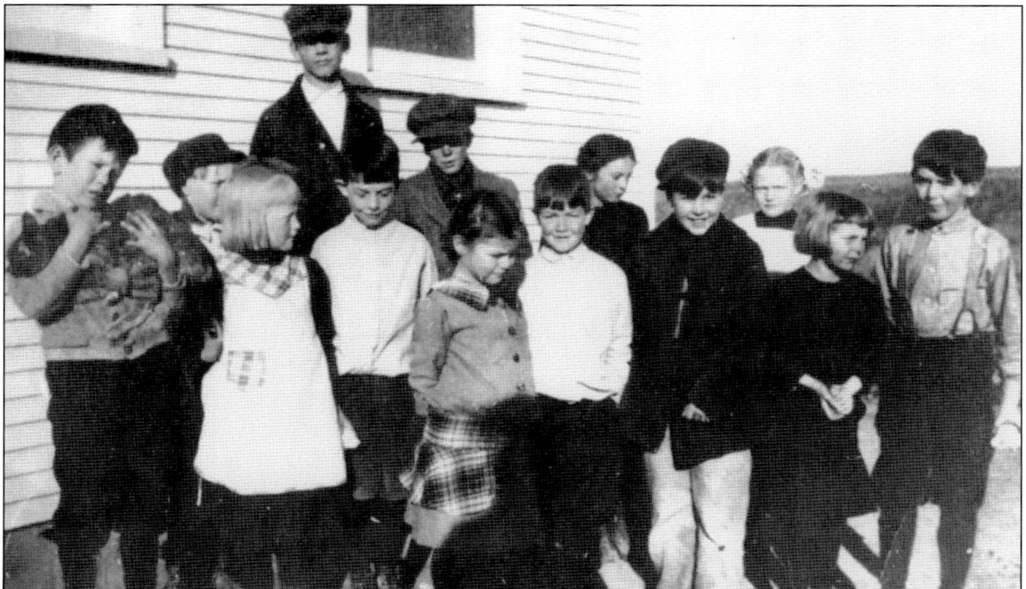

Pictured here is the Guffey School in 1915. Guffey was located at the mouth of Rabbit Creek on the Snake River. Its primary reason for existence was that it served as the terminal point of the Boise-Nampa-Owyhee rail, becoming Owyhee County's only railroad town. (Courtesy of K.O. Richards.)

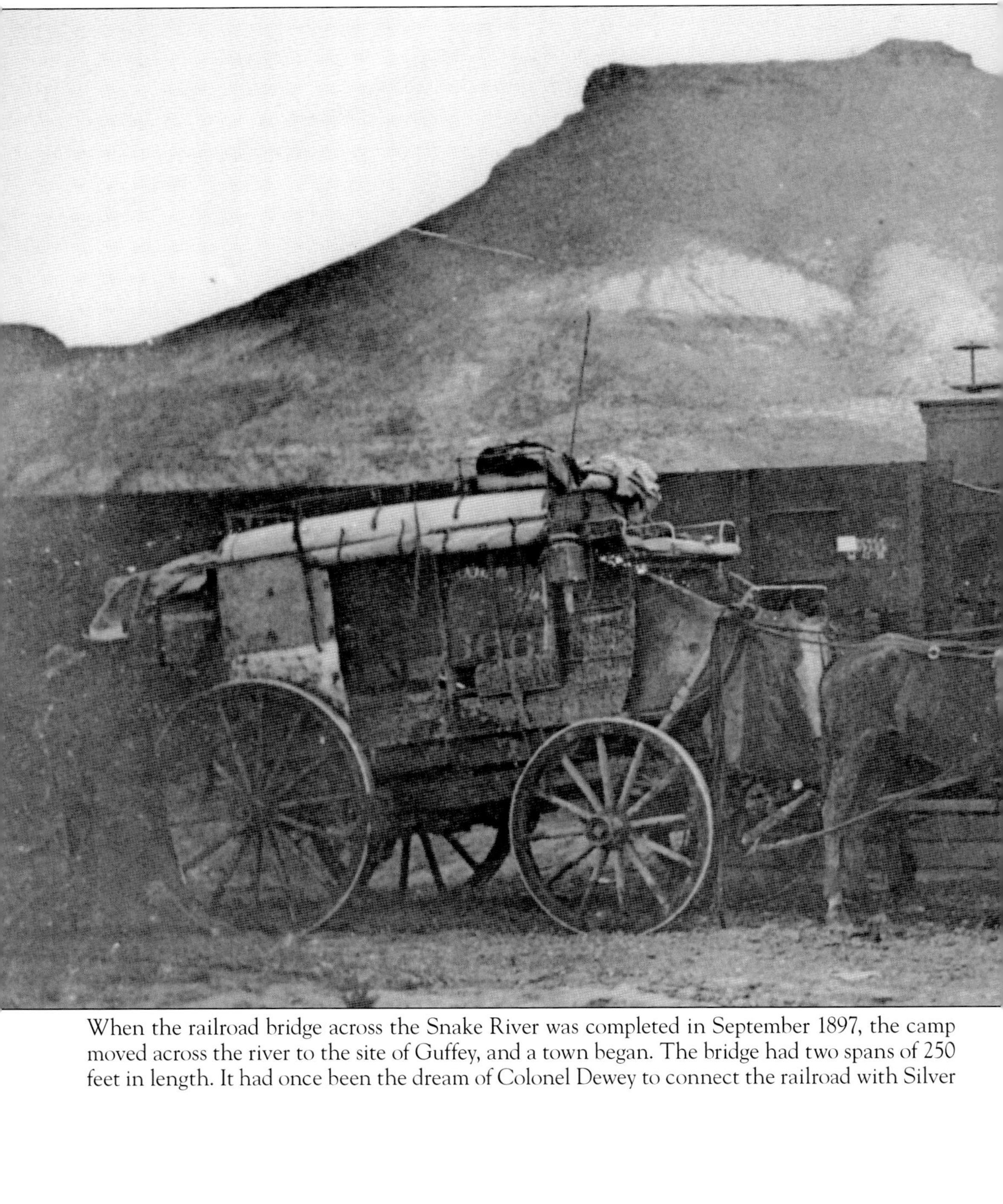

When the railroad bridge across the Snake River was completed in September 1897, the camp moved across the river to the site of Guffey, and a town began. The bridge had two spans of 250 feet in length. It had once been the dream of Colonel Dewey to connect the railroad with Silver

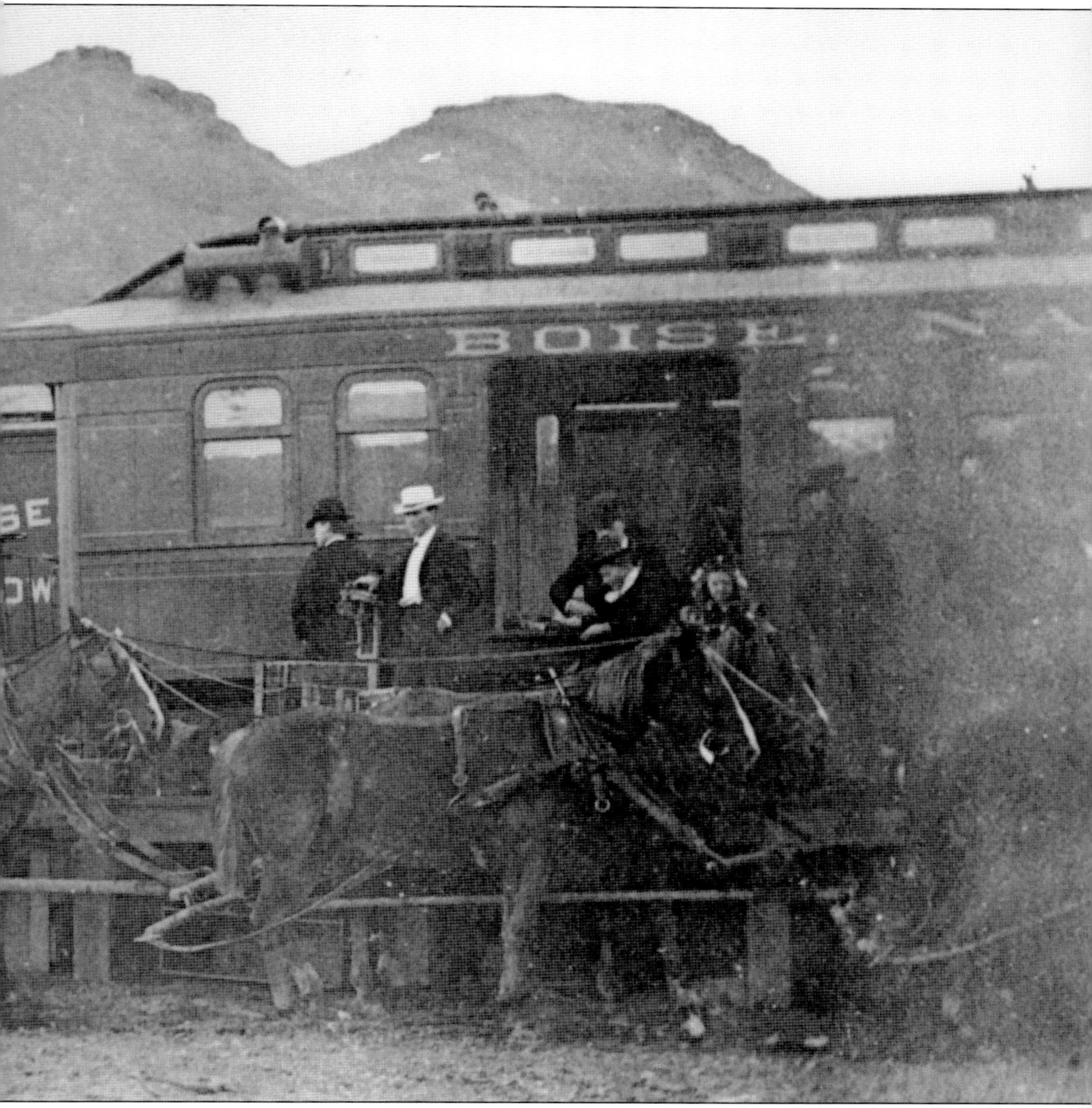

City and ultimately Winnemucca, Nevada, but these hopes came to nothing, and Guffey became the end of the line. Nearby Murphy, today the Owyhee County seat, also owes its existence to the original hopes of the failed railroad. (Photograph by Edith Farrer.)

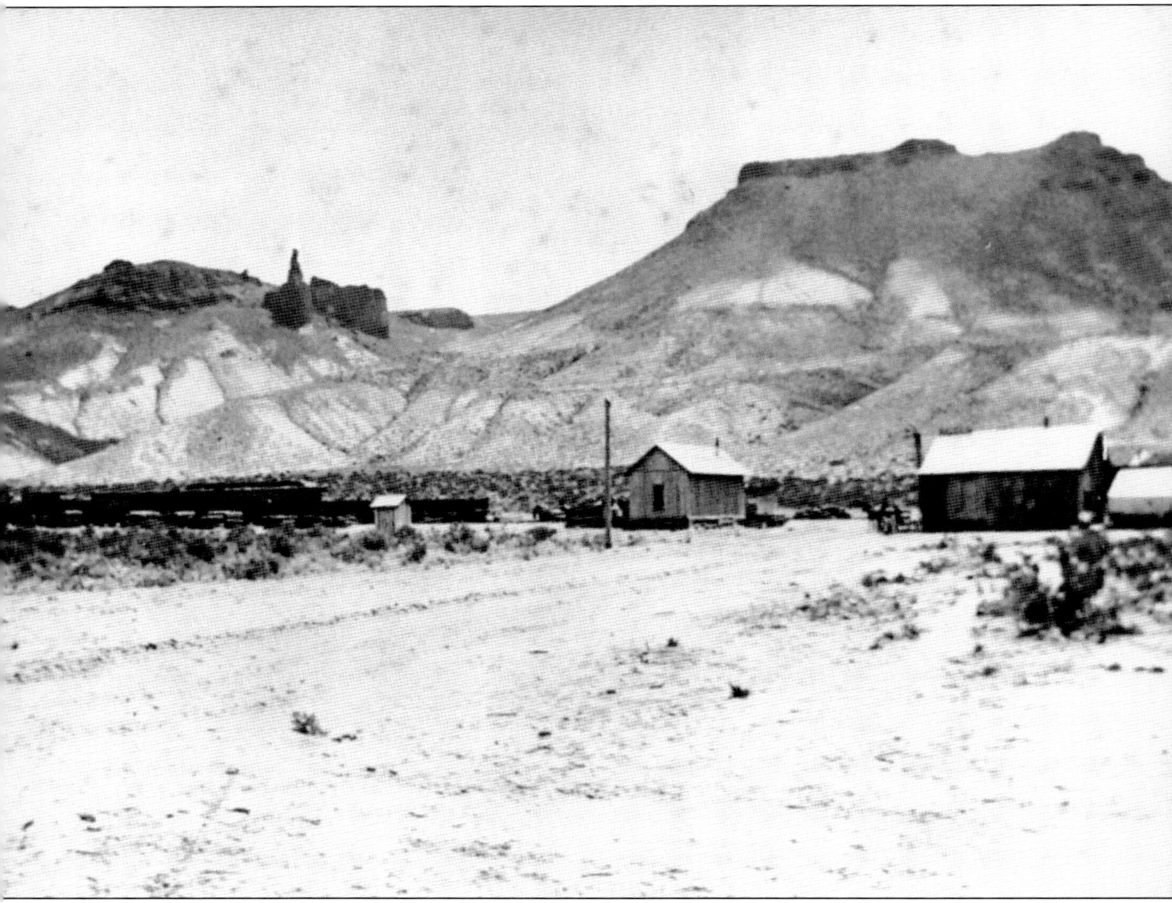

Pictured here is Guffey as it appeared in June 1898. The building on left is the depot, and the post office is on the right. The population expanded to 100 by 1898, with freight being hauled up to the mountain mining camps. The stores also served local ranchers. For a short time, Guffey was a beehive of activity, with materials coming through to extend the rail line to nearby Murphy. As hopes for an extended railroad faded, and with it the building activity, Guffey slowly faded away, as so many mining communities had. Eventually, the schoolhouse was the last remaining building, and when it too was moved, Guffey became one more Owyhee community that existed only in memory. (Courtesy of Henry R. Griffiths.)

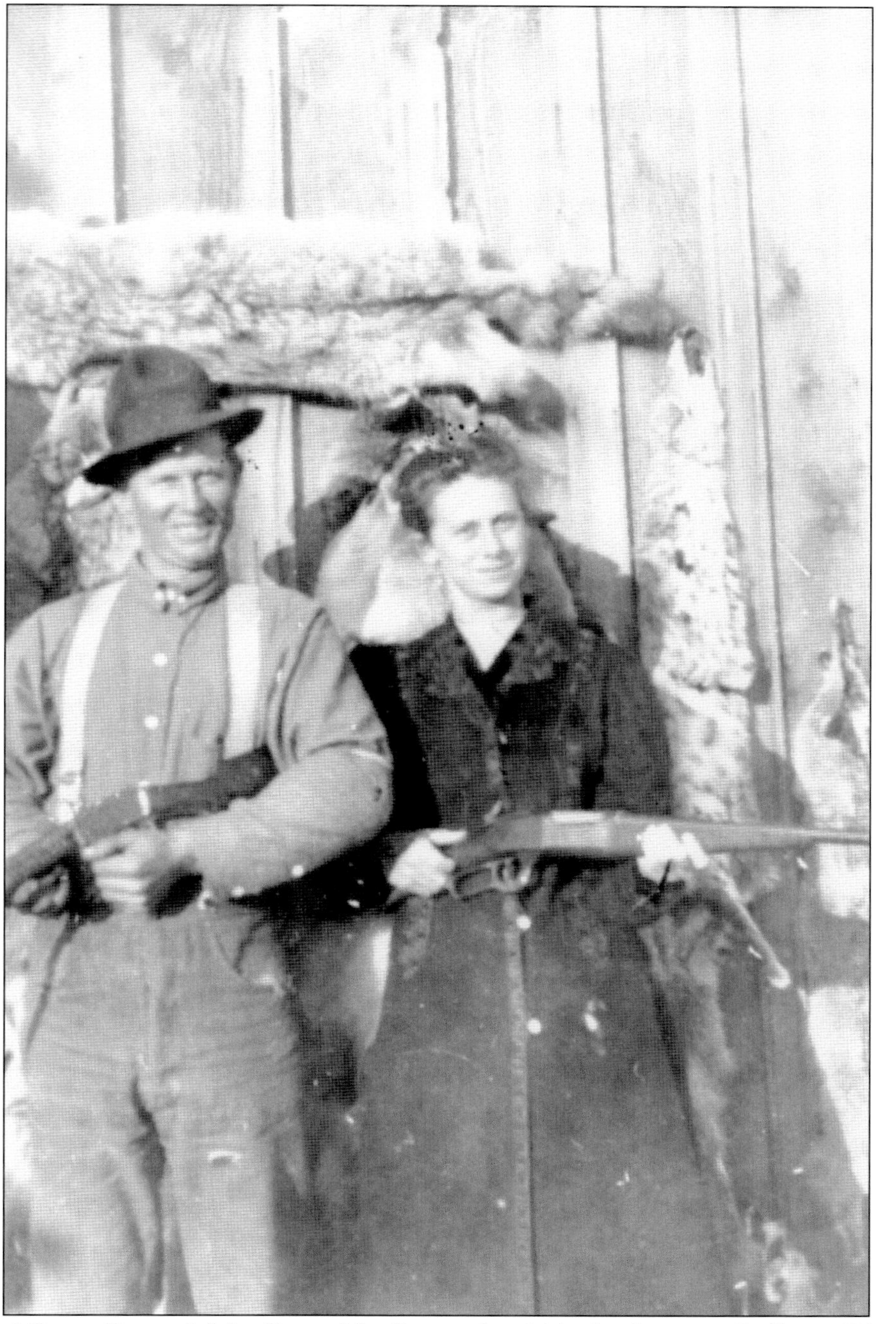

Guy and Carrie Givens (of the Givens Hot Springs family) built a house in Guffey in 1911. Guy trapped during the winter for coyotes and bobcats. Originally named Riva, the town was renamed in honor of Pittsburgh capitalist and investor J.M. Guffey, who was a friend (and financial backer) of the indefatigable promoter of Owyhee County, Col. W.H. Dewey. Long before the railroad and town were even imagined, the large, flat area where it was located was a resting spot for weary immigrants on the Oregon Trail. The spot was the first available water after a long dry stretch of travel, and records from the period tell of numerous persons being buried there, succumbing to drinking too much water after a long thirst. (Courtesy of Mildretta Adams.)

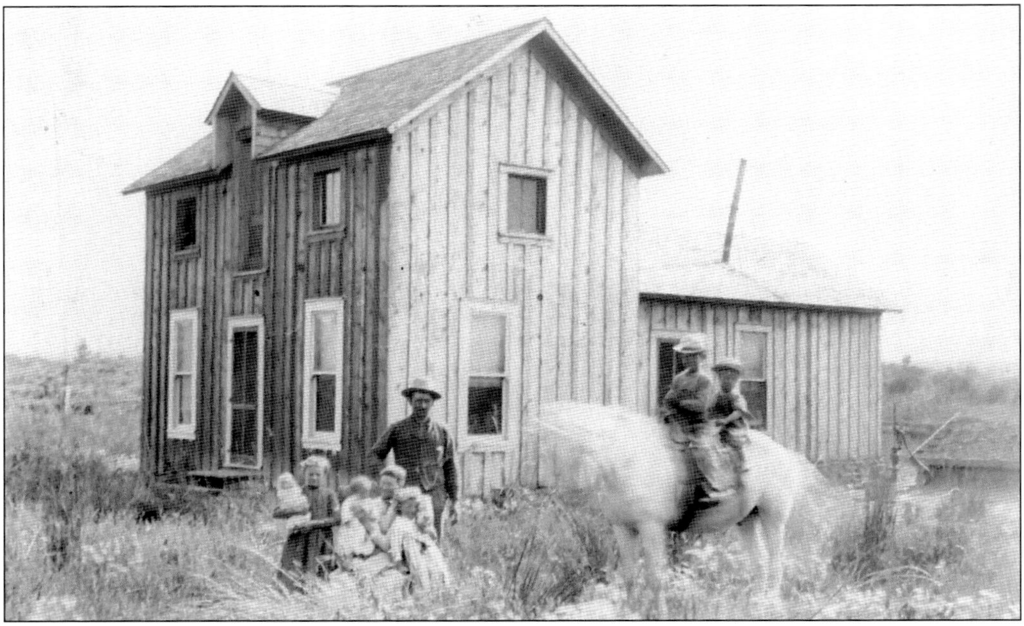

Lyse Bernard built this house on Reynolds Creek in 1900. Walter and Earl Bernard are on the horse. The community was established as Reynolds from 1884 to 1913, changed to Brunzell from 1913 to 1919, and returned to Reynolds in 1920. (Courtesy of Velma Bernard McKee.)

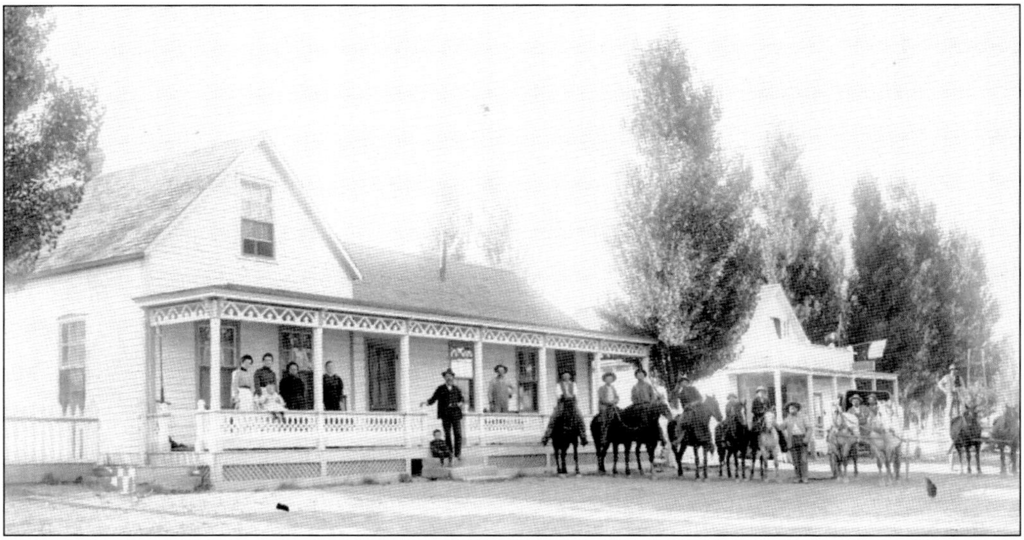

This was the Brunzell Hotel as it looked in 1900. The Brunzell family was prominent in the local communities of Murphy and Reynolds Creek for many years. Alvin Brunzell became the first postmaster in 1899, and Carl Brunzell, Carrie Brunzell, and Eva Brunzell all served as postmaster and postmistresses. As Guffey dissipated nearby, Murphy grew in stature, eventually becoming the Owyhee County seat. The town was named by Colonel Dewey in honor of an Eastern railroad magnate who was a financial backer of the ill-fated railroad line from Nampa. Designed to climb to the mountain mining communities above Murphy, and ultimately stretch all the way to Winnemucca, Nevada, the plan ultimately failed. The lonely, abandoned railroad bridge at the former site of Guffey is the only reminder of the colonel's ambitious plans. (Courtesy of Velma Bernard McKee.)

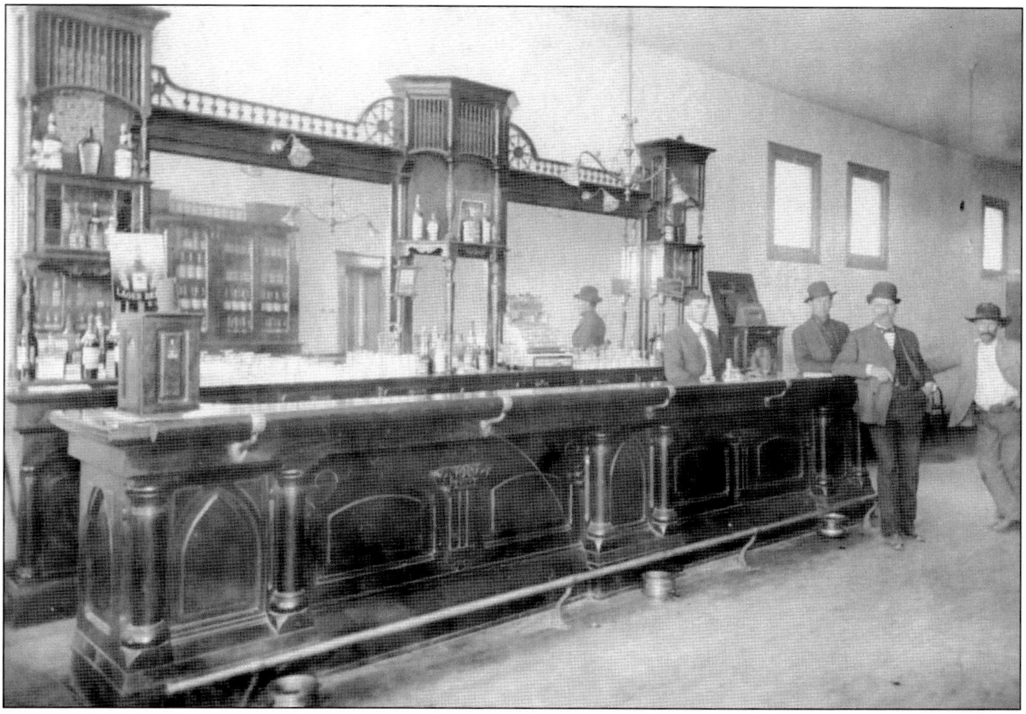

Pictured here is the Brunzell Bar in Guffey. The first building erected at Guffey after the railroad bridge was completed contained a saloon, house, and ferry office. It was built by J.R. Brunzell, who managed the ferry prior to the coming of the railroad. On the Canyon County side of the Snake River, the temporary railroad camp was known as Stoddard.

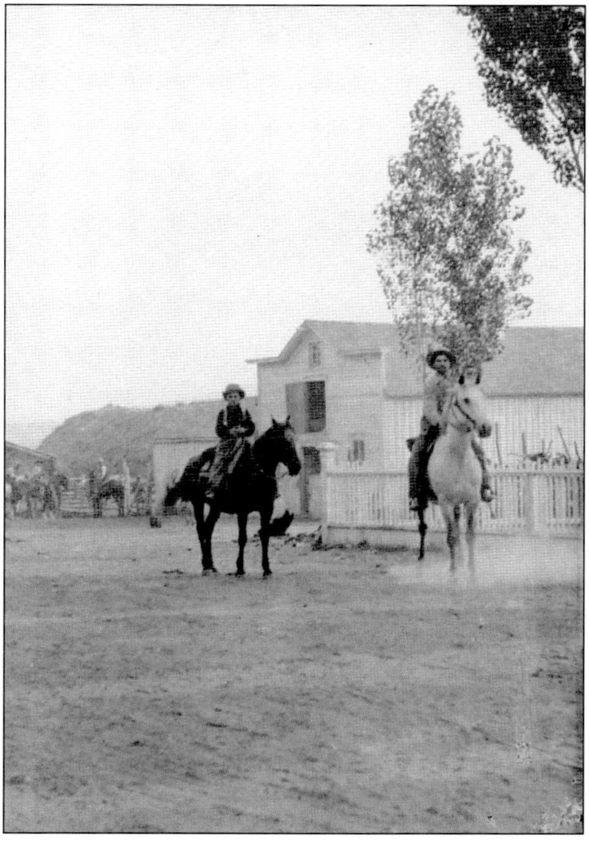

Reynolds Creek cowboys pose at the J.R. Brunzell barn, which also served as a stage stop. Reynolds Creek was established in 1884 but had its name changed in honor of the prominent Brunzell family in 1913. The name was changed back to Reynolds Creek in 1920. Reynolds Creek was on the main route to Murphy, and large herds of cattle, horses, and sheep passed through the area after Murphy became the railhead. Cowboys were a familiar sight on the streets at all times of the year.

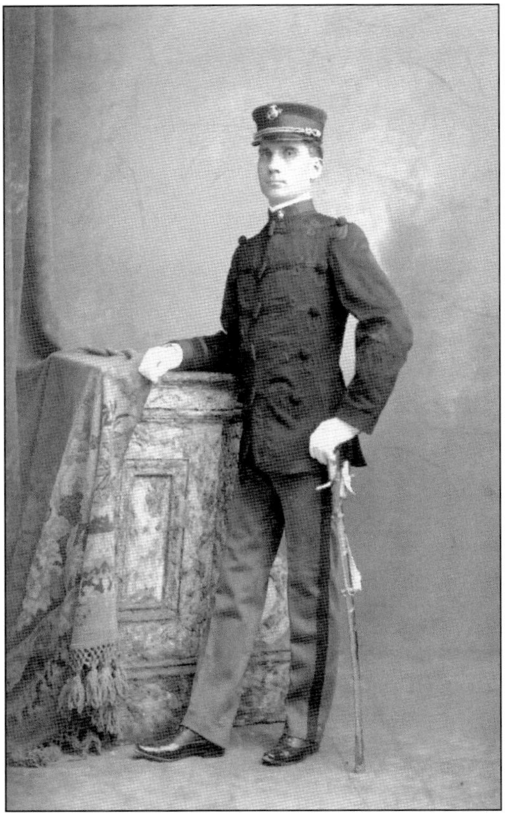

J.R. Brunzell's son Albert poses in his Marine Corps uniform (note the Mameluke officers' sword). Brunzell was born in Sweden, served in the Swedish Army, and then came to America in 1868. He went first to Silver City, where he and his brother Fred operated a mercantile business. He then purchased the old Booneville Hotel and engaged in ranching at Reynolds Creek. He erected a two-story hotel and residence, a post office building, barns, and stables. Brunzell's Saloon was a part of the hotel operation.

Clint Wroughton and Ciola Foreman Wroughton ride herd near Oreana. A visitor, Alva Read, described her first impression of Oreana in 1906: "Ulrich & Mike Hyde's Saloon was the extent of Oreana proper. Down the road a piece was the schoolhouse. A long row of stately poplar trees lined the road to the Hyde ranch about a mile below town." Harry Nelson, a Silver City businessman, purchased the Owyhee Exchange building in Silver City in 1882 and moved the structure to Oreana, where he converted it to the Oreana Hotel. (Courtesy of Roland Foreman.)

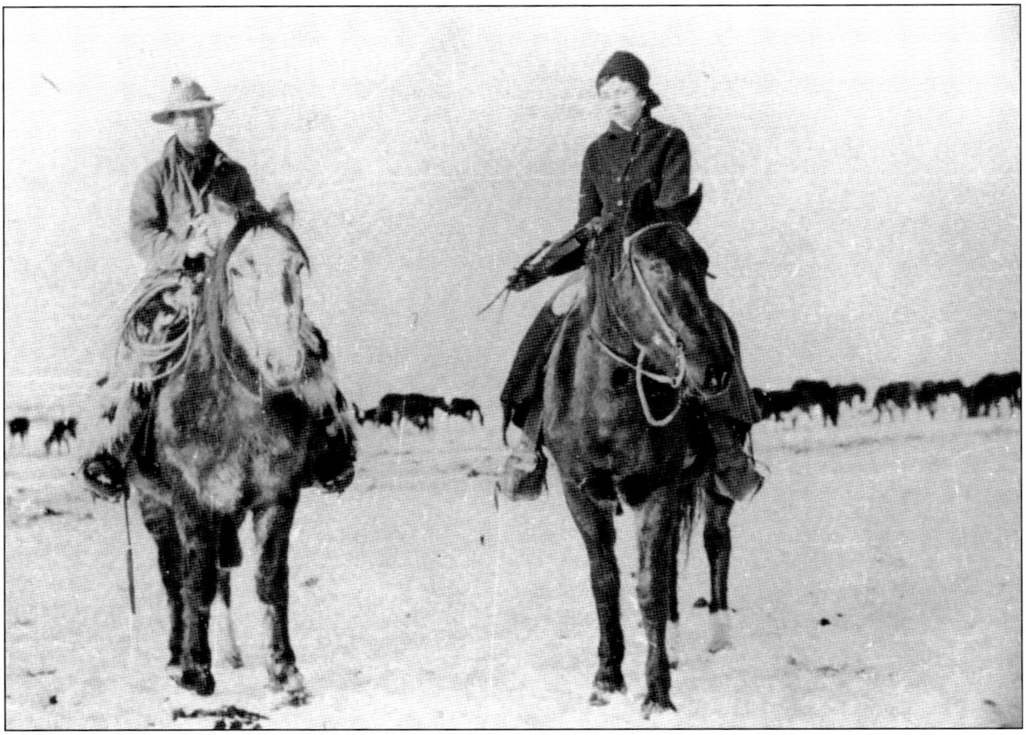

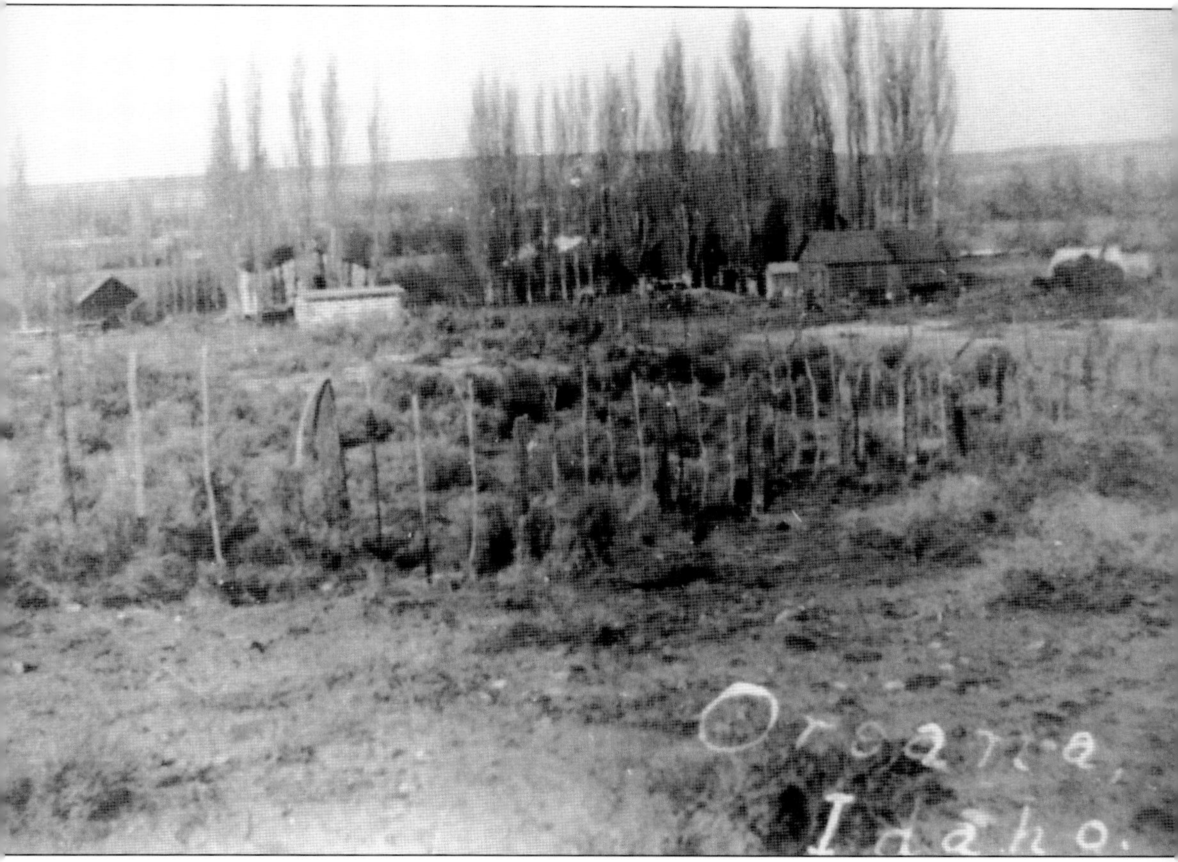

The town of Oreana is about 25 miles from Reynolds Creek. The saloon is on the left, and the hotel is in the center. Oreana Valley features Picket, Hart's, and Catherine Creeks with Castle Creek on the eastern side of the valley. The town was laid out in the center of the valley in the 1880s. (Courtesy of Roland Foreman.)

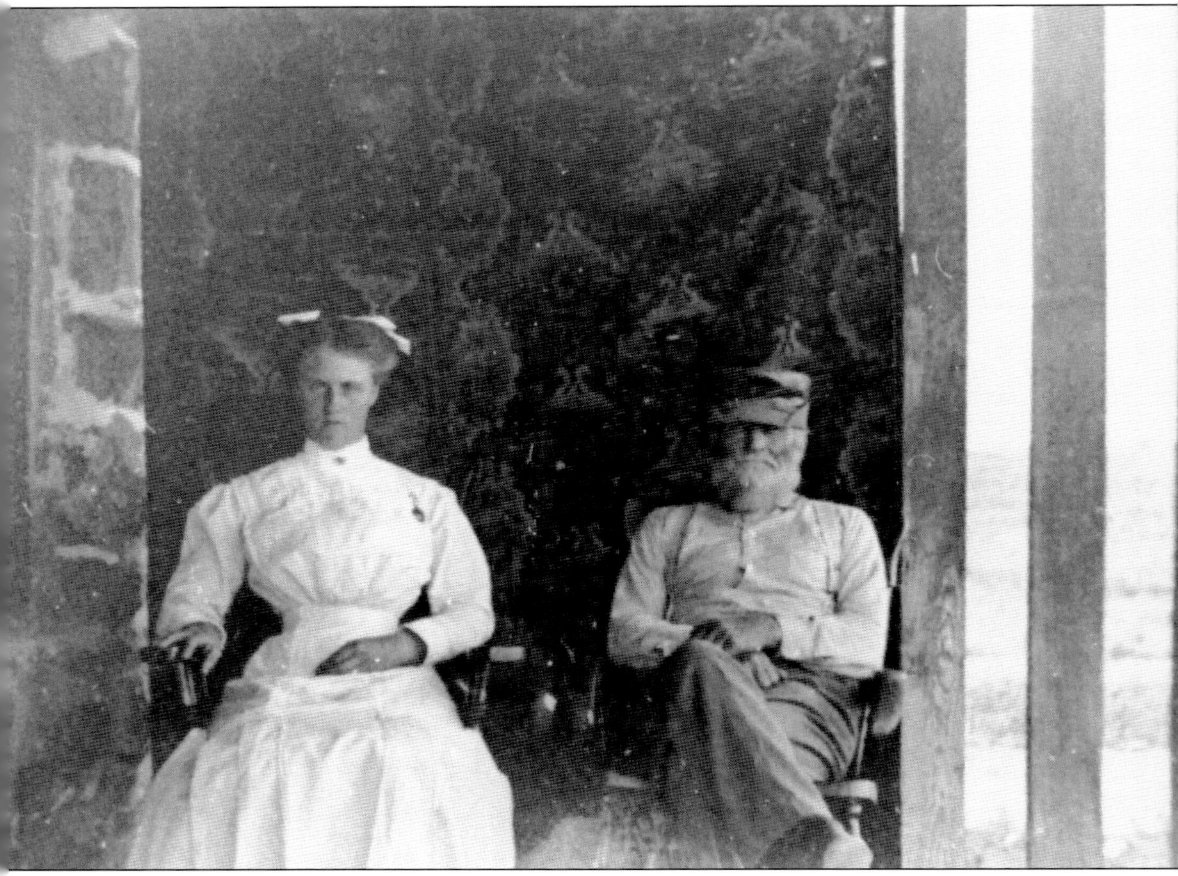

Zella Foreman and "Granddad Ratliff" pose near Castle Creek in 1910. From the 1867 *Owyhee Avalanche*, "The locality furnishes a great area for stock raising, affording an abundant supply of excellent bunchgrass, and the vast plains of white sage furnishing an inexhaustible supply of winter forage." A letter written to the *Owyhee Avalanche* on April 22, 1867, described the Castle Creek area, "The valley is geographically located 20 miles east of Silver City and about 60 miles southwest of Boise City, and has no greater altitude than the latter place. The main creek and its tributaries flow through arable land having an average width of 80 rods for 14 miles. The locality furnishes a great area for stock raising, affording an abundant supply of excellent bunchgrass, and the vast plains of white sage furnishing an inexhaustible supply of winter forage." (Courtesy of Roland Foreman.)

About the Owyhee County Historical Society

The purpose of the society is to investigate and reserve for future generations any kind of historical records, documents, sites, building, articles, oral histories, and artifacts pertaining to Owyhee County, provide a library and museum complex, and promote interests in and a concern for Owyhee County history.